Global governance is here to stay. Challenges facing our modern world are far beyond the capacity of single nations to handle and overcome. This book is about seeking new balance in a chaotic world. It is an excellent assembly of provoking ideas, critical views, and examples on building new global arrangements. An essential reading for those who study, examine, and simply care about safeguarding civilization by new enterprises of collaboration in a global realm of perplexity.

Eran Vigoda-Gadot, *University of Haifa, Israel*

With globalization increasing the interdependence of governments, NGOs, and private firms responsible for delivering services and conducting business and policy across borders, John Forrer's *Global Governance Enterprises* offers seasoned experts and newcomers to these ideas an accessible and compelling overview of the causes and consequences of globalization. Applied to very specific contexts, the book sees a way through the complexity in the development of enterprise networks.

Christopher Koliba, *University of Vermont, USA*

John Forrer's book brings needed illumination to the uncommon collaborations now becoming common—partnerships to solve societal challenges amongst civil society, the private sector, and sometimes government. New skills and knowledge are needed to make these partnerships effective and John Forrer shows us the way.

Tensie Whelan, *NYU Stern, Center for Sustainable Business, USA*

John Forrer's thoughtful and in-depth analysis of global governance enterprises highlights, in a clear and succinct manner, real opportunities for state and non-state actors to make a positive impact on society. Today's global challenges cannot be solved by one government or entity alone—they require multi-level collaboration across sectors and regions. The 2030 Agenda for Sustainable Development (SDGs) can best be achieved through innovative partnerships and alliances, combined with a transparent and robust governance mechanism. Forrer's book is an excellent pathfinder and a must read for *all* disciplines. I applaud him for this important work.

Amir A. Dossal, *President, Global Partnerships Forum, USA*

GLOBAL GOVERNANCE ENTERPRISES

Global Governance Enterprises focuses on a specific multisector collaboration—the formation of an entity that carries out global governance—providing a detailed analysis of the context of their emergence, as well as how they are created, managed, and sustained.

Forrer considers the growing challenges to successful global governance and the role of multisector collaborations in overcoming these challenges, arguing that such partnerships should be considered successful only when they meet specific conditions that ensure they are "doing well" and "doing good." By establishing a coherent framework to define global governance enterprises across a wide span of sectors, the book develops a strong theoretical foundation for this type of partnership and provides the reader with an understanding of the practical, operational realities of organizing, financing, and sustaining global governance enterprises. It includes a full section of case studies, ranging from healthcare to environmental organizations, providing practical insight into this form of governance and its function.

This book should be on the shelf of any professional or student interested in global governance, public–private partnerships, or public management.

John J. Forrer is Associate Research Professor in the Department of Strategic Management and Public Policy, and Director of the Institute for Corporate Responsibility at The George Washington University, USA. His expertise includes CSR and global governance, public–private partnerships, governance networks, and globalization.

GLOBAL GOVERNANCE ENTERPRISES

Creating Multisector Collaborations

John J. Forrer

Routledge
Taylor & Francis Group

NEW YORK AND LONDON

First published 2017
by Routledge
711 Third Avenue, New York, NY 10017

and by Routledge
2 Park Square, Milton Park, Abingdon, Oxon OX14 4RN

Routledge is an imprint of the Taylor & Francis Group, an informa business

Library of Congress Cataloging in Publication Data
A catalog record for this book has been requested

ISBN: 978-1-138-81211-6 (hbk)
ISBN: 978-1-138-71289-8 (pbk)
ISBN: 978-1-315-74895-5 (ebk)

Typeset in Bembo Std
by Swales & Willis, Exeter, Devon, UK

CONTENTS

FIGURES

TABLES

ACKNOWLEDGMENTS

This book is based on 15 years of research, teaching, and practice, focused on understanding globalization and what now should constitute good global governance. There are countless colleagues, students, and friends whose insights and ideas provide invaluable building materials that support the architecture used to organize the discussion presented here. The claims and propositions in this book have been sparked and nurtured through serious scholarly works, interesting academic panels, impromptu discussions in airports returning from conferences, long-threaded emails, friendly arguments over meals and drinks, and casual yet profound office and hallway chats. Some contributors require particular acknowledgement for their openheartedness in sharing their wisdom and experiences.

Colleagues who were invaluable contributors and generous listeners include James Rosenau, Jan Aart Scholte, Mark Amen, Ed Keller, Barry Gills, Peter P. Mandaville, Ronald Stade, Rafael Lucea, Hossein Askari, and James Kee. Many concepts that inform the definition of Global Governance Enterprises were cultivated while writing *Governing Cross-Sector Collaboration* with James Kee.

Graduate and undergraduate students whose research made essential contributions include: Ridhima Kapur, Leilani Greene, Karen Mo, Andrea Devis, Ole Mohr, Maria Alejandra Porras Santolamazza, Kerry Scanlon, and Drew Nichols. Jake Braunsdorf, Whitney Milliken, Kelly Pernia, Adriel Pond, and Mark Vincent made important contributions to Chapter 15 through their research on business participation in multisector collaborations.

The case studies of Global Governance Enterprises presented in Chapters 5 through 11 were made possible by a grant from One Earth Future Foundation. Ridhima Kapur made invaluable contributions developing the interview protocol, conducting interviews, and writing up the case studies.

Putting the concepts and principles about Global Governance Enterprises into practice provided invaluable feedback for capturing the real world experience that is described in Part III: Building GGEs. Practitioners whose experiences and collaborations were especially valuable include: Amir Dossal, David Berdish, Gloria Cabe, Thomas Niemann, Cheryl Self, and Meghan Chapple.

Patti Niles provided indispensable administrative and copywriting support.

Lastly, I wish to express gratitude to my wife, Sharon Forrer, for her enduring patience and love throughout the many late nights, early mornings, and weekends of research and writing. I dedicate this book to her.

John J. Forrer

INTRODUCTION

Globalization is transforming our world so quickly that the conventional and familiar approaches to global governance are being rendered ineffective. For those who study globalization, this is only to be expected. Globalization is changing everything rapidly while international institutions remain wedded to ideas about governance that are rooted in a post-WWII paradigms. Contemporary crises such as European Union (EU) migration or the Ebola, Zika, and Middle East Respiratory Syndrome (MERS) pandemics illustrate the insufficiency of our global governance institutions to react adroitly and effectively. Persistent global problems such as poverty, environmental degradation, and the massive inequality of the haves and have-nots reveal the outdated structures, methods, and ideals employed to solve our pressing global problems. Whatever views people hold about the merits and shortcomings of our current efforts at solving global problems, it is increasingly apparent that our basic presumptions about what makes for good global governance are becoming outdated and ineffectual. The world has moved on.

The international institutions that comprise the central actors of contemporary global governance remain firmly established in their leadership roles. Yet, the necessary predicates for effectiveness and legitimacy have been undermined by globalization. Weaker, fragile, and failed states have a difficult time representing their own people's interests. They fall short of providing the types of basic social services, safety and security, well-being, and social and economic justice to their own citizens. The porosity and permeability of borders challenges governments to maintain the policies they might choose within their own country. These conditions fester poor governance, corruption, the high cost-of-doing-business, and a "green zoning" of society that protects the wealthy and influential at the expense of the majority of the citizens who find themselves marginalized and disregarded. Increasingly, nations are poor representatives for the interests of the vast at-risk and underserved global population.

These conditions are not unique to a globalized world; however, accentuated global problems are caused by globalization. These same conditions have existed in various degrees throughout time, but the awareness of the scale and scope of global problems is unprecedented. Dictators and autocrats may have ruled in the past to protect the interests of the ruling elite at the expense of a disenfranchised citizenry and in conspiracy with other interested political and economic actors. Today, these circumstances are the topic of global media outlets and social media. The more aware people are of global problems, the harder it is to deny an effort to make them right. As a whole, the world may be no worse off than at other times in history, but knowing so much more about it creates a moral and political imperative to take action.

Re-Imagining Good Global Governance

Fortunately, scholars and practitioners became aware of the profoundness of this disconnect in the early 1990s and have been developing new theories and practices that contribute to the creation of a new "partnership paradigm" to guide how good global governance could be conducted in the future. Some have documented the failed efforts of development, international institutions, and the wasted funding on programs and projects that principally benefitted government officials and contractors. Others have begun to sketch out what a new 'good global governance' would look like that did not follow the past practices and norms of the Bretton Woods institutions and their more modern embodiments. The weakening of international institutions creates new opportunities to adopt global governance processes that are far more democratic, give a stronger voice to citizens about the form and substance of global policies, and take urgent actions that are grounded in a global perspective, not the narrow interests of a small number of countries or multinational corporations (MNCs). Good global governance serves the broad interests of diverse communities with shared interests in solving global problems, no matter what political boundaries, social divisions or economic interests may separate them.

At more practical levels, scholars and practitioners began exploring an emergent form of global governance: multisector collaboration. Researchers began to study this new approach where non-state actors (e.g., business, non-governmental organizations [NGOs]) played a much more influential role in the design and implementation of efforts to solve global problems. This new form of "network governance" attracted attention and investigation: What different types were there? What did they do? What role did government play? What made them different from conventional approaches to governance? The practice of multisector collaboration has since spread and gained interest and accolades. Partnerships are now the governance approach of choice and multisector collaborations that take on global problems have become showcased as the preferred way to solve them.

Enthusiasm for multisector collaborations has never been stronger. Yet, the rapid transition of multisector collaboration from a global governance novelty to a mainstay has left several unresolved issues in the wake of its ascendance. First, what is the justification of multisector collaboration as an appropriate approach to global governance? Many have questioned the appropriateness and legitimacy of expanded influence of non-state actors on governance. Second, scholarly support for the advantages to multisector collaboration are substantial, but how do we identify which subset of all the multisector collaborations (i.e., global governance enterprises [GGEs]) embody the characteristics that enable success in practice that researchers have singled out in theory? Third, how do people go about building multisector collaborations in such a way as to give them the best chance to be successful?

This book addresses these three questions. Multisector collaborations in general, and GGEs specifically, offer the most promising opportunity to develop approaches to good global governance that can help solve global problems as outlined by the United Nations Sustainable Development Goals (SDGs). Yet, without locating a clear and decisive definition of GGEs, expressly supported by scholarly research, and without a clearer understanding of what makes GGEs different from other multisector collaborations, there is no guidance on which of these countless partnerships that populate the global governance landscape should be supported and applauded and which should be disregarded. Without a detailed description of the processes that can be used to build successful GGEs, well-intentioned efforts will be wasted by seeking to duplicate what cannot be duplicated and re-inventing the "flat tire."

This book assembles and synthesizes research on, and experiences working with and building, multisector collaborations. It is a diverse set of scholars and practitioners who provide the conceptual building blocks that are used here. Areas of study include globalization, global governance, public management, public–private partnerships, network governance, economics, business management, corporate social responsibility, finance, and international development. Most importantly, good global governance is about people agreeing to work together on behalf of a shared interest to achieve some agreed upon outcome. Learning how to bring people together from diverse backgrounds and with different goals, into a situation that supports and empowers people to act as trusted partners and encourages participants to work simultaneously for their shared interests while transparently capturing benefits for their organization (and themselves), is the "secret sauce" of successful GGEs.

Organization of the Book

This book is organized into three parts. Part I is a description of the changes globalization has made in the world and how conventional approaches to developing global policy and implementing them through global governance are being rendered ineffective in a globalized world.

It sets out the advantages and challenges of a different approach to governance—multisector collaboration. Further it introduces and describes a specific form of multisector collaboration—GGEs—that anticipates the consequences of globalization and provides a viable alternative today to addressing global problems while upholding the values of good global governance.

The four chapters of Part I lead the reader through a series of discussions and justifications for embracing new approaches to global governance. Chapter 1 presents an overview of the rise of globalization and the economic, social, and political transformations it has caused. Chapter 2 discusses the challenges governments and international institutions face designing and implementing global policies. Chapter 3 describes the emergence of multisector collaboration as an innovative approach to solving global problems and their limitations. Chapter 4 presents a theoretical justification for a specific form of multisector collaboration—GGEs.

Part II builds off the theoretical justifications for GGEs and presents profiles of seven GGEs in Chapters 5 through 11. The profiles differ from previous case studies on multisector collaborations as these focus on each of the GGEs' "origin stories." What GGEs do and how they do it is very much grounded in the process that came to be used to create them in the first place. These GGEs were formed without a blueprint on what typical GGEs look like or recipe on how to actually create them. Each of the GGEs takes a different approach to addressing global problems and is distinctive in how it organizes and operates. However, they all share a faithfulness to the four criteria that define which partnerships qualify as GGEs. Chapter 12 provides a short summary on lessons learned about the organization and leadership of these seven GGEs.

Part III sets out an ambitious agenda for future governance. It argues that GGEs—when done right—have a good prospect of not only filling a global governance gap, but also to address global problems. It provides a practical guide to building GGEs that can make the world a better place by addressing the global problems identified in the SDGs. Drawing from research on multisector collaboration and the documented experiences of GGEs co-creating themselves, it describes in detail a five-stage process that can be used to build successful GGEs. Chapter 13 discusses creating a clear vision for bringing about real change in the world. Chapter 14 describes how to develop a change model that guides GGE partners in ways to achieve the vision. Attracting and leveraging contributions of potential GGE partners is presented in Chapter 15. Chapter 16 describes techniques for creating and capturing value and its importance in building GGEs. Chapter 17 discusses four design principles and four collaboration principles to guide the assembling of the GGE. Finally, Chapter 18 argues that GGEs have the potential to be an effective and impactful approach to global governance and identifies changes in conventional approaches to global governance needed to unleash the power of partnerships.

The three parts of this book, taken together, hopefully entail a journey of discovery and inspiration. It begins with the most abstract concepts about globalization and its transformational powers, explores and addresses the daunting theoretical and practical challenges of conceptualizing and conducting good global governance, and arrives at eight organizing principles that can guide the building of future GGEs that will be successful in helping to solve global problems.

The frustrations of those early anti-globalization protestors that took to the streets at the turn of the millennium are no less palpable today as global problems mount and threaten the health, security, and well-being of communities, nations, and the world. GGEs are not the last word on good global governance. We need new theories about global governance to catch up with the social innovations that have already been developed and implemented to help clarify what is working and what is not. Multisector collaboration should have no preferences given to them if they do not embody good global governance.

GGEs are not the best global governance approach to use for every global problem. It is one approach. It is a modest contribution that clarifies the prospects for GGEs to be a force in helping to solve global problems, shows the success of early pioneers trying to do just that, and provides guidance and lessons learned for governance entrepreneurs to co-create their own GGEs and make the world a better place. Hopefully, it offers inspiration to a younger generation—or an older generation young at heart—that have less attachments to, and investments in, how we have thought about global problems and global governance in the past and can forge innovative ways looking forward.

PART I

Globalization and the Emergence of Global Governance Enterprises

OVERVIEW

A principal theme of this section reveals a paradox: as global problems become more vexing and threatening due to globalization, our global governance capacity to solve them is diminishing rapidly. This fading capability of global governance is due in part to globalization itself. The world is transforming in ways that outstrip the experiences and, in some cases, the time to grasp and react to these changes. The rapid pace of globalization has accentuated our modern governance gap to the point where long-standing global governance approaches to solving problems seem less relevant to the global problems and crises we hear about every day. Whether it is in the areas of combating terrorist organizations, preventing human trafficking, fostering development in poor communities, responding to pandemics such as Ebola, Zika, or flus, relief and recovery efforts in the aftermath of natural disasters, curtailing greenhouse gas (GHG) emissions, preserving tropical rainforests, etc., global events seem to be happening quicker, on a larger scale, and with more profound implications—and sometimes larger unintended consequences—than we can comprehend.

If we are to formulate and become comfortable with approaches to global governance that are more effective and purposeful, they must be grounded in an understanding of the transformative nature of globalization and why it has rendered the familiar approaches to global policy and global governance not only less consequential, but less relevant. Turning away from the conventions of our contemporary practice of global governance to an approach that celebrates partnerships, collaboration, and network governance opens up unforeseen opportunities for social innovations that help solve global problems.

If global governance enterprises (GGEs) are to be accepted as a desirable approach to global governance, we need to explain how democratic accountability will still be respected. What roles do business and non-governmental organizations (NGOs) play in these new arrangements? Where are limits set on business influence in the formulation and execution of global policy and global governance? How do we measure success? How is it possible to have global governance initiatives of billions of dollars spent on social problems with limited government involvement? How do the real differences between the public values we advance through collective actions led by government agencies and the pursuit of profits by business that trumps everything else in the bottom-line be reconciled?

One nagging concern about the expansion of multisector collaborations that have emerged to fill a yawning global governance gap is the "corporatization of society." As businesses, and particularly large multinational corporations (MNCs), become more involved in global governance, will public values be eroded at the expense of private sector values? Will pursuit of profits and responsiveness to shareholders demanding market-rate return-on-investment dominate the design and delivery of public goods and services? Countervailing these concerns is the prospect that engaging business more closely in helping to solve global problems could advance the "socializing of the corporation." MNCs have adopted corporate social responsibility policies and activities addressing sustainability, human rights, and ethical practices in response to stakeholders who want corporations to take greater account of their impact on society. As multisector collaboration takes on activities that supplement and sometimes supplant government operations, it is critical that these global governance arrangements be held accountable for their actions—no less than would be wanted for government.

These are important challenges that are addressed in Chapter 3. Before that, it is important to describe the emergent forms of multisector collaboration that have grown in popularity so quickly. It is critical that we understand why these new forms of governance have emerged, and the logical basis for accepting them as proper forms of governance is discussed in Chapter 2. Prior to fully understanding the popularity of multisector governance, it is important to comprehend why our conventional approach to global policy and global governance have become less effective and how urgent is the need to develop new approaches to governance.

Multisector collaboration in general—and GGEs in particular—offer a bold and exciting new approach to global governance. They are born out of an awareness that globalization is transforming our markets, institutions, engagements, ideas, judgments, and a need for adapting to and harnessing this change. It leverages resources, shared interests, and a recognition of the growing interdependencies that globalization has wrought. Understanding how globalization is changing the world and making current practices less potent is addressed in Chapter 1.

Persuading potential partners that GGEs are an attractive global governance approach means convincing people who are largely unfamiliar with such a collaborative approach. Making a convincing case on behalf of GGEs requires an understanding of why they have been created and how to justify their positioning in the global governance landscape to those who are familiar with conventions and hesitate to embrace such an untested and implausible approach—at least when viewed through the lens of traditional governance.

1

GLOBALIZATION AND GLOBAL PROBLEMS

Globalization has changed everything. It has propelled us into a world of rapid change and transformation. We are used to generation gaps and the emergence of new ideas and practices that shake-up established norms by a younger genera-tion. Globalization is changing our world so rapidly, it seems there is no time for generation gaps; now we only have time for evolving cohort slices of Gen-X, Gen-Y, and Gen-Z parsed by single decades, each with their own particular identities. It appears there simply is not enough time to establish traditions as people are compelled to adapt to a world in constant change.

In the short span of a few decades, so many markets, institutions, norms, trends, and identities bear little resemblance to what they looked like in the past. Our markets and global supply chains are so dense and intertwined that sea scallops caught off the coast of France are flown to China to be processed and then sent back for sale in Paris in ready-to-prepare meal packs. Approximately 17 million people fly on commercial airlines every day (3.1 billion a year), more than double the number in 2000 (International Air Transport Association, 2013). Starbucks has 21,000 stores in over 65 countries; in 1987, it had 17 stores (Starbucks, n.d.). Airbnb, founded in 2008, is now the largest lodging company in the world with over 1,500,000 listings in 34,000 cities and 190 countries and yet it owns zero properties (Airbnb, n.d.). In August 1991, there was one web-site and now there are over 1 billion (Internet Live Stats, n.d.). There are more mobile phones on the planet than people (7.68 billion) (Shontell, 2011). The first text was sent in 1992 (it read "Happy Birthday"). Today, 23 billion texts are sent every day (Tumbleson, 2015). Seasonality in foods is dwindling, with an array of fruits and vegetables available year round. The Blue Revolution means globally, aquaculture supplies more than 50 percent of all seafood produced for human consumption (National Oceanic and Atmospheric Administration, n.d.). Just 1 percent of the world's population owns over 50 percent of all the world's wealth (Bentley, 2015).

These examples are just a speck of how globalization has changed the planet and its people. Globalization does not present itself evenly across the globe. At one end of the spectrum globalization has fostered global "cosmopolitans" who live in the major cities around the world. They share a similar world view and experiences: flying to similar destinations, watching the same movies, reading the same news reports, shopping at the same websites and stores, drinking the same wines, and making similarly large salaries. These global cosmopolitans have much more in common with each other than the citizens of their own countries. At the other extreme are a few communities who have experienced little of the changes brought about by globalization, living their traditional lives as did their parents and their parents before them.

The majority of the world's population lives in state of flux that is a strange globalization cocktail: a mix of modern and traditional social, economic, and political realities that are in a constant state of conflict, confluence, and reconfiguration. The mixtures are different all around the world, but the reason for this state of mutability is the same for all: globalization. The most obvious manifestations of globalization—such as those cited above—are just the expressions and representations of a turbulence that globalization has brought about: not as a one-time event that helps segue history from one era to another; globalization is remarkable by its constancy of fostering ever more rapid and dramatic change, which itself creates the conditions which are disposed to changing again, with no end in sight for this globalizing swirl.

One consequence is globalization has exposed communities to global threats as never before. Global pandemic episodes such as avian flu, Ebola, and the Zika virus spread through global travel and transportation networks with little advanced warning or predictability. The disintegration of the Soviet Union suggested a reprieve from the threat of a future World War III, only to be replaced by global terrorist acts and the growing eruption of more violent conflicts around the world. Global financial crises have wiped out trillions of dollars in value and peoples' savings in a matter of only a few days. Fossil-fuel energy systems supporting worldwide growth have spewed sufficient carbon emissions into the atmosphere to escalate global climate change concerns about ever more imminent rising ocean levels and ocean acidification.

The need to do a better job at solving global problems is obvious and needs to be expedited. The frustrations many feel with our inability to adequately respond to our most challenging global problems is matched by the enthusiasm many feel for employing a new, multisector, collaborative approach to global governance. The potential for collaborative global governance to unleash the full value of social innovation created through partnerships is tantalizing. However, it is critical to recognize that both sensibilities are deeply rooted in globalization.

Having a clear view of what globalization is about, how it is transforming our world, and its implications for global policy and global governance are prerequisites for establishing support for collaborative global governance and creating new approaches that work.

We increasingly recognize how the world is being bound together in a global community and, at the same time, more torn and threatened by war and violence, resulting in destruction and displacement of communities. The current migration crisis involving Middle East and North Africa (MENA) and the European Union (EU) exemplifies the porosity of borders that is a signature trait of globalization. The openness of the borders meant an overwhelming influx of desperate and needy people into EU countries that were ill-prepared to accommodate this migration crisis. The suffering of those dislocated by the wars in Syria and Iraq as well as other conflicts across the MENA region, or those leaving to avoid poverty, desperation, and human insecurity and relocating has been met with compassion, sympathy, and an understanding that these migrants' suffering was not of their making. At the same time, the violence and despair that is goading such frantic migration was not of the making of those providing shelter. The closing of nations' borders to immigrants only concentrates the suffering to refugee camps, with no practical global policies adopted about what to do next. It has also inflamed a radical nationalism and a resident and latent ethnic and racial hatred that has engulfed the EU and put it in such a tumult as to threaten the EU's cohesion and future.

Our abilities to cope with the rapid changes globalization has introduced into people's everyday lives and to tackle the significant global problems that it has fostered is predicated on understanding globalization. Effective global policies and global governance require a clear comprehension of what are the forces of globalization, the ways in which these forces are affecting our world, and what actions will be purposeful and impactful when there is a need to bring about real change. However, it is the same rapid transformation of the world that globalization brings about that makes understanding globalization such a struggle.

James Rosenau attempted to capture the paradoxical character of the changes generated by globalization in his book *Distant Proximities* (2003). Looking back on the early studies of globalization—himself a trailblazer in the field—Rosenau identified three dynamics he believed have been spawned by globalization. He called them: (a) distant proximities, (b) fragmegration, and (c) macro structures. *Distant Proximities* reflects the view that any event in the world—however remote or insignificant—could be expected to have consequences for people anywhere in the world. *Fragmegration* refers to two simultaneous forces: the never-ending fragmentation of what exists now and the on-going reintegration that creates new arrangements. Fragmegration occurs on a scale applicable to communities as well as globally. *Macro structures* suggest that governments and corporations will play a lesser role in shaping history, eclipsed by the actions of individuals who will have greater influence.

These are broad, sweeping claims and there are exceptions and relative degrees of applicability to be expected. They set out the new ways of thinking about how globalization has changed some of the most fundamental ideas upon which conventional approaches to designing global policy and implementing global governance have been based. *Distant Proximities* proposed that the traditional focus on government and multinational corporations (MNCs) to explain how power and wealth are created and distributed in society is misdirected. Efforts to preserve familiar global governance institutions through reform and re-missioning are misguided. Shaping and framing global policy and global governance through bounded rationality and respect for borders and boundaries—geographic, political, or conceptual—is fruitless.

The only rational way we can formulate purposeful and impactful approaches to global policy and global governance is to accept "the globalization of all things." This means that at any point in time, the understanding we gained from studying and experiencing the past has limited value for addressing global problems today. The changes brought about by globalization are not incremental adjustments to accepted ideas and practices. They are a radical transformation of global realities that have rendered our current ideas about global problems and what we might do to solve them, inapplicable and, therefore, ineffective. Looking forward, good global governance requires the creation of a new set of global governance standards and approaches that stay aligned with the new realities that are constantly being reinvented by globalization. The first step to accomplishing this goal is to understand globalization.

Globalization Emergent

Views of globalization have been contested and controversial ever since the concept was first popularized. Its origins are contested as well. In one version, according to the *Oxford Dictionary*, the word globalization was first employed in the 1930s. It entered the *Merriam-Webster Dictionary* in 1951. However, it was not widely used by economists until the late 1980s. It was a convenient way to think of events as being on a worldwide scale, reflecting awareness of the planetary scale and scope of specific issues.

Rosenau's (2003) characterization of globalization has given the word a far more sophisticated and profound meaning than its more humble origins. A more robust conception of globalization views the world changing in fundamental ways—not just markets and trade (what some refer to as economic globalization)—but culture, travel, identity, knowledge, and technology. These changes are occurring at unprecedented levels of scale, intensity, and speed. The consequences of these changes are profound and important to recognize, document, and comprehend as a way of understanding the new realities created by globalization. However, the transformational powers of globalization mean that by the time we recognize, conceptualize, document, and validate such changes, there is a prospect that what we think we learned has lost its relevance because the world has already changed again. It is the "process of globalization" which must be grasped and understood if we are to construct the new approaches to global governance that address global problems in a way that are rational, purposeful, and impactful.

Given this more holistic conceptualization of globalization as background, Levitt (1983) was among the first (along with sociologist Roland Robertson) who invoked "globalization" in its modern scholarly incarnation in a paper in the *Harvard Business Review*. He argued that new technology, which has "proletarianized" communication, transport, and travel, has created the emergence of global markets of unprecedented size for standardized consumer products. According to Levitt, the future belongs to the "global corporations" who are emerging as dominant economic forces as the era of the multinational corporations is winding down. Differences in local consumer preferences and tastes are not the focus of global corporations. Success for global corporations is based on marketing low-cost, standardized products and utilizing enormous economies-of-scale in production, management, distribution, and marketing. This new era of "homogenized demand" was seen by Levitt as hegemonic: no sector is exempt. Over time, all products would be standardized and sold in global markets to global consumers. Local preferences for product variations will lose to low-cost alternatives and eventually will disappear (Quelch & Deshpande, 2004).

Levitt's predictions have not yet fully come to pass. In retrospect, his assessments come across as exaggerated and overreaching. The power of his ideas was grounded in the recognition of the transformational force of globalization. He sensed that something fundamental was changing in the structure and operation of corporations and markets that, in turn, would usher in profound changes for society, government, markets, and the environment. His portrayal of globalization was as a sweeping force, rapidly reorienting people's lives across the globe in similar ways. Levitt considered the nature of globalization through the lens of international business, but it introduced a concept of globalization as more than just the scale and scope of change (i.e., globalism). To be globalized was a phenomenon unto itself. Globalization is its own process of change. The prognosis of the impending "globalization of all things" made some howl with disapproval, some cheer in celebration, and some, perplexed by the prospect of such all-pervasive force of change, tried to understand more thoroughly what globalization was all about.

Takin' It to the Streets

Today, now that globalization has permeated all aspects of our everyday lives and we experience it on a daily basis, it is accepted that we live in a globalized world. It was not so long ago that the idea of globalization was the center of controversy: on the streets and among academics.

Twenty years ago, concerns began to grow over how "globalization"—a relatively new term at the time—was ruining national economies, encouraging environmental degradation, impoverishing workers, fostering worldwide financial crises, and stripping indigenous peoples of their rights. It inspired street protests. Protestors blamed large MNCs for abusing excessive economic power, amassed from financial deregulation and so-called "free-trade" agreements. The expanded powers of MNCs were seen to undermine government authority, effective regulations, and the voice of local communities, thereby leaving MNCs free to make risky investments that generated superprofits. As a result, when the economies of the "Asian Tigers" failed in 1997–8, the "Dot Com Bubble" burst in 2000, and the "Great Recession" of 2008 hit, the MNCs were bailed out by governments, while national economies and their citizens were left to suffer the consequences.

Not only was globalization viewed as driving a greater inequitable divide between the wealthy and powerful, and the poor and disenfranchised, it was transmogrifying capitalism into a distorted caricature of itself: *Casino Capitalism* (Strange, 1986); *McWorld* (Barber, 1995), and *Disaster Capital* (Klein, 2007) are some of the better known derisive monikers. The argument was made not only that globalization was causing world-scale problems, but that it was itself a world-scale problem. Many anti-globalization protestors called for new global governance activism—including transnational democratic movements—that provided heightened participation and democratic representation, advancement of human rights, fair trade, and sustainable (i.e., inclusive) development. Many activists would say they were not only anti-globalization, but also pro-social justice.

People began to organize around these claims and assertions and organized street protests at meetings of international organizations (see Table 1.1). One of the earliest and most publicized anti-globalization protests targeted the World Trade Organization (WTO) Ministerial Conference of November 1999 in Seattle, Washington. The demonstration is sometimes referred to as the "Battle of Seattle." Protestors blocked streets, and some targeted and damaged the storefront windows of corporations such as a large Nike shop and many Starbucks. Police arrested hundreds of protestors with widespread injuries. The movement gathered momentum and the next protest was held in April 2000. Protestors gathered to demonstrate at the joint-International Monetary Fund (IMF)/World Bank (WB) meeting in Washington, DC. The protests were largely peaceful and garnered tremendous press coverage. A little over a year later, the protest movement was carried over to The Group of Eight (G8) Summit in Genoa, Italy. There, protests turned violent, as peaceful activists were joined by more radical groups who incited violence. Protestors and police alike were injured and one death resulted. The violence drew extensive media coverage for the protestors.

TABLE 1.1 Protests against Globalization

Date	Event	Place
1988	Meetings of the International Monetary Fund (IMF) and the World Bank	Berlin
1989	The G7 Summit	Paris
1994	The 50th anniversary of the IMF and the World Bank	Madrid
June 1999	25th G8 Summit	Cologne
November 1999	World Trade Organization Ministerial Conference	Seattle
April 2000	Meetings of IMF and World Bank	Washington, DC
September 2000	Meetings of IMF and World Bank	Prague
2001	27th G8 Summit	Genoa
2002	Meetings of IMF and World Bank	Washington, DC

Today, the meetings of the WB, the IMF, the G8, and other international organizations are held regularly without protesting placards and with limited public notice. Many former protestors (and their children) are likely to be satisfied customers of Nike and Starbucks. The protests targeted international institutions because of their belief that policies supported and/or implemented by these international institutions were a cause of the global problems they were protesting; and a change in those policies could alter the world's fortunes and future. There is no doubting the influence international organizations have on a host of global problems. Over time, it became more apparent that these same international institutions were themselves at the mercy of the globalization forces that inhibited their own performance and prevented them from achieving their goals. The end of large street protests should not be taken to mean people started to care any less about global problems and their linkages to globalization. The violence in Genoa, and perhaps the recognition of the utter enormity of globalization, suggested the futility and dangers of such forms of protest, and the need to channel passions into other ways of bringing about change.

One outlet has been the World Social Forum (WSF). The first meeting was organized in 2001 in the city of Porto Alegre, Brazil and was a counter-event to the World Economic Forum held in Davos, Switzerland at the same time. The slogan of the WSF is "Another World Is Possible." In June 2001, the World Social Forum Charter of Principles was adopted. It provides a framework for addressing global problems for international, national, and local Social Forums worldwide. The WSF has held meetings since, the latest (at the time of writing) in 2016 in Montreal, Canada.

Perhaps the anti-globalization (or pro-social justice) movement was a victim of its own success. As public awareness of the globalization debate grew and evolved, it attracted an ever larger amalgam of issues to protest by assigning blame to "globalization." The anti-globalization movement became the repository for so many complaints about the way things were, and "globalization" became the "whipping-boy" to blame for all manner of discontent. Globalization gave a name to myriad global problems that coalesced under one cause to rally around and protest. While this raised awareness of globalization as an issue and potential problem, the sum of the anti-globalization protests may have been less than the sum of its parts.

The large protests came and went. They introduced "globalization" to the public through extensive media coverage and launched a debate about whether people should be for or against globalization. They began a global dialogue on what globalization was about and not about, whether it was a positive or negative force in people's lives, and whether they were for it or against it. Everyone agreed: globalization was here to stay.

Grappling with Globalization

Since the mid-1980s, books and articles on globalization have proliferated almost as rapidly as the process of globalization itself. The globalization literature covers a wide range of descriptions, interpretations, and analyses of its implications and meanings. Several schools of thought have emerged about what is globalization, what it means for people and the planet, and what to do about it.

Globalization Alarmists

A large number of books critical of globalization were published in the 1990s, many of them providing the incendiary fuel that fed the anti-globalization protestors' ire. They generally shared the presumption that globalization is a force that is expanding the power of the haves over the have-nots and with the support and empowerment of MNCs who, in turn, are favored by Western elite politicians in governments (national and international) and corrupt leaders in developing countries. They described forces of globalization that confirmed some people's worse fears about powerful institutions—public and private—cooperating to accelerate wealth creation for a small elite class at the expense of working conditions, human rights, culture, and the environment. The arguments were inflammatory and rhetorical as well as thoughtful and scholarly.

Globalization was a massive machine that was swallowing up everything local and homogenizing it into global products and brands. The production and supply chain practices of MNCs were decimating the environment and entrapping workers in perpetual poverty and unsafe working conditions. Human trafficking enslaved people into forced labor. The drive for profits was spoiling the earth and translating them into an uber-rich class at the expense of people, their cultures, lands, freedoms, and identities.

International institutions such as the IMF or the Bank for International Settlements (BIS) were not trying to stabilize nation's economies and help them grow and develop, but were, in fact, working to enforce neoliberal economic policies that tolerate poverty and protect the investments and held debt by the wealthy elites. In this view, globalization is just another way of pointing out that the worse traits of capitalism have expanded to a global scale and were freer to operate with fewer regulatory mechanisms to tame it. National leaders were corrupted to let global corporations have access to land and resources with little social regulation. Human rights abuses expanded with the influence and greed of business and the corruption of state-owned enterprises.

The authors protested against injustice, unfairness, and the homogenization of human culture, paired with calls for reversals of current international economic policies and practices and the institutionalization of "democracy and economic justice" for a more just and environmentally friendly world. If corruption, self-serving ideologies, and unfair policies have propelled and fostered globalization, alternative policies could arrest and reverse these circumstances and redirect us towards a better world. A sample of publications reflecting the globalization alarmist view is presented in Table 1.2.

Globalization Defenders

Partially in response to these critiques, others presented globalization as a powerful force of change and change for the good overall, although acknowledging it was not without its issues. From this view, globalization was the logical extension

TABLE 1.2 Globalization Alarmists

Date	Author	Title
1993	George Ritzer	*The McDonaldization of Society*
1997	Hans-Peter Martin and Harald Schumann	*The Global Trap: Globalization and the Assault on Prosperity and Democracy*
1999	Naomi Klein	*No Logo: Taking Aim at the Brand Bullies*
1999	Amartya Sen	*Development as Freedom*
2000	Noam Chomsky	*Profit Over People: Neoliberalism and Global Order*
2000	David C. Korten	*The Post-Corporate World: Life after Capitalism*
2000	Antonio Negri and Michael Hardt	*Empire*

of national market forces and liberal economic policies. Expanding markets and trade between nations and global capital markets were a historical trend, traceable back to the industrial revolution, with antecedents even evidenced before that. The result is growth, development, and modernization. The benefits are improvements in people's lives in terms of raised standards of living, increasing democratization of nation's governments, longer and healthier lives, and access to life-enhancing technologies.

Yes, global change and transformation caused dislocation and disruption, but this has always been the nature of growth and progress. Expanding markets should be understood as bringing greater access to jobs, technologies, medicines, culture, ideas, mobility, and opportunities to more people than ever before. The reach of globalization to the most remote communities brought benefits they had not experienced before. Globalization is forcing national economies to open up, lessen trade barriers, and adopt responsible fiscal and monetary policies. Globalization forces could be blunt instruments of change, but the changes they bring are far superior to neo-mercantilist policies that seek to delink with globalized markets. Globalization is inevitable, and efforts to slow it down or to become disengaged from it are not only unwise and counterproductive, but also futile. Globalization should be embraced as the best chance people have to bring prosperity and wellness to the entire world's population.

Defenders of globalization are not unaware or insensitive to the human suffering that can come from the dislocations of the transformations of economies and societies. They are passionate about their belief that the best remedy to address the suffering that exists among populations today is *more* globalization, not less. Efforts to adopt policies intended to stop the macro forces driving globalization and untangle global networks will only make matters worse, not better. Globalization should be accepted and appreciated for the opportunities it brings to global communities, while helping and being compassionate about people who suffer from profound dislocations brought about by globalization. A sample of publications representing the globalization defender view is presented in Table 1.3.

TABLE 1.3 Globalization Defenders

Date	Author	Title
2002	Douglas Irwin	*Free Trade Under Fire*
2003	Johan Norberg	*In Defense of Global Capitalism*
2004	Jagdish Bhagwati	*In Defense of Globalization*
2005	Martin Wolf	*Why Globalization Works*
2010	Bruce Greenwald and Judd Kahn	*Globalization: n. the irrational fear that someone in China will take your job*

The Middle-of-the-Roaders

Some authors found comfort with one foot in each of these two schools of thought on globalization. They felt a strong solidarity with protestors, understanding that the benefits of growth and modernity were unavailable to certain segments of society—often the poor, powerless, and marginalized. At the same time, they could not agree that dismantling basic international economic and development institutions and global governance arrangements of the international system would lead to some better future for those global communities under duress. Therefore, there was some solidarity in agreeing to policy changes addressing the negative impact globalization could have on people and the environment, but not to reverse or derail globalization itself.

They also agreed with globalization defenders that there were historical precedents to the forces driving globalization and they concurred that those macro forces were largely inevitable and beyond the powers of governments to reconfigure or redirect. They believed that specific policies needed to be adopted to assure global communities experienced more fairness, protection, compensation, and equity than was currently the case. Drastically improving transparency, debt relief, land reform, and restructuring corporate accountability systems are supported. Increasing capacity in fragile states to foster development, greater access to technologies, expansion of microfinancing, and improving educational opportunities are proposed. Support for sustainable supply chains, corporate social responsibility programs, enhanced philanthropy towards development, and public private partnerships are endorsed. Using the power of markets and "bottom of the pyramid" strategies are supported. All these efforts are made to counteract the acknowledged negative consequences of globalization, in short: globalization with a human face. A sample of publications representing the middle-of-the-road view on globalization is presented in Table 1.4.

It is critical to recognize and appreciate these views on globalization when advocating for specific global policies and approaches to global governance to address global problems. The different camps have very clear ideas about moving forward.

TABLE 1.4 Globalization Middle-of-the-Roaders

Date	Author	Title
2000	Adrian Wooldridge and John Micklethwait	A Future Perfect: The Challenge and Hidden Promise of Globalization
2005	Kemal Derviş	A Better Globalization: Legitimacy, Governance, and Reform
2005	Thomas Friedman	The World Is Flat
2005	Stuart Hart	Capitalism at the Crossroads
2006	Joseph Stiglitz	Making Globalization Work

- The harshest critics of globalization propose significant shifts in the distribution of power and wealth through government intervention to assure greater development and economic justice, less power in the hands of MNCs and international institutions, taxing global financial transactions, and more democracy.
- Defenders of globalization advocate for more market openness, more free-trade agreements, lower taxes on business, encouraging global investing, and continued liberalization and rationalization of regulatory regimes.
- The middle of the roaders want both at the same time in somewhat diluted forms. Support markets and corporate expansion and leave intact the basic financial policies and institutions that are now in place. Expand humanitarian aid, protect the environment, global public services, and encourage social entrepreneurs, impact investing, and opportunities for small businesses and communities.

There is no real prospect for resolving the debate over globalization by scholars and pundits. For all the fervor and sanguinity about globalization and the claims and counterclaims made about its impact on the world, globalization is here to stay. If Rosenau and other globalization scholars are correct that globalization is shaping our world into fundamentally new and largely unrecognizable realities, less time is needed on excoriating globalization or cheering it on and more time should be spent actually understanding the changes globalization is bringing about, and how it is affecting everyone now and in the future. Such a foundational understanding is essential if rational and purposeful revisions of how to better conceptualize good global governance are to be designed and instituted.

The Globalization of Everything

Despite disagreeing about almost everything to do with globalization, there is a consensus around an undeniable phenomenon that is at the root of globalization and its impact on the world: the thickening of global networks that has weakened nations' powers (Ritzer, 2007) and facilitated people feeling more connected due to a worldwide diffusion of practices, expansion of cultural relations across continents, organization of social life on a global scale, and growth of a shared global consciousness along these same networks (Lechner, 2005).

The growth of global networks is among the most recent and profound changes that have occurred in the modern world. They are expanding, growing denser and thicker every day, connecting us together in global communities; sometimes in ways we want and do on purpose and other times in ways we do not want and without our knowledge. Being connected in global networks can be tremendously beneficial and be highly threatening and deleterious. Some of the interesting areas where networks have developed are listed in Table 1.5.

TABLE 1.5 Global Network Examples

Areas of Global Networks	
Transportation	Airlines
	Container ships
	Intra-modal shipping
Telecommunication	Internet
	Satellite
	Cell phones
	Cable/Fiber optics
Business	Mergers and acquisitions
	Innovation partnerships
	Global supply chains
Social Media & Communities	Digital diasporas
	Trans-boundary democratic movements
	Facebook
	Twitter
	Bandoo

With these global networks in place, global traffic began to increase rapidly. Put simply, global networks foster more things being in more places around the world more quickly and more cheaply than ever before. Trade in goods and services are not the only traffic that clutters global networks. Engaging with the traffic that travels on global networks is an aspect of globalization that puts people in greater contact with other people, ideas, and experiences outside the normal encounters of their physical community, yet begins to bring them closer to many different global communities. Examples of the types of traffic moving along these global networks are:

• Goods and services
• Technology
• People
• Ideas
• Images
• Data
• Flora and fauna
• Disease
• Capital
• Currency
• Culture
• Information

People's global connection through the internet is a major force creating new global communities and breaking up existing local communities. Engagement in social media networks is now prolific and commonplace, with active users on a global scale. The top three leading social networks worldwide ranked by number of active users are Facebook (1.55 billion), WhatsApp (900 million), and QQ (860 million) (Statista, 2016). It appears that one could just sit in their room all day and still feel linked together with the whole world—as long as they had an internet connection. Television has gone global. Not just BBC News or CNN, but MTV has over 40 stations, broadcasting on every continent (except Antarctica) and the content has become more global with stories from around the globe, reflecting the suspicion that what happens in the world—even in remote areas—affects global events (Statista, 2015). The internet is the global portal through which news, entertainment, and sports are transmitted. Top Gear is watched by 350 million people every week. The 2014 World Cup final had nearly 10 percent of the global population watching. The movie *Avatar* (not including pirated copies) has grossed 2.8 trillion U.S. dollars—only 30 percent in the U.S. YouTube has nearly five billion videos watched *every day* in 54 languages (Statistic Brain, 2015).

Engagement with the global community also comes from global travel and encounters with those from other countries. Global migration has increased by 65 percent in the Global North and by 34 percent in the Global South since 1990 (International Organization for Migration, 2014). New peoples, manners, and cultures are encountered in people's hometowns, when they travel abroad, and when work assignments take them abroad. The emphasis on diversity and inclusion policies in schools and firms reflect the globalizing of casual and professional engagements. International students typically comprise 25 percent of U.S. university student bodies (Martin, 2010). Study abroad has become a common event during a student's third year of college. Professionals travel the world to attend conferences and training sessions. The U.S. was once noted for being a "melting pot": now the whole world itself is becoming a melting pot.

The daily engagement of global communities through networks has raised global awareness. It simply comes from living enmeshed in networks, which brings a feeling of connectedness with millions, perhaps billions, of people who have shared interests, tastes, passions, values and who, despite sharp differences in age, culture, and life-styles, for some inexplicable reason simply cannot get enough of watching "Gangnam Style." Global engagement has been used to expand access to education and education through Massive Open Online Courses (MOOCs) and other online courses, do-it-yourself (DIY) videos, music, movies, and videos and information to answer whatever question you may have.

One of the most ubiquitous ways people encounter globalization is through commerce. The reduced costs of production and shipping means products from around the world can be sold in global markets, inviting introductions to new products, and changing tastes and fashion. It also has raised awareness of the conditions in which products are grown, manufactured, harvested, refined, and processed as they work their way through global supply chains. Campaigns have been organized to raise awareness of the economic, social, and environmental consequences of products made abroad including: "Blood Diamonds," "Conflict-Free Minerals," "GoodWill Chocolate," and more generally, fish, tropical timber, cotton garments, and a host of other commodities. Growing awareness of sustainability and human rights concerns is moving people to see more clearly the global connection between what they buy and how that influences how products are grown and made. Global standards are emerging—not without controversy—around responsible business practices that affect labor, development, environmental damage, diversity, and gender equity to be enforced in corporation's supply chains.

Social media sites unite millions in shared experiences who have never met each other—and feel no need to do so. These global communities are also powerful instruments of social and political destabilization. Some are used in the name of promoting democracy and government accountability, like the so-called Arab Spring, or used to advance product safety in China, or, more recently, #Telema to change governments in the Democratic Republic of the Congo, or used to recruit youth to join the Islamic State of Iraq and the Levant (ISIL).

The metastatic forces of globalization have profoundly changed our encounters with the world and expanded global awareness. Globalization has brought about a networked life for many, although still many more are waiting to be connected. It has created and invited people to be a member of an inchoate global community. This global engagement and the raised global awareness it has fostered has changed the world and what it means for identifying and addressing global problems.

Implications of Global Networks

One of the implications of living in a networked world is that it has had a profound influence on changing how we think about global problems, what should be done about them, and our ability to address them. This tetrad phenomenon—expanded *global networks* encourage *increased global traffic* across the networks, which increases people's *global encounters* and expands their *global awareness*—is a cornerstone to how globalization requires a new approach to global governance when addressing global problems. Greater global connectivity has changed the world in numerous and important ways.

Volatile and Uncertain Global Systems

On the one hand, the expansion of global networks has created a new capacity to connect and to move, unprecedented in human history. Yet, these same networks are less stable, more volatile, and more at risk than in prior times. Due to the interconnectedness, a failure in one part of the network can threaten the performance of the entire system. Based on conflicts in the Middle East,

U.S. crude futures dropped as much as 5 percent in one day, driving prices below $27 a barrel, the lowest point since 2003. In total, crude oil plunged an incredible 75 percent from its June 2014 peak of almost $108 (Riley, 2016). Unexpected declines in Chinese stock markets starting in the summer of 2015 depressed stock prices around the world. The annual GDP growth rate in China averaged 9.88 percent from 1989 until 2015 (Trading Economics, n.d.). The sudden Chinese stock market collapse, and a possible slow-down in China's domestic economy, threatens the health of the entire global economy. Global supply chains are vulnerable to localized events that cause disruption worldwide. Typhoon Halong hit southeast Asia in August 2014 causing US$10 billion in global business revenue losses and required 41 weeks to repair damage caused to supply chains (Snell, 2015).

Expanded global networks are more unstable and volatile because of the adding of more pathways and increased traffic without centralized command and control. That means poor or failed performance of one node could shut down major sections of a global network: a satellite, a server farm, an oceanic fiber optic cable, an international canal, a currency, a nation's economy. There are limited ways to ensure the proper precautions and procedures are followed to reduce network volatility. The world's population is more reliant on global networks and that same reliance and expanded use adds to the networks' vulnerabilities.

Risk-Intense Environment

The legacy of many of the world's biggest problems has expanded the risks people face today from new global problems. The risks of pandemics have increased due to expanded travel and migration. At the same time, the legacy of inadequate healthcare services leaves many countries unprepared to curtail diseases from spreading in their earliest days. This makes the risks even greater. Access to inexpensive arms and the lack of governance in fragile states has made violent rebellion and conflict easier to foment. The impoverished and desperate lives faced by many communities with no reasonable prospects of change makes people—particularly youth—more susceptible to recruitment for violent conflict. Environmental crises such as climate change, ocean acidification, oceanic micro-plastics, and tropical timber destruction threaten to usher in major ecological disasters. The insistence of operating global supply chains that preference profit over people and planet has set in motion global imbalances that may be impossible to bring back into equilibrium.

Weakened International Governance

The increased permeability of nations' boundaries to the traffic that journeys on global networks reveals the growing ineffectiveness of nations to effectively represent and protect their own citizens' interests. Expanded global networks mean nations cannot protect their borders as before and have disrupted and undermined the traditional roles of governance. The weakening of the state has meant the growth of fragile states, states in conflict, hollowed-out states, and failed states where governance, public service delivery, and policing and security are problematic on their best days. With weaker states, the international system, and the international institutions it established, faces diminished capacity to conduct good global governance.

The United Nations and many other multilateral organizations share similar characteristics: (a) their members are states where non-state actors have limited influence, (b) the non-intervention in the internal affairs of other states and sovereignty remain core beliefs of the international system, (c) the international system is based essentially on voluntary acceptance of common norms across nations with few tools to penalize non-adherents, and (d) internationally agreed upon goals and strategies are underfunded for what is needed for implementation. Preoccupation with concerns of legitimacy, representation, accountability, and efficiency are used to avoid taking decisive action. Decision-making is slow and cumbersome. National preoccupations usually override common interests, and institutional reform is even more difficult to bring about than in national institutions. There are fewer opportunities to shape the world to reflect the values and interests of nations. Actions and policies conceived around national borders are increasingly less relevant and effectual.

Globalization(s)

Globalization should be understood as both a condition and a "supraterritorial" process (Scholte, 2000). We live in a world that is both globalized and still globalizing. Its constant reformulation of itself fosters new opportunities and closes off others. The consequences are harmful to some and beneficial to others. It presents a chaotic and confusing picture to those who look at it compared to the past, and an open canvas of opportunity and creativity to those imagining how the future might look. It presents the unavoidable challenge of managing the unmanageable. Globalization is not anything to be for or against; it simply exists.

Its antecedents are located in history, a series of isolated and interactive events that shaped and codified the forces of globalization, buffeting our world today (O'Rourke & Williamson, 1999). No doubt, there were moments in time when different public policy decisions could have been chosen and they would have altered the arc of globalization's metamorphosis. However, foresight is not 20/20 and such moments are lost to us now. Many forces are driving globalization's reconstruction of our societies, but the expansion and thickening of networks is a leading factor and the most conspicuous.

Unfortunately, overlaying the conventional paradigms and narratives around global governance, international relations, new world orders, and the international system onto what we observe about globalization makes understanding globalization only more difficult. The disparity between what the world had been like prior to the post-World War II invention of Bretton Woods' institutions and how it is today continues to widen rapidly.

The profound changes brought about by globalization makes the world increasingly unrecognizable. As a result, the prevailing wisdom about what causes global problems and what can be done to solve them is becoming less and less relevant. It is not that people do not know what changes globalization have wrought, although many still perceive the world to be as it used to be 30 or even 70 years ago. Public policies about foreign affairs in democracies are typically grounded in a combination of some perceived self-interests of that nation's leaders, constituencies, and citizens. The rationales for adopting many of our current global policies are grounded in ideas from generations ago. Without leadership to translate new ideas into new policies, the old rhetoric and narratives drive our thinking and actions. There is always a natural "lag effect" between generations and their world views. Globalization is changing the world so rapidly even major generational reassessments of the "given wisdom" are outdated before they get a chance to be implemented.

The traditional instruments used to conduct global governance are becoming dulled and losing their efficacy. Successfully addressing our biggest global problems—such as the Sustainable Development Goals (SDGs)—means governance models cannot be successfully built on broad global policy, but guided by what will work for a community at that specific place in time and space. Future global governance is not about accepting or rejecting globalization, but understanding what to do differently to make it a better world. Such approaches to governance will need to be just as adaptive, responsive, and resilient as globalization is dynamic and transitive.

Global problems need fresh observations and new ways of thinking about problem solving. It is a challenge for a younger generation to take a fresh look at solving the most pressing global problems. Given the pace of change of globalization, the long-maligned "short attention span" of Millennials may be a decided advantage. Giving less credence to the lessons of history, accepting the globalization of all things, and recognizing the limitations of best practices and lessons learned are just the attitudes needed to see more clearly why global problems exist and what can be done about them.

2

GLOBAL PROBLEMS, GLOBAL POLICY, AND GLOBAL GOVERNANCE

Global Problems

At the Millennium Summit in September 2000, perhaps the largest gathering of world leaders in history adopted the United Nations (UN) Millennium Declaration, committing their nations to work on achieving eight specific development goals and setting out a series of time-bound targets. It was a bold initiative that called for action to address endemic problems that were plaguing a majority of the world's population; most having existed since people walked the earth (see Figure 2.1).

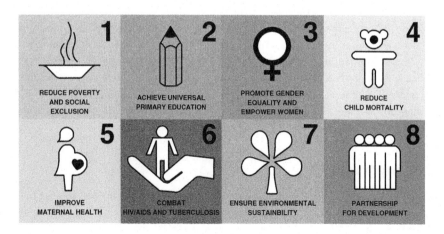

FIGURE 2.1 Millennium Development Goals

Source: http://www.un.org/millenniumgoals/.

The Millennium Development Goals (MDGs) pointed a bright spotlight on a diverse set of intransigent global problems and set out a pathway for progress on specific, quantifiable metrics associated with those goals to be achieved by 2015. The MDGs gave visibility, energy, and impetus to UN agencies and offices, local and big international non-governmental organizations, corporations, government agencies, investors, development contractors, other international organizations, and communities to work together to strengthen existing programs and develop new innovative approaches for solving global problems. Fifteen years after the initiative, the success in meeting MDG goals presents a mixed story.

The mixed reviews on the actual impact of the MDGs can be explained away in part by their good intentions. A case can be made that the specific goals set out for the MDGs were in fact only symbolic targets; their purpose was to galvanize attention to the problems, marshal resources, and renew efforts. Given that interpretation, it could be said that the MDGs were successful. The failure to achieve some goals by the 2015 deadline was well eclipsed by the accomplishments made in other areas. The progress that was made achieving the MDGs was, in all likelihood, more than would have been accomplished otherwise. Without the MDGs to draw attention and drive efforts to meet the goals, the progress that has been made would never have occurred.

Yet the shortcomings of the actual impact of the MDGs against their targets cannot be dismissed entirely by this argument. Successful global policies must be purposeful and impactful in their design. Just because there are global problems that are significant or deserving of attention, does not mean that we know what steps are required to solve or mitigate them. Are the keys to solving our most pressing global problems to spend more money and try harder? Good intentions are commendable, but what success did the MDGs actually have in alleviating the targeted global problems they set out to redress?

The progress made on meeting the MDGs is an encouraging sign, and should lend support to those who advocate that focusing on global problems can have success. A closer look at some of these assertions of success tells a different story. Closer examination of the claims for success achieving some MDG goals reveals not only an overstatement of their impact compared to their targets, but also exposes limitations that are more serious. In some cases, claims were made for their effectiveness that are unwarranted and cast doubts on whether the policies employed to achieve the MDGs were effective.

Poverty Reduction

The World Bank is claiming significant poverty reduction has taken place since the 1990s. According to their data, the percentage of people living in absolute poverty has gone from 37.1 percent to 9.6 percent from 1990 until now (BBC, 2015). The World Bank (WB) claims this trend is due to strong growth rates and establishing better educational, health, and social safety nets

GOAL 2 | Achieve universal primary education

| Goals and Targets | Africa | | Asia | | | | Oceania | Latin America and the Caribbean | Caucasus and Central Asia |
	Northern	Sub-Saharan	Eastern	South-Eastern	Southern	Western			
Universal primary schooling	high enrolment	moderate enrolment	high enrolment	high enrolment	high enrolment	high enrolment	high enrolment	high enrolment	high enrolment

The progress chart operates on two levels. The text in each box indicates the present level of development. The shades show progress made towards the target according to the legend below:

■ Target met or excellent progress.   ▦ Poor progress or deterioration.
▦ Good progress.   ▥ Missing or insufficient data.
▦ Fair progress.

FIGURE 2.2 Millennium Development Goal 1 Progress Report, 2015

Source: http://www.un.org/millenniumgoals/2015_MDG_Report/pdf/MDG%202015%20PC%20 final.pdf.

in developing countries. This data seems to suggest the programs that the WB and United Nations Millennium Campaign have implemented since the 1990s will have a hand in completely eradicating absolute poverty in the not so distant future. As demonstrated in Figure 2.2, a further examination of the issue shows this is not so black and white.

The main goal of the UN Millennium Campaign when it was created was to cut absolute poverty in half by the year 2015 (Hickel, 2015). By examining the data on a global scale, it seems as if the UN has reached their goal. On the other hand, looking at absolute poverty statistics country by country paints a very different picture than it does globally. Globally, the percentage of people living in absolute poverty is 9.6 percent, but when you look at how many people living just in the Sub-Saharan region of Africa are in absolute poverty, the percentage grows to 35.2 percent (BBC, 2015). This is because the Millennium Development Goal 1 (MDG 1), which plans to eradicate extreme poverty and hunger, was altered to account for people living in extreme poverty by proportional numbers instead of absolute numbers. By doing this, the target numbers became much smaller and made their goal of cutting absolute poverty in half from 1990 to 2015 much easier to achieve. In fact, these new proportions, when put into place, automatically reduced the target numbers to reach MDG 1 by 167 million people.

Paradoxically, by measuring problems in global aggregate, progress in one area of the world can mask serious shortfalls in others. MDG 1 was altered even further when it was redefined from halving poverty for the population of the world to halving poverty for the population of developing countries (Hickel, 2015). In addition, the UN Millennium Campaign extended the analysis baseline from 2000 back to 1990, therefore including China's progress in reducing abject poverty, which the campaign had no hand in helping. The International Poverty Line (IPL) also further complicates the assessment. The analysis accounting for people who live at or under the IPL suggests that the numbers are growing instead of decreasing when it comes to absolute poverty (Hickel, 2015).

Five-Year-Old Deaths

MDG 4, to reduce child mortality as an example of global policy, attempted to cut infant mortality by two-thirds for children between the ages of one and five by 2015. The UN prides itself on the fact that despite population growth, the number of deaths in children under five has been reduced by about 66 percent (UN, n.d.). It is suggested global governance plays a role through the UN to provide more primary care for these children. Additionally, the UN administers HIV/AIDs treatments, which, consequently, reduce mother to child transmissions. Lastly, the widespread usage of mosquito nets in risk areas such as Zambia helped reduce the spread of malaria. However, it should be noted that these improvements are temporal. The assessment of progress on MDG 4 (Figure 2.3) conveys that the number of deaths in children declined from 11.9 million in 1990 to 7.7 million in 2010 (UN, n.d.). The UN statistics paint an encouraging picture that the declines in child mortality are as a result of its aforementioned interventions.

Even yet, in the face of all the UN's progress displayed by its reports, there are converse ways of reading its statistics. When looked at closely, over that time period there are new methodologies that measure the scale of child mortality, which was less than had been thought originally. In addition, reduced birth rates occurred during this time, which directly decreased the number of deaths in children. In addition, along with reduced birth rates, there was an increase in two-year birth intervals. Babies born within two-year birth intervals have higher survival rates than babies born with shorter birth intervals. These factors, taken together, tell a different story about the achievements of MDG 4. There is no doubt that efforts made to reduce child mortality were on behalf of achieving MDG 4. But the assessment above shows clearly that several other important factors—some related to how the numbers were calculated and some related to broader social trends—help explain the reduction in child mortality.

These two examples raise important questions, not about the good intentions of those who work hard to solve global problems but of the efficacy of the global policies and approaches to governance employed. The widespread accolades regarding the success of the MDGs, the selective reporting of the

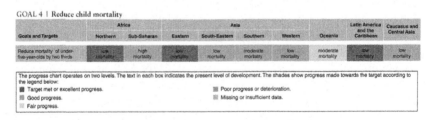

FIGURE 2.3 Millennium Development Goal 4 Progress Report, 2015

Source: http://www.un.org/millenniumgoals/2015_MDG_Report/pdf/MDG%202015%20PC%20 final.pdf.

FIGURE 2.4   Sustainable Development Goals

Source: http://www.un.org/sustainabledevelopment/sustainable-development-goals/.

metrics, and the general effort to "put the best face" on the MDG campaign grants an endorsement of the current global policies and the conventional approaches to governance.

However, a "deeper dive" into the reasons behind the incidence of global problems in 2015 compared to 2000, as articulated by the MDGs, suggests that the enthusiasm for the efficacy of the efforts made by the UN and others to achieve the MDGs is misplaced. That assessment raises serious concerns about the efficacy of the conventional approaches now directed at solving global problems.

Nonetheless, building off several years of global committees and consultations, a new, expanded action agenda, *Transforming Our World: The 2030 Agenda for Sustainable Development* (or Sustainable Development Goals [SDGs]) was adopted by UN member states at a summit in New York, September 2015. The 17 topics and 169 targets of the SDGs (Figure 2.4) replace the MDGs.

As the MDGs officially expired in 2015, their renewal in the form of the SDGs is a logical progression. Since the MDGs were not all accomplished, it would be unusual for the UN simply to stop their efforts, just because the target date came and time ran out. Continuing the commitment to solving these global problems and establishing a new timetable were not difficult choices. However, 15 years later, the adoption of the new SDGs reflects an expanded recognition of problems that should now be considered global. The "doubling-down" on the MDGs and the expansion to addressing 17 issues reflects an acknowledgement of the global nature of our biggest problems.

Paradoxically, the adoption of the SDGs and acceptance of another 15-year term of performance are an implicit acknowledgement that conventional global policies and global governance will not be sufficient to bring about success. The MDGs could not be achieved in 15 years, even with the most generous interpretation of their effect. At least some claims for MDG success can be explained away by exposing clever accounting techniques or economic and social forces well beyond the control of the UN. The SDGs may be the equivalent of proclaiming the goal of running a marathon when 10 k is the farthest we have ever been able to run. While 15 years may not seem like a long time given the drawn out negotiations that are the typical experiences for many international treaties, that timeframe no longer aligns with the scale or scope of these problems and the negative impact they can have worldwide. The SDGs lack a critical component of success: urgency.

The SDGs—set out so clearly and with such detailed goals and targets—require an effective and expedient approach to developing innovative global policy solutions and effective global governance. We can no longer afford to have individual nations pick and choose which global issues they want to address while ignoring others. The interconnectedness and interdependencies of nations, communities, and people requires an integrated approach to problem solving with clear outcomes, setting strategies for actions to achieve those results, committing resources and collaboration, and executing to success. Global problems left unresolved put us all at peril. More problems are now global and everyone's problems. What are the prospects that the same global policies and approaches to global governance that fell short in meeting the MDGs will be successful in achieving the new SDGs by 2030?

Global problems may not be so tractable to our conventional ways of designing global policy and implementing them through conventional global governance.

Globalization and Global Problems

Given our current conditions of a globalized world, globalization, and the changes it has fostered, shines a new light on global problems and how we might address them.

- With economic, social, and political networks expanding and thickening, the events in one part of the world have more significance for other areas. Globalization has knitted us together in a web of networks that are trafficked more heavily, faster, and to more locales than ever before.
- Nations are less able to manage their borders.
- Problems themselves are getting more complex.
- Everything is moving at a faster speed.

It only makes sense to seek out more rational and comprehensive formulations for global policies that incorporate the complexities and anticipate the interdependencies. The very idea of global policy is that we have a worldwide shared experience or interest that transcends our individual interests.

Rationales for Global Policies

There are several reasons why making policy for a wider geographic area can result in better outcomes. Public management has long understood the advantage of reaching out geographically for a regional approach or collaborating with other governments for an intergovernmental approach to designing policies. Making policy that strives to include forces beyond a government boundary can be good public management practice.

The nature of these global problems is so different—affecting communities directly and then spreading out their impact through worldwide networks, overwhelming a nation's capacity to address issues within their own borders and outside them, presenting a stark complexity due to our existing interconnectedness and interdependencies, and the rapid rate with which conditions change and re-express themselves—that each cascades into a new set of problems, so that addressing them through global policies appears as an attractive option. There exists a "global community" (Lomborg, 2004) who share interests beyond those articulated by nations' institutions and leaders and have "global concerns that cannot be successfully addressed unilaterally, bilaterally, or even regionally" (Simmons & de Jong Oudraat, 2001). Many global problems exceed the capabilities of nations to mitigate or solve them. In some instances, the causes of global problems are located outside the control of individual coalitions of nations. Other times, the problems are outside the power of one or more nations to address.

Externalities

Externalities are a type of market failure and many global problems are fostered by them. They are consequences of market exchanges that affect others, but the costs or benefits of those consequences are not accounted for in the price of the product or service. Typically, they are the movements of cross-border pollutants, such as climate change, ozone holes, oceanic micro-plastics, space junk, and the consequences of unsustainable global supply chains.

Exporting Problems

One nation adopting a policy may end a certain practice within its borders. While that might possibly end the problem within the nation, it may simply shift the problem elsewhere. For example, in the U.S., using high-sulfur coal has been outlawed as a way to reduce air pollution. Now, since it is illegal in the U.S., this same coal is exported to South Korea, which does not have a similar ban, and the coal is burned there in its power plants. Another example, imposing tougher international adoption standards in one country shifts the demand for adoptable children to other countries where standards are less strict. An additional example, destroying poppy, marijuana, or coca crops simply raises the price of the associated drug, encouraging others to fill this temporary supply shortfall. New communities that were never affected by illegal drug trade now suffer the consequences.

Global Commons

The "Tragedy of the Commons" is a familiar dilemma, made famous by Garrett Hardin (1968) (and later by Elinor Ostrom [1990]) by formalizing the logic of how depleting a shared natural resource made economic sense, for if one firm were to halt its activities, it would not redress the problem while leaving that firm to suffer economic losses. One country or even a few agreeing to restrictions on fishing only leaves the schools of fish at-risk to those nations' fishing fleets that have not adopted such restrictions. Threats to animal extinction, preserving tropical rain forests, overfishing, or overharvesting seafood are all global commons problems.

Global Corporations, Global Markets

The growth of multinational corporations (MNCs) and the expansion of markets have left countries unable to impose their own ideals about corporate governance and acceptable business behavior. Corporate taxation policy in one country is left at-risk by profits being repatriated to another nation that has lower tax rates. MNCs have moved their headquarters or operations when differentials in corporate tax policies are too generous to pass up. Antitrust policies are nearly impossible for one country to enforce when other countries have adopted different standards.

Global Crime

Criminal activities have gone global. Black markets for gambling, drugs, prostitution, slavery, smuggling, selling contraband, kidnapping for ransom, counterfeiting, and pirating expand across the global. The efforts of one country will not be effective in enforcing laws to stop these global crimes. The nations with weak enforcement capabilities allow crime to survive and thrive, making enforcement all the harder in countries that have stronger legal systems and more effective enforcement.

Global Democracy

With weak or non-existent democratic institutions, some nations will represent only a narrow spectrum of their citizens' interests. The voice on behalf of marginalized populations, whether based on race, ethnicity, income, religion, or gender, is frequently too faint to gain notice in the cacophony of diplomatic posturing and debate.

Global policy seeks to consider a more inclusive set of interests that may be expressed by non-state institutions (Scholte, 2000). Global policy seeks to enlarge and enhance the pluralism that advances our shared interests; not based on negotiations among nations, but on a true reflection of what benefits all who live on this planet. Nations retain an important role in creating global policies, but the prerogative they enjoy in international policies to hold exclusive franchise in representing their citizens' interests and claims is foregone.

What Makes a Problem Global?

Many good reasons exist for global policy, but which problems are actually global and what does it mean to classify a problem as being global—what policies would be different? Are the approaches different? Are responses designed differently or implementation different? The global nature of many problems facing the world is obvious. The SDGs are a definitive, but not exhaustive, list of problems that threaten the world's population, economies, societies, and/or environments. Surely not all problems are global problems, are they? We still recognize that some problems are local and particular to geographic regions, ethnic and/or religious norms and traditions, natural resources, and geography.

How are we to judge when problems are of such a nature that they should be deemed "global"? Looking for an answer through metrics is not very promising. Should global problems be determined by the number of countries involved, the percentage of the population affected, or the percentage of the population at-risk of being affected? If we were to employ such a method, what levels trigger the global problem classification—50 percent? If a condition or affliction affected 49 percent, is that 1 percent really the difference between global and local?

Such metrics are arbitrary at best. In addition, such quantifications take no account of intensity of certain problems. Would not the concerns over such events as initiation of mass atrocities, the rapid collapse of food production leading to famines, and/or outbreaks of highly lethal diseases qualify as worthy of being global problems and deserving of a global response, overriding some formulaic classification grounded in some calculus addressing just quantity? Would not populations at-risk, with few resources available to them, engender more sympathy for a global approach beyond just numbers? Worldwide humanitarian responses to natural and man-made disasters—even when isolated geographically—give evidence of a sense that intense problems that overwhelm local capacity deserve a collective response, even when the total population at-risk is less than 1 percent (and sometimes 1 percent of 1 percent) of our global population.

Determining which problems should be granted "global problem" status cannot be solved unequivocally. There will always be room for a debate over whether specific conditions are global problems.

Yet, understanding differences in problems around the world and providing a reasonable rationale for addressing them as global has the advantage of helping to marshal support for global policies. Explaining to constituencies and interested parties why a problem is global and why it is only rational to address it through global policies is a necessary aspect of building support for global policies. Just claiming problems to be global—even when it is done through the UN's SDGs— has limited power of persuasion to people and groups who have to make practical decisions about what type of actions they are and are not willing to support.

Getting nations to agree to act together and craft and support global policy is not easy. Just because issues are identified as being global does not mean that automatically there will be support in developing and implementing a global policy in response. While numerous issues may be claimed as global issues, support for global policies will differ according to the nature of the global problem.

The nature of the global problem—what makes it global—is useful in several ways.

- It makes clearer the justification of a problem being addressed by global policy.
- It anticipates the likeliness of global policy support.
- It clarifies how global problems could be approached through different policy designs.

Four basic types of global problems have been identified. They are not defined by their scope or scale, but on two factors: (a) the way in which the global problem affects people; and (b) the source of the cause of the global problem. The four types are described in Table 2.1.

Shared Global Problems

Climate change is an issue that affects people around the globe similarly and is the result of the same phenomenon. The rise in the earth's atmospheric

TABLE 2.1 Types of Global Problems

Types	Nature of Global Experience and Cause	Examples
Shared global problems	• Experiencing the same problem • Cause of the problem is the same	Climate change
Common global problems	• Experiencing the same problem • Cause of the problem is different	Poverty
Related global problems	• Experiencing different problems • Caused by another problem	Corruption
Connected global problems	• Experiencing same problems • Caused by another problem	Financial crises

temperatures is associated with rising sea levels, extreme weather events, ecological disruptions, threats to species, and higher risk of pandemics. The rising temperatures are linked to the increase in anthropomorphic carbon emissions, especially fossil fuel power plants, manufacturer plants, and gasoline engine vehicles. The causes of climate change come from global sources: a long list of countries across the world. The problem of rising temperatures and its impacts are universal.

The shared experiences and sources of climate change would appear to make it an excellent candidate to be addressed by global policy. The 21st Conference of the Parties (COP 21) to the 1992 United Nations Framework Convention on Climate Change (UNFCCC) without a firm policy of action suggests otherwise. The costs of reducing emissions are very different among the Global North and the Global South nations. The projected negative effects of rising temperatures affect different countries in different ways and some sooner, some later. The need to incur costs now to address climate change, but only realize the benefits in avoided costs, makes for difficult choices. The lack of certainty around whether climate change can be curtailed undermines full commitment to global policy.

Common Global Problems

Poverty is found around the world. While it is found more frequently in some countries than in others, the experience is very global. Causes of poverty are many: lack of natural resources, corrupt governments, fragile nations, persistent droughts, persistent conflict, concentration of low-wage industries, poor economies, weak education systems, debilitating diseases, and urbanization. The experience of poverty in nations all around the world is a common problem, acknowledging that the relative states of poverty vary widely. The causes of poverty differ across nations, but there are many commonalities.

Related Global Problems

Corruption is a global problem because it has so many negative consequences for business transactions and good governance. The corruption in one country does not affect others around the world directly, but it is related to many other problems that have global consequences. Financial investments can be captured and deterred by corruption. Investments for good projects are redirected to other countries in return for pay-offs. Corruption can impede access to funds to those most in need—corrupt cooperatives mean higher prices paid for more sustainable products that do not always make it to the farmers. Corrupt government officials steal millions intended for development projects. Lack of economic and social justice sustains inequalities, and stagnant growth can foster violence. The global problem is the same, but the consequences are very different for different communities.

Connected Global Problems

Financial contagion means the crisis in one country brings a financial crisis in others. The financial health of a country can be sound and well managed. That provides limited protection from a financial crisis in some other country, or even in one sector in one country, from starting a cascade of financial problems that brings economic damage to other countries. The focus of the global policy would be to identify and reform those economies that pose the greatest risks to financial failure. The global problem is the failure of good governance in one country that spreads to other countries.

Once these types of global problems are considered, it is easy to imagine disagreements and stimulating debates over how any given problem might be classified. While it may not matter which reason is invoked, as long as it is clear, it is global. Why a problem is deemed to be global is important as it informs the types of actions that are needed to respond. Of course, people will debate which problem is of which type, and it can be more than one. This is critical, because why it is a global problem guides the scale, scope, and rationale behind a global policy that is needed to address it.

Looking more closely at the four different types of global problems shows that the consequences of the problems are felt with much more irregularity and disparity than the general notion of a global problem suggests. Global problems are far more diverse in the effects on global communities. A call for global policies to be developed to address a global problem would benefit from understanding the different natures of global problems and recognizing how different global problems can be from one another.

Impediments to Good Global Policy

A global approach to solving problems is not welcomed by all. It infringes on a basic notion of sovereignty and self-determination. It limits the power of the nation's leaders to shape public policy. Nation-states still look to advance their interests in the context of global issues, the options for actions, the winners and the losers, and the consequences for constituencies. Using foreign policy—and thereby prescribing participation in, and support for, global governance—is not an unreasonable tactic. The matter is that globalization continues to limit the efficacy of that approach. The demands of global problems—stretching across national borders and requiring quick and comprehensive responses—are not addressed well by unilateralism or actions taken by agreement only by NATO, the G-7/8, or even the UN Security Council.

When global policies are examined in the context of a globalized world—networked, rapidly changing, and weakened state governance—it makes what is already difficult to do when traditional global institutions are engaged, even harder. There are several reasons why good global policies will be a limited option for solving global problems.

Takes Too Long

The slow and deliberative processes of international institutions are not well-suited to the rapid changes brought about by globalization. For all the enthusiasm around the COP 21 meeting in Paris, France and the efforts to reduce carbon emissions, the "21" means that is how many times this UN initiative has met. The UNFCCC is an international environmental treaty negotiated at the Earth Summit in Rio de Janeiro in June 1992. The COP first convened in Berlin in 1995. The World Trade Organization (WTO) procedures for resolution of disputes reflects a similar lack of urgency. In February 1996, a complaint was filed with the WTO by Ecuador, Guatemala, Honduras, Mexico, and the United States against the European Union and was resolved over 15 years later. While it is the longest dispute process to date, complaints filed at the WTO typically take years to resolve, and that schedule is being delayed even more from resource shortages (WTO, 2012). Needing 15 years to work on such important issues may not seem so unusual to the international community, but those rhythms are too slow paced for what is needed to address the global problems we face.

Too Much Log-Rolling and Too Many Logs

Building a consensus among nations with diverse interests will always be a challenge. The growth of the economies of many nations has raised their influence in international forums and makes the process of agreeing to global polices even more difficult. The Doha Development Agenda, more often referred to as the Doha Round, is the latest cycle of trade negotiations under the umbrella of the WTO, the Geneva-based arbiter of global trade. The Doha Round is working to help developing countries join the global marketplace and boost their economies as a result. The round was launched in November 2001—and it is still not over (*The Guardian*, 2012). The idea of bringing all 155 WTO members together to agree on complex global trade rules is a mammoth task, with so many interests and counter interests affected by any given rule. The prospects for all these interests and disputes being aligned is poor and the time taken so far on it provides testimony to its impractibility.

No New World Order

In an address before a Joint Session of Congress (September 11, 1990), President George H. W. Bush called for a "New World Order." The U.S.-led coalition had just invaded Iraq in response to its invasion of Kuwait. The then Soviet Union was disintegrating piece by piece and total dissolution seemed inevitable. The call sought to set out an intellectual template for major new alignments of national interests and allies in the imminent end of the Cold War. While the recognition of new global alignments was timely, the presumption that a nation's shared values provided a sufficiently solid platform on which coalitions and mutual interests could be convened proved ill-fated. Fifteen years later, people and communities are finding shared interests and mutuality through global communities; globalization appears to be fracturing the strategic interests of nations.

The Cold War drove nations together in coalitions for shoring up security, fighting proxy wars, and waging competition over markets and claims of ideological superiority. Post-Cold War, the reduced threat of nuclear holocaust appeared to have given nations more room to maneuver and represent their national interests in other alliances. However, the porosity and permeability of states' borders is more likely convincing many of the need for stronger national representations of national interests rather than subsuming them under some new world order coalition. The hoped for alliances, based on shared values around democratic and market-based ideals espoused by the U.S., has less resonance with other nation's leaders than President Bush had believed.

Unfortunate Theory of Global Policy

Few matters are more characteristic of globalization than the speed at which news travels on the internet. Smart phone photos and videos are staples of the breaking news stories. Television news programs, bloggers, and news sites are providing analysis of news before more conventional news outlets get to do interviews in the "spin room." One ramification is the shorter length of time between an event happening and people having the issue framed for them: was the airplane crash the result of terrorism? Did government officials know about a threat prior to it happening? Are attacks on a village the work of a known rebel group? Are the military actions by other nations a threat to other countries' security? The speed at which news travels means little or no time for fact checking. Modern news is more about reporting what someone saw or thought they saw and the comments of others on what might or might not have been seen. With so many news outlets, it is easy to see how one event could be represented in numerous different ways to many different communities.

Purposeful and impactful global policy, even when done in response to an emergency or unforeseen event, requires fact checks, review of claims and their legitimacy, and assembling many different reports, even before a possible response or approach is proposed. Rationales for actions need to be crafted and grounded in reasonable expectations. Justifications for how nations will benefit need to be affirmed.

By the time a thoughtful policy proposal is developed and vetted, people and communities already have it framed the way they heard it. That makes persuading people to support a global policy all the harder, because many more people have a clear idea about some of the issues and its implications.

In theory, global policies are needed if significant global problems are to be addressed effectively. Once the realities of designing and carrying out global policies are clarified, the chances for success are diminished significantly. In a highly globalized world, the prospects for success are even lower. The problem is not in designing global policies that would help, but fewer reasons to believe in significant enthusiasm to build a coalition around supporting such policies. Global policies are not defined as to what is and what is not—but who is included in the decision and whose interests are taken into account when policies are developed. That dimension reflects both the promise and the pitfalls of global policies.

The Future of Global Policy and Global Governance

Global policy suggests a unity of purposes and interests, an awareness of the interconnectedness of our lives, and the need to address global problems with a global policy that captures a shared experience. Globalization has indeed stitched us together, not into a seamless sheet of cloth, but rather into a patchwork quilt. It turns out that globalization has made people feel more alike through engagements in global communities, and nations more aware of their differences and how globalization is challenging their governance. We are too diverse for one size fits all global policies to garner much real and sustained support.

No doubt, there are numerous opportunities for global policies to be crafted and adopted by international institutions. Globalization is bringing change so quickly that the alignment of deliberative processes of policy formulation and urgency to act, as global problems express themselves in unexpected ways and with unforeseen speed, has only a small window of opportunity for conventional global policy, and with it conventional global governance, to be deployed.

There will always be a gap between the ideal of policy and ambition, as well as inspiration, and the realities of what can be accomplished on the ground given seen and unforeseen constraints and barriers. Edwardian England acknowledged these prospects in the phrase "noble failure," not accomplishing what was sought after, but seeking to accomplish them for all the right reasons and intentions.

This ideal allowed for recognition of the value of those who tried to do something extraordinary, heroic, game changing. The failure to achieve should not be allowed completely to eclipse the qualities it takes in people to tackle challenges and problems that are too big, too daunting, and too intimidating— but strive to attain the goal anyway. Many may see a resonance with the MDGs and SDGs. While ambitious, you cannot fail if you do not try.

Globalization is making the gap between conventional global policy ambitions and global governance impact so large it cannot be assigned to the usual reasons of why we fall short of ambitious goals. The rapid transformations of globalization on society, communities, markets, values, and expectations have left solutions that are developed in the realms of policy formulation to have limited relevance on the ground. The assumptions and assertions behind too many policies are far flung compared to what is really happening. As long as the funding is sustained, the speeches are made, and good intentions are hoisted above outcomes and impact, social innovations will be crowded out. New approaches to solving global problems not only need fresh thinking, but the flexibility to conduct global governance in a new way as well. We need to invent and develop new ways of responding to global problems that are effective, purposeful, and have sufficient support.

The very forces of globalization that are posing challenges, leaving established institutions, ideas, and theories diminished and less powerful, are the very ones that can be tapped to develop new, innovative, and inspiring approaches to global governance. To achieve these new ways, we have to set aside many ideas about governance, the roles played by different sectors, and what it means to be accountable, successful, and impactful.

3

GLOBAL GOVERNANCE AND MULTISECTOR COLLABORATION

The need for better global governance has been called for alongside the organization of anti-globalization protests. Stiglitz (2002) provided a scathing critique of the poor performance and misguided policies of international institutions, based on his inside view with positions in the White House and the World Bank. Murphy (2000) offered a scornful assessment of the state of global governance, calling it crowded, chaotic, and done poorly. Easterly (see Easterly & Easterly, 2001, 2006; Easterly & Levine, 2001; Easterly, 2007, 2014) has made himself a one-man global governance wrecking machine in his many writings on the utter failure of international institutions and their efforts to stimulate growth and alleviate poverty in developing countries. He argues that the tools of development such as promoting education, providing foreign assistance, investing in infrastructure and equipment, curtailing population growth, and making loans and then forgiving those same loans, have failed. They have not resulted in the hoped for benefits to poor countries as promised because of the failure to apply proper economic principles in such global governance efforts.

An assessment of the efficacy of multilateral aid organizations finds them weak on good global governance. They are composed of states as members with limited influence from non-state actors. Notwithstanding approval of military incursions by the United Nations (UN) Security Council in nations contending with internal conflicts, the sanctity of sovereignty and non-intervention in the internal affairs of other states is the core principle of the international cooperation system. Financial resources are inadequate for implementing international programs and administrative services. Their overall impact is small compared to global needs. These organizations are challenged over issues of legitimacy, fair representation, accountability, and efficient operations. Decision-making is slow and cumbersome. National preoccupations usually trump common interests, and reforms of any kind are difficult to implement as national interests always trump global interests (Fréchette, 2007).

Many serious prescriptions have been offered on how to improve global governance in response to the challenges it faces in light of globalization. Nye and Donahue (2000) were early to make the call for fundamental change in the conduct of global governance, although only as far as it did not challenge national sovereignty. Held (2004) and his colleagues (Held & McGrew, 2002) and (Held & Koenig-Archibugi, 2005) have focused their attentions on how to design global governance practices so social democratic values are advanced and to ensure greater accountability from the multisector institutions that are now conducting global governance. Dervis (2005) proposes reforms to existing international institutions that would rejuvenate their relevance and effectiveness in a globalized world, as does Stiglitz (2006) who seeks a reformed and more democratized international system.

More effective, more accountable, and more democratic are the dominant themes for improving global governance. None of the authors argues that their proposed reforms for multilateral institutions to promote good global governance have prospects to be adopted anytime soon. Assessments of the reasons why conventional global governance is so poor and fails to meet program goals is invaluable for informing how alternative forms of global governance—such as multisector collaborations—might be designed and organized. Prescriptions for curing international institutions of their "governance sclerosis" have few realistic hopes of being adopted. It appears that at this point, as a response to global problems, our global policy grasp exceeds our global governance reach.

Global governance is a logical and reasonable response to global problems. Achieving good global governance will need to be animated other than through conventional global governance. The efforts span beyond the power and influence of any one power, ally, regional government, or multilateral organization. As we invent those new forms of governance that recognize Rosenau's distant proximity realities, we: (a) anticipate that remote events will be consequential, but once anticipated, they will no longer be remote, just one more usual part of the new global governance landscape; (b) expect volatility and instability, but once resilience, adaptation, and flexibility are built into the arrangement, organization, and management of global governance, they are no longer volatile, just a new-normal part of the globalized world; and (c) rely less on governments and corporations and more on global citizens to lead change and be the social entrepreneurs and social innovators, and seeing governments and corporation in a supporting role will be normal.

We are at a juncture in time when globalization has knitted us together through networks, awareness, and a growing sense of affiliation, but we remain tethered to international perspectives that see the interests of the nation first, even when the efforts to protect those interests only make global problems worse and/or more difficult to solve.

The Rise of Multisector Collaboration

Multisector collaboration has gained popularity as an approach to global governance. Today, they are a common feature on the global governance landscape. This willingness to accept corporations and non-governmental organizations (NGOs) into activities traditionally assigned to governments represents a significant change in the approach to global governance. Businesses, NGOs, and other constituencies are expected to participate in policy formulation within their own nations, and these interests are carried through to the formulation of global policy and global governance interests. The emergence of transnational democratic movements, global NGOs, and global corporations have added new global governance actors whose activities, programs, and influence sometimes complement, sometimes compete with, and sometimes contradict global policies of nations and international institutions.

The emergence of multisector collaborations has been welcomed by governments and international institutions. The leading development institutions promote multisector collaboration as a mainstay of their global governance approach. For example, the UN Foundation was created in 1998. Ted Turner provided $1 billion to the UN Foundation in support of its efforts. The main issue areas that the Foundation addresses are child health, climate change, energy, sustainable development, technology, women and girls, population, and supporting the UN (UN Foundation, n.d.). They explain their approach as a dynamic partnership organization that brings together a diverse set of stakeholders to take on some of the most pressing global challenges. UN Foundation corporate partnerships link the entrepreneurial spirit and expertise of the private sector with the social, economic, and environmental objectives of the UN. The partnerships are results-driven and include scientists, foundations, membership organizations, and faith communities to make a difference in the important work the UN does across a broad range of issues (UN Foundation, n.d.). Some of the biggest global campaigns that the UN Foundation has been involved in include Polio Eradication Initiative, the Measles and Rubella Initiative, the Global Alliance for Clean Cookstoves, Sustainable Energy for All, Nothing but Nets, Girl Up, Shot@Life, and the Better World Campaign, among others (UN Foundation, n.d.).

The United States Agency for International Development (USAID) has embraced the opportunities for multisector collaboration and made it a central theme for improving agency performance. Former USAID Chief Administrator, Dr. Rajiv Shah, stated, "This agency is no longer satisfied with writing big checks to big contractors and calling it development." By contrast, the reform process is supposed to establish a "more strategic, focused and results-oriented approach" at USAID. As part of this reformed approach, USAID aims to strengthen its cooperation with "institutions, private sector partners and civil society organizations that serve as engines of growth and progress for their own nations." To achieve sustainable development, USAID plans to combine this novel approach with "increased investment directly to partner governments." Furthermore, by collaborating with research universities and facilitating innovative solutions "to intractable development challenges," USAID attempts to stay ahead of the curve in the development world (Nixon, 2014).

The World Bank describes the value of their efforts to promote partnerships as follows:

> There are tens of thousands of donor-funded development projects worldwide, each governed by countless demands, guidelines and procedures designed to protect the projects and ensure that aid gets to the poor. Experience shows that capacity in developing countries can be improved and strengthened quickly when donors better coordinate their activities and harmonize their procedures. As such, the World Bank works with other international institutions and donors, civil society and professional and academic associations to improve the coordination of aid policies and practices in countries, at the regional level and at the global level.
>
> *(World Bank, 2015)*

Despite the non-conventional approaches to global governance that multisector collaboration offers, the enthusiasm and support for them has become the convention for international development agencies.

Defining Multisector Collaboration

There is no agreed upon definition that clearly distinguishes multisector collaboration from other forms of partnerships. Some generalized descriptions of multisector collaborations capture the basic idea.

Governance scholar, Robert Agranoff (2006), suggests that new approaches to governance that involve networks of actors have become a mandatory tool of the trade. Today's public administrator must engage other governments, businesses, and NGOs in order to effectively respond to the complexity and urgency of problems in the globalizing world. As Eva Sørensen and Jacob Torfing (2009) further explain, new forms of negotiated governance through the formation of public–private partnerships, strategic alliances, dialogue groups, consultative committees, and interorganizational networks have burgeoned to compensate for the limits and failures of both state and market regulation. In essence, the goal of the global governance networks is to "produce the maximum possible public value, greater than the sum of what each lone player could accomplish without collaboration" (Kooiman, 2008).

Reinicke and Deng (2000) described such governance networks as melding the advantages of three different sectors: nations and international organizations bring capacity-building skills, coordination and enforcement, and rule-making power. Civil society brings voluntary energy and legitimacy. Business brings financial resources.

In fact, there is a plethora of terms used to describe the concept of organizations working together to address global problems: multisector alliance, cross-sector alliance, network governance, governance networks, multisector alliances, multisector governance, multisector networks, multisector governance, multisector partnerships, network minimalism, trans-sectoral governance, public–private partnerships, cross-sector collaboration, megacommunities, global alliance networks, and corporate responsibility coalitions. There are several reasons for this growing inventory of names used to describe multisector collaboration.

First, as a new area of research, many scholars and practitioners have discovered and explored the idea independently and simultaneously. Over time, some terms should begin to find favor and become the labels of choice. Second, a clear distinction is not always made between multisector collaboration as an approach to global governance and the formation of an entity that carries out that approach. Third, the concept itself—multisector collaboration—is very broad, allowing for many variations and permutations of the same basic idea. For example, is there a difference worth noting between an alliance, a network, a partnership, or a coalition in the context of global governance? They are generally just a different word for a similar idea. Despite the variations among the definitions of multisector collaborations, a commonality undergirds the concepts. The basic notion is that organizations from different sectors will agree to work together to address some global problem.

The common sectors that are anticipated to be involved are government, business, and nonprofit. Government also refers to international organizations or regional political entities like the European Union. The nonprofit sector includes NGOs, community organizations, churches and religious groups, or volunteer organizations. Business can be firms of all sizes, but also banks and investors, and those interstitial companies—social enterprises or benefits corporations.

A Typology of Multisector Collaborations?

Unsurprisingly, there have been attempts to develop taxonomies of the multisector collaboration landscape. Among other benefits, a taxonomy could help potential multisector collaboration partners to discern which multisector collaboration would be the best "fit" in order to achieve their objectives. Malena (2004) argues that an "exhaustive typology" of the multistakeholder partnerships landscape is not possible. She suggests that "ideal types" are a better way to create a structure that describes the multisector collaboration environment. Malena also provides a summary of the most common ideal types from the multisector collaboration literature. According to her, the most prevalent ideal types make a distinction between "primarily operational v. advocacy-oriented partnerships or between process, project, and product-oriented partnerships." Additionally, frameworks that separate between "negotiation, coordination, and implementation" as the function of multisector collaborations are also popular. Yet, if we take a step back, and reflect upon what constitutes a multisector collaboration, it becomes clear that the question that we should be asking instead is: what benefit do people, organizations, institutions, businesses, and governments collaborate in the first place?

Multisector collaborations tackle a wide variety of issues in many different ways. It is important to note, however, that the multisector nature of these novel governance entities should not have any value in and of itself. It's not about their function, but how they help those participating in the partnership. The bottom line should be that collaborative approaches are justified because they create better results for all involved parties. This is not always the case. Partners often decide to collaborate in the same multisector collaboration for different reasons. Hence, many multisector collaborations raise questions about the real motivations of the members who join that particular partnership. Are partners involved for legitimate global governance purposes or are they merely practicing a form of window dressing? These concerns frequently arise when large corporations decide to become part of a multisector collaboration.

Multisector Collaboration in Action

Multisector collaborations represent a diverse range of entities that have come together to address a global problem. They take different approaches, are organized in different ways, use different forms of governance, and establish different types of relationships among their members and/or partners. Illustrative examples of multisector collaborations are described below.

UN Principles for Responsible Investment

The first example, the Principles for Responsible Investment (PRI), is a multisector collaboration between "the global investment industry, intergovernmental organizations, civil society and academia." First and foremost, PRI is the result of private sector actors (institutional investors) collaborating with public sector entities (the UN Environment Programme Finance Initiative and the UN Global Compact). The partnership's goal is to "help investors integrate the consideration of environmental, social and governance (ESG) issues into investment decision-making and ownership practices across all asset classes and regions, and in so doing, help contribute to the creation of a sustainable financial system." As of July 2016, PRI had 1,553 signatories (i.e., asset owners, investment managers, service providers) that manage $45 trillion in assets (Principles for Responsible Investment, n.d.). It is important to note, that PRI's private sector stakeholders are at the helm of this multisector collaboration. Apart from institutional shareholders, "asset owners such as pension fund trustees" also have considerable influence within the multisector collaboration's governance structure through seats on PRI's advisory board (Waddell, 2011). Moreover, the multisector collaboration gains greater reach and legitimacy by collaborating with the UN Environment Programme Finance Initiative and the UN Global Compact.

Fair Labor Association

The Fair Labor Association (FLA) focuses on auditing and advocacy efforts in order "to promote and protect workers' rights and to improve working conditions globally through adherence to international standards." Instead of focusing on developing collaboration between the private and the public sectors, the FLA connects businesses, NGOs, and colleges/universities. Consequently, the board of directors of this nonprofit multisector collaboration is made up of "six business representatives, six Labor/NGO representatives, six university representatives and a Chair." Companies that want to sell clothing and other products at colleges/universities that are collaborating with the FLA, are required also to participate in the multisector collaboration. In turn, these businesses have to "commit to the 10 Principles of Fair Labor and Responsible Sourcing and agree to uphold the FLA Workplace Code of Conduct throughout their entire supply chain."

Global Fund

While private sector entities and NGOs were mainly responsible for launching the two multisector collaborations described above, the UN was the driving force for the establishment of the Global Fund. "It was the dream of Kofi Annan, former Secretary-General of the United Nations, to establish a 'war chest' of funds to fight [AIDS, tuberculosis, and malaria]." Thus, the Global Fund is not an implementation agency. Instead, it operates as an "international financing institution" that works with governments, private sector entities, NGOs, and communities, which are affected by AIDS, tuberculosis, and malaria. The Global Fund has a Secretariat, based in Geneva, that handles the daily operations of the private foundation. Similar to the first two multisector collaborations, the Global Fund's governance is administered by a diverse board, "which is composed of representatives from donor and recipient governments, civil society, the private sector, private foundations, and communities living with and affected by the diseases."

Forest Stewardship Council

After the 1992 Earth Summit in Rio failed to produce an agreement to stop deforestation, a group of businesses, environmentalists, and community leaders came together to create the Forest Stewardship Council (FSC). Gathered in the first FSC General Assembly in 1993 in Toronto, Canada, the group set out to create a voluntary, market-based approach that would improve forest practices worldwide. At the time, FSC represented an alternative to boycotts of forest products, which were shown to be counterproductive since they devalued forestland.

Originally headquartered in the forested region of Oaxaca, Mexico in 1994, the FSC Secretariat was relocated to Bonn, Germany in 2003. In 1995, the US chapter of the FSC was established, and is now headquartered in Minneapolis, Minnesota. Today, FSC operates in more than 80 countries, wherever forests are present (Forest Stewardship Council, n.d.).

Kimberley Process Certification Scheme

In May 2000, responding to a growing grassroots movement on "blood diamonds," governments and the diamond industry came together in the South African town of Kimberley to combat the trade in diamonds from conflict zones. The result of these negotiations was the Kimberley Process Certification Scheme (KPCS), setting up an internationally recognized certification system for rough diamonds and establishing national import/export standards. In November 2002, 52 governments ratified and adopted the KPCS, which was fully implemented in August 2003. The Kimberley Process is made up of 80 participating countries representing most of the nations involved in the diamond trade. It also includes participation from advocacy organizations and the diamond industry (Global Policy Forum, n.d.).

To belong to the Kimberley Process, member countries are supposed to meet certain requirements. They are not supposed to produce conflict diamonds. They must trade diamonds only with each other. They must also attach Kimberley Process certificates to their exports of rough, or uncut, diamonds. By these arrangements, it is hoped that conflict diamonds will be kept out of the global diamond supply chain. Regrettably, however, the Kimberley Process is easily evaded by diamond smugglers. Worse, it is so limited in scope that it grants "conflict free" certification to diamonds mined in violent and inhumane settings (Brilliant Earth, n.d.).

The U.S. President's Emergency Plan for AIDS Relief

The U.S. President's Emergency Plan for AIDS Relief (PEPFAR) is the U.S. Government's initiative to help save the lives of those suffering from HIV/AIDS around the world. Founded in 2008, funding of $48 billion was provided by U.S. Congress over the next 5 years to combat global HIV/AIDS, tuberculosis, and malaria; $39 billion for HIV and the Global Fund, $4 billion for tuberculosis, and $5 billion for malaria.

PEPFAR continues to be a cornerstone of U.S. global health efforts. As a component of the Global Health Initiative, PEPFAR works with other health and development programs and coordinates these efforts. The goal of the coordination is to further the reach of bilateral assistance, leverage the work of multilateral organizations, promote country ownership, and increase the sustainability of national health programs.

Why Has Multisector Collaboration Become So Popular?

The idea of multisector collaborations has gained popularity as an alternative approach to addressing global problems. This is surprising in several ways. What has made people more receptive to businesses playing a bigger role in global governance? How do organizations with such different goals find common ground? Why would businesses volunteer to help solve global problems? There are several reasons that help explain their favorable reputation.

Fragile Failed States

The world is in a state of conflict and poor governance beyond doubt. A measure of the state of governance of nations presents gloomy findings. The Fragile State Index counts 38 nations as being in one form or another of alert. Most of the countries are in Africa or the Middle East (The Fund for Peace, 2015). Another 27 nations are on high warning. Together, that is around one-third of all the nations in the world that are too fragile to provide security, prosperity, and well-being for its citizens. An important aspect is the failure of government agencies and state-owned enterprises (SOEs) to provide basic public services for its citizens. Looking for other institutions such as global NGOs that provide humanitarian relief and development support for needy communities and tapping into the power and influence of global corporations through their foundations, investments and supply chain operations is a logical response.

Failed Privatization

Privatization and deregulation welcomed industries to operate and provide services that were once thought of as the prerogative of governments. Privatization has been implemented in many sectors with mixed results, but the water sector is the poster child for its failed efforts and generation of political backlash. It has limited support today as a global governance approach, especially associated with the Sustainable Development Goals (SDGs). Many cities that signed 20-year or longer concessions with private water companies have terminated these agreements and returned to municipal control of urban water provision. Buenos Aires, Johannesburg, Paris, Accra, Berlin, La Paz, Maputo, and Kuala Lumpur are among the 180 cities that have all "re-municipalized" their water systems since the mid-2000s (Vidal, 2015).

Corporate Social Responsibility

The efforts made by global corporations to promote sustainability, education, health and safety, and well-being in the name of corporate responsibility have risen dramatically in just this century. Examples include Unilever:

> Unilever has world-class research and development facilities, but we are constantly looking to work with partners with great technical solutions, whether they are individuals, businesses, existing suppliers, universities or NGOs. We will work with anyone who has an idea that will help us achieve our ambition of doubling the size of our business while reducing our environmental footprint and increasing our positive social impact.

And Johnson & Johnson:

> The Johnson & Johnson Family of Companies recognizes the importance of building strong working partnerships that can advance the quality of health care globally, respect the environment, and support local communities. Whether you are a research scientist working on an innovative concept, a biotech/pharma company in search of a development partner for your product, a business professional interested in exploring creative commercialization solutions for your company's product, or a supplier with materials, goods or services that can potentially benefit our companies, we can shape the future of healthcare. At our corporate headquarters and at our Family of Companies around the world, we work closely with scientists, technology experts and other professionals from the global academic and business communities to develop and market new products every day.

These are illustrations of the expansion of global corporations into addressing global problems affecting people and communities. The focus on corporate responsibility is more popular in the U.S. and the EU, but India's Companies Law (2013) now requires firms to spend 2 percent of their net profits on corporate social responsibility activities.

Foundations and New Corporate Philanthropy

The best-known foundation is the Bill & Melinda Gates Foundation Partnerships:

> We do all of our work in collaboration with grantees and other partners, who join with us in taking risks, pushing for new solutions, and harnessing the transformative power of science and technology. We strive to engage with our grantees and partners in a spirit of trust, candid communication,

and transparency. Our collective efforts also depend on the support and resources of governments, the private sector, communities, and individuals.

They gave $3,320,725,374 in 2013, eclipsing all other foundations. The remaining nine largest foundations gave a combined $6 trillion that same year. Corporate philanthropy has also grown dramatically. As shown in Table 3.1, the top ten corporate philanthropies gave over $1.3 billion in 2013. Private philanthropists also contribute their share.

Those funding levels may pale in comparison to the total needs of people in communities, and not all of this giving is directed at SDGs. However, it is a major reason for the rapid rise of multisector collaboration: gifts from philanthropists are funding these partnerships. Without this giving, where would the partnerships get the funds to support their efforts? Non-government funding directed to solving global problems is a major reason for the emergence of multisector collaborations.

Multisector collaboration presents both a challenge and an opportunity for those looking to improve global governance and advance the SDGs. On the one hand, they do not conform well to the accepted views on the role of government and good governance. On the other, they present one of the most promising approaches in helping to solve our most pressing and difficult global problems.

Clearly, more research is needed to better understand governance networks and to make more coherent and comprehensive assessments about their legitimacy in taking on governance responsibilities in what has traditionally been thought of as within the government's prerogative.

TABLE 3.1 Top Foundational Giving

Rank	Name/(state)	Total Giving ($)	As of Fiscal Year End Date
1	Novartis Patient Assistance Foundation, Inc. (NJ)	452,981,816	12/31/2013
2	Wells Fargo Foundation (CA)	186,775,875	12/31/2013
3	The Wal-Mart Foundation, Inc. (AR)	182,859,236	01/31/2013
4	The Bank of America Charitable Foundation, Inc. (NC)	160,479,886	12/31/2013
5	The JPMorgan Chase Foundation (NY)	115,516,001	12/31/2012
6	GE Foundation (CT)	124,512,065	12/31/2013
7	The Coca-Cola Foundation, Inc. (GA)	98,175,501	12/31/2013
8	Citi Foundation (NY)	78,372,150	12/31/2013
9	ExxonMobil Foundation (TX)	72,747,966	12/31/2013
10	Caterpillar Foundation (IL)	55,998,836	12/31/2013

Source: Foundation Center's database as of September 19, 2015.

Solving the Fukuyama Paradox

In his 2004 book, *State-Building: Governance and World Order in the 21st Century*, Francis Fukuyama clarified a difficult dilemma that hung heavily on the enthusiasm to bring about change through the Millennium Development Goals (MDGs) and now the SDGs. He keenly posited two observations about development efforts and institutional capacity building that seemed to remove any hope in advancing development and making a better world for those in underserved communities.

First, he considered the relationship between any given nation's provision of social services in terms of: (a) the scope of state functions, and (b) strength of state institutions. Fukuyama argued that it is simply good governance for states not to provide more complex and expansive social services than they have the capacity to support and administer properly. He explained that it is this consideration, more than any other, that explains failed development policies and efforts to bring inclusive growth to so many developing economies. Fukuyama's claim underscores the increased emphasis on capacity building as a key element to successful development.

> Specifically, capacity building encompasses the country's human, scientific, technological, organizational, institutional and resource capabilities. A fundamental goal of capacity building is to enhance the ability to evaluate and address the crucial questions related to policy choices and modes of implementation among development options, based on an understanding of environment potentials and limits and of needs perceived by the people of the country concerned.
>
> *(United Nations Conference on Environment and Development, 1992)*

Many of the SDG targets are aimed specifically at building capacities in developing countries. Fukuyama's second point spoke specifically to the idea of capacity building. He argued that past efforts to enhance "local" capacity have not only failed but have made matters worse. First, he argued that technology and

TABLE 3.2 Transferability of Capacity Building Factors

Component	Discipline	Transferability
Organizational design and management	Management, Public administration, economics	High
Institutional design	Political science, economics, law	Medium
Basis of legitimization	Political science	Medium to low
Social and cultural factors	Sociology, anthropology	Low

Source: Francis Fukuyama, *State-Building: Governance and World Order in the 21st Century.*

expertise does not transfer easily from developed to developing societies. Although capacity building is now a central component of global development strategies, they cannot be effective no matter how it is tried. As shown in Table 3.2, he identified four types of knowledge and technologies associated with capacity building and ranked them according to how difficult they are to transfer.

Fukuyama considered such governance capacities to take many years and the result of a more organic development of institutions, public norms, and local political economy. Second, he suggested, paradoxically, that making efforts to transplant Western-style technical, management, business structure, and approaches only crowds out the establishment of local capacities. As long as money and institutions are brought to countries, it impedes the authentic establishment of capacity that works well in individual countries. If true, Fukuyama's thesis is a depressing and sobering assessment of the poor prospects for developing countries and those communities to achieving better conditions any time soon.

Multisector collaborations offer the perfect antidote to Fukuyama's trenchant indictment of conventional global governance efforts to bolster states' capacities and to support development. The operations and successes of multisector collaborations are not dependent on local government capacities. They are intended to fill the very governance gap that Fukuyama speaks to. Since local capacities, customs, and norms are critical considerations in achieving good global governance, designing activities to align with these factors is what successful multisector collaborators do. One possible objection to multisector collaborators playing such a role is the fact that they are not government-centric forms of global governance. For Fukuyama, such a condition invalidates the legitimacy of many multisector collaborators, but how many people in underserved communities would choose his ideological purity regarding issues of legitimacy over working with multisector collaborators to provide the basic services needed so desperately? Building strong multisector collaborations provides a great opportunity to fill the global governance gap and to answer Fukuyama's well-placed critique.

The Promise and Pitfalls of Multisector Collaboration

The general view is that the three main sectors—government, business, and nonprofit—bring complementary strengths to solving global problems. The government brings legitimacy, funding, administrative staff, and program goals. Business brings funding, management, and technical expertise. Nonprofit offers knowledge of community needs and institutional history of past efforts and experiences (Forrer et al., 2014). Given the "wicked" nature of many global problems today (Kolko, 2012), understanding and solving problems requires multiple perspectives.

TABLE 3.3 Perspectives in Multisector Collaborations

	Nonprofit	Business	Government
Types	• Indigenous/local, regional, state, national, international • Formal/informal community groups • Issue-oriented/task-oriented • From broad public interest perspective to private narrow focus	• Local, regional, corporations, and multinational • Micro, small, medium, and large	• Local, regional, state, national, international and regulatory entities
Organizational goals	• Fulfilling mission and values • Pursue principled beliefs	• Profit • Pursue material interest	• Delivery of public goods and services/meeting public needs
Factors that limits actors' influence	• The size and diversity of the NGO community, leading to fragmentation • Financial resources • Representation, accountability, and transparency • Increased competition for limited resources	• Limited understanding of the social issue at hand • Potential distrust by NGOs, including watchdog and consumer groups • Suffer from negative stereotypes, such as being considered hegemonic and exploitative	• The traditional roles of government were no longer sufficient to carry out its responsibilities in an increasingly globalized world (Salamon, 2002) • Impediments include insufficient budgets, absent training, unreasonable policy expectations • "Hollowed-out" government (referring to a government with little or no capacity to manage its partners, let alone deliver services itself) (Goldsmith & Eggers, 2004) • Lack of financial and human resources
Governance functions of each actor in GGEs	Can also serve the role of integrator, which serves to connect the components of the network, facilitate interaction, and resolve problems (Goldsmith & Eggers, 2004)	Can also serve the role of integrator, which serves to connect the components of the network, facilitate interaction, and resolve problems (Goldsmith & Eggers, 2004)	• Can serve as administrative core • As facilitators and conductors, rather than implementing and dictating policies and program approaches (Salamon, 2002) • Typically serves the role of integrator, which serves to connect the components of the network, facilitate interaction, and resolve problems (Salamon, 2002)

Developing solutions to global problems could mean addressing issues that fall outside the mandates of many government agencies and expertise. Employing partnerships opens up avenues to bring in experts to work together on solving global problems. Multisector collaboration can introduce new information and new ideas that are needed to address difficult global problems. Table 3.3 describes some basic characteristics of organizations in these different sectors that proffer diverse perspectives and approaches and offer opportunities for synergies.

Using multisector collaboration as an approach to solving global problems does not guarantee success. Unless properly designed and managed, they may end up benefitting only a single group out of all their partners. Multisector collaboration has been criticized for only promoting the interests of their corporate participants. The FLA, described above, falls squarely into this category. While the FLA's mission is to "promote and protect workers' rights," "its board of directors includes no actual worker representation or union" (Finnegan, 2013). The FLA has a board that is supposed to be evenly split between members from the business, NGO/labor, and university sectors. Yet Brian Finnegan, who is the Global Workers' Rights coordinator at the American Federation of Labor-Congress of Industrial Organizations (AFL-CIO), argued that the only labor rights group deserving the name, the Maquila Solidarity Network (MSN), left the multisector collaboration in February 2013. As a result, the FLA is firmly controlled by its commercial interests that are shared by the business and university representatives. In addition, the FLA relies on its corporate members for two-thirds of its revenues. Put simply, the FLA has an agency conflict because it is financially dependent on the very companies whose factories it is auditing with the help of contractors. Finnegan asserts that the "overwhelming influence of the company bottom line has dominated the agenda[s] of the FLA . . . while the workers who are supposed to benefit . . . have been marginalized or altogether ignored." He elaborated that the FLA has not "demonstrated results regarding their ability to improve workplace standards, respect for rights like freedom of association or to bring wages above poverty level."

The KPCS is a multisector collaboration that has also been criticized (Choyt, 2013). It has struggled with conflicting agendas of its members. KPCS's main objective is to "stop the trade in 'conflict diamonds' and ensure that diamond purchases are not financing violence by rebel movements and their allies seeking to undermine legitimate governments." To achieve this goal, KPCS brought together the diamond-producing countries, the international diamond industry, and civil society organizations. KPCS states on its website that it "imposes extensive requirements on its members to enable them to certify shipments of rough diamonds as conflict-free." However, in 2011, the NGO Global Witness left the KPCS because of its "refusal to evolve and address the clear links between diamonds, violence and tyranny [that] has rendered it increasingly outdated."

Global Witness cited Zimbabwe as an example of a diamond-producing country that continues to increase its export of diamonds with a Kimberley certificate, despite widespread "government-led human rights abuses, smuggling, and weak internal controls" (IRIN, 2009). Attempts by Global Witness to reform KPCS in concert with other NGOs failed because any reform proposal requires approval from all governments that take part in KPCS. Zimbabwe, among other African governments, evidently prefers the KPCS in its current form and therefore President Mugabe shows "no interest in reform" of the existing situation (Global Witness, 2011).

Concerns about Multisector Collaborations

There are general concerns about the basic presumptions of multisector collaboration that go beyond the success of any individual partnership. As with both FLA and the KPCS, global corporations can have undue influence on the decisions and actions of the collaboration. It could lead to the corporatization of global governance and public values.

Another concern is multisector collaboration has no clear governance anchor that provides political legitimacy. If governments are not playing a strong role in guiding the actions of these partnerships, whose interests are being represented? A related concern is the lack of tangible lines of accountability: to whom are the multisector collaboration and its partners accountable? What standards are to be used? How transparent are they?

Finally, multisector collaboration may undermine or "crowd-out" more effective existing development activities, make less efficient use of scarce resources or increase dependency. Some multisector collaborators—specifically those addressing global disease—have been challenged for distorting local market incentives or national development priorities by going around official processes, favoring single issues and vested interests, or focusing on "quick-win," media-friendly, but unsustainable successes. There are concerns in certain quarters about the influential role that individual celebrities and philanthropists are playing in shaping global and national public policy agendas when they are neither elected nor appointed officials. Few of these high-profile multisector collaborators have achieved national or global scale to date, and in many cases their methodologies are still being tested and their impact evaluated (Nelson, 2007).

Davies (2011) puts forward several critiques of the claims made about the admirable—and sometimes preferable—traits of global governance that have been claimed for multisector collaborations. Many theorists have focused on the advantages of network governance with limited critical examination of the sign of the underlying governance theories. Davies claims that network governance theory is too utopian and that it does not justify arguments of significant transformation from government-centric governance to network-centric governance. He also argues that there remain serious institutional and legal barriers to networks carrying out the actions that scholars suggest are possible in theory. The popularity of network governance has become an ideology and a more careful examination of its real advantages and disadvantages is warranted.

Kouzmin *et al.* (2011) take an even harsher view of network governance—they use the term public–private partnerships (PPPs). To them, PPPs are an arrangement that facilitates State Crimes against Democracy (SCADS) and Economic State Crimes against Democracy (E-SCADS). The concern is that multisector collaboration would be more accurately described as political and financial conspiracies involving elites and other self-serving interests. As this criticism relates to multisector collaboration, the concern is that such governance structures open up possibilities to "antidemocratic" manipulations without proper checks against such violations. Such multisector collaborations should not be accepted based on their form of governance, but rather only on a case-by-case basis to ensure they are accountable to the public interest (Thorne & Johnston, 2012).

Waddell (2011) points out the possibility that one partner participating in a multisector collaboration may not have the goal of success of the partnership. One partner may have only the goal of promoting its own interests. He cautions there may be cases when partners attempt actively to impede the efforts of multisector collaborations to achieve their own organizational goals. Simply put, some stakeholders only cooperate with a multisector collaboration to "defend their interests," either encouraging or discouraging action based exclusively on how the partner itself fares.

The Future of Multisector Collaboration

Multisector collaboration is here to stay. It is too popular, too useful, and too pregnant with possibilities to lose favor. Organizations, partnerships, and alliances will continue to be created reflecting this global governance approach. Multisector collaborations may be inevitable fixtures of the global landscape, but their success and efficacy are anything but assured. There should be no preference for multisector collaboration as a form of governance, only when it carries out good global governance and helps solve global problems should it be embraced.

The opportunities for partners to collaborate in ways that generate new synergies for solving global problems are significant. However, putting the idea of multisector collaboration into practice turns out to be more difficult than some first imagined. In fact, multisector collaborations present a serious "clash of cultures" among the partners. The differences between the government, business, and NGOs are profound and do not dissolve when they are assembled in a cooperative venture. Experiences of the FLA and KPCS demonstrate that simply collaborating does not guarantee success.

The suspicions and concerns raised about multisector collaboration are warranted and deserve to be heeded. The challenge remains to understand how multisector collaborations could be created so they are successful and persuade doubters that "governance without government" can address global policy issues with the same concern for accountability and public values as we wish governments to honor. How can multisector collaborations overcome the "clash of cultures" and blend the interests of the different members into success performance?

4

DISCOVERING GLOBAL GOVERNANCE ENTERPRISES

With the end of the third decade of the twenty-first century as the target for accomplishing the Sustainable Development Goals (SDGs), current global governance efforts to solve the world's greatest problems are facing a "perfect globalization storm": an inflection point regarding what constitutes good global governance, how it will be done, and by whom.

People are more aware than ever about the scale and scope of the environmental, social, economic, and political problems that afflict a majority of the world's population. They realize how failing to solve many of these problems not only perpetuates suffering and conflict on a global scale, but also that these conditions pose a clear threat to those who live in communities that are safer, healthier, and more prosperous; even when living on the other side of the world from where the problems reside.

The legacy of poor and inadequate governance that is the experience of so many fragile and frail states has increased the risk of global problems expanding and spreading beyond the local conditions. Efforts to increase and energize our efforts at establishing good global governance as a means for combating global problems are left with a weak and ill-equipped foundation to build upon. Not only has this neglect made it more difficult and more expensive to solve global problems, but also it puts into serious question the likely efficacy of these efforts employing conventional approaches to global governance.

We can better appreciate the advantages of thinking about global problems and appreciating how complex and deleterious they are through a lens of "global policy" that anticipates a more interconnected and comprehensive set of actions. That is, "think local, act global." Yet, as we make a transition from global policy, organized around our current international system, to one where global institutions, global problems, and global citizenship are the dominant perspectives, there is neither an obvious global-wide consensus on how to address these same global problems, nor an acceptable set of institutions and political processes that could legitimately forge and confirm a popular global consensus.

We have seen an explosion of innovative approaches to global governance and a radically reshaped landscape that has expanded the roles and leadership of global corporations and global non-governmental organizations (NGOs). At the same time, there is no accepted standard to use as a basis for determining which multisector collaboration is successful, should be welcomed, and supported as one way to fill the global governance gap. There is no framework for designing new multisector collaborations that are sure to "do good and do well."

All of these trends and developments herald an untimely crisis in global governance: the SDGs have been established with higher levels of ambition for solving global problems just at the time when the capacity to design and implement good global governance is rapidly diminishing. We need to discover new ways of solving global problems, accounting for the influence of globalization. It is time now to rethink and recreate good global governance if there is to be a reasonable chance at making progress at solving global problems as prescribed by the SDGs.

The expansion of multisector collaboration provides the best opportunity to address global problems in the face of these trends and conditions. They do not conform well to the accepted views on the role of government and good global governance. They present significant difficulties to those who struggle with the diminished role of governments and the ascendant influence of global corporations in global governance. They present serious challenges to those who support these new approaches to global governance to defend their effectiveness and legitimacy. There is limited evidence to support the claim that the multisector collaboration approach by itself ensures better global governance. It is difficult to separate the hopes and "boosterism" for multisector collaboration from demonstrable and valid documentation of the efficacy of such an approach to global governance.

Global Governance Enterprises (GGEs) and Good Global Governance

The global problems that are most pressing have been set out and articulated by the SDGs. Multisector collaboration is the popular approach to global governance that could be used to improve the chances of helping to solve these and other global problems. What is needed now is to establish a clear and credible definition of GGEs that would qualify as undertaking good global governance: global governance enterprises (GGEs) Currently, claims of successful multisector collaborations addressing global problems are case-based. Recent assessments (Waddell, 2011; Grayson & Nelson, 2013; Forrer *et al.*, 2014) of partnerships typically have high praise for the cases they present. These studies offer valuable insight on how such partnerships are organized and what traits they share in common. For example, Waddell (2011) identified characteristics shared by Global Action Networks (GANs), including global and multi-level coordination, diversity embracing boundary spanners, interorganizational networks, systematic change agents, entrepreneurial action learners, voluntary leaders, and global public goods producers. While each GAN does not possess all of these characteristics, they all possess at least three. However, no evidence is offered as to how, or even if, these characteristics are linked to GAN performance.

These studies provide a reasonable justification for endorsing these specific partnerships as being successful, but they do not include any particular standards that could be employed to assess other multisector collaborations. The assertion of good performance is based on researchers' observations, but there is no way to determine what reasonable expectations should be for their performance. Defining GGEs in terms of the way in which they are structured, organized, and conducted provides a more systematic way of assessing whether any given multisector collaboration could be considered a GGE.

The challenge is to discern what are the characteristics of a GGE that are related to good global governance. If GGEs are filling a global governance gap, they should be expected to perform at a level that meets expectations of what constitutes success. With partners from different sectors, success is going to be measured in different ways in terms of the partner's particular perspective. What is success in terms of using this form of global governance? What should reasonable expectations be about this approach in helping to solve global problems? One answer is found in an analogous situation involving business. When considering the reasons to support efforts by business to have a positive impact on society, two typical rationales are cited, (a) doing good by doing well, and (b) doing well by doing good. The first rationale emphasizes the commercial aspect of the activity and sees the positive consequences for society when business thrives in communities. The second rationale emphasizes the commercial benefits business can accrue by having a positive impact on the communities in which they work.

For GGEs, the aim is to do good *and* do well at the same time—one dimension is not isolated from the other. In fact, they are mutually reinforcing. The GGE should do well, which means it has set out to make changes that will improve people's lives and make for a better world, and it is successful in bringing about these changes. Doing well is not about having great goals, but having an important, sometimes profound, effect on the people who need help: goals do not help people, but outcomes do. Doing good means that the GGE is conducting its operations with an awareness of the public values governments, business, and NGOs should honor. GGEs need to be well run and well organized, but not at the expense of adhering to traditional organizational standards such as efficiency, effectiveness, and equity.

Ideally, GGEs should provide a better approach to global governance than the current practice. Murphy's (2000) observations on the poor state of global governance explain the need for an aspiration that GGEs should not perform on the same level as conventional global governance, but rather develop approaches that are superior to past practices. The ascribed benefits of multisector collaboration in general and GGEs in particular—innovative, flexible, adaptive, and responsive—have the potential to solve global problems, invigorated by the promise of good global governance that GGEs promise. It also provides the analytic foundations for an understanding of how proactively to build GGEs. What is required is a clearer articulation of the theory that justifies GGEs before anything can be said about their practice.

Network Governance as Good Global Governance

The literature on the effects of globalization on public management suggest the need not only for a significant reconceptualization of what it means to govern in a globalizing world, but for better understanding of how to organize governance in ways that adapt to the changes brought about by globalization. Provan and Milward (2001), in their early efforts to contribute to a framework for the evaluation of the efficiency and effectiveness of governance networks, traced the origins of this field of study back to the 1960s. Business and organization scholars, Lawless and Moore (1989), situated themselves as advancing the study of a particular conceptual framework begun earlier in the 1980s. Attention to networks, both in organization and management theory in general, and in the field of public administration and global governance in particular, is no longer novel, and has become commonplace. Rizvi (2008) saw the evolving idea of network governance as a profound change, explaining:

> [h]ierarchical governments are being replaced by interlinked webs or networks of agencies within government and often linked beyond government to the civil society organizations and the market. The core responsibility of the government has shifted from managing people and programs to coordinating resources for producing public value.

This evolution in thinking about network governance has rapidly taken place, and scholars have responded with investigations, attempting to describe the changes they are seeing and the ways in which we should seek to adapt to and influence those changes.

Scholars have spent the last 20 years investigating multisector collaboration as a new form of governance, describing them, discerning different types, and theorizing over what different traits are understood to be associated with them to carry out those operations. The research has examined many different types of partnerships and arrangements. Network governance is the term of art. The research on network governance is rich and an innovative approach to governance. It informs both the expectations for and definition of GGEs.

Riggs (1991) explicitly drew the connection between the phenomenon of globalization and its consequences for the study of public administration, suggesting that analysis of governance and administration will of necessity be "comparative," requiring a "comprehensive ecological understanding" of global public administration, as opposed to "American" and "foreign" public administration. Clearly, new institutional and social arrangements made by public administrators perpetuate the cycle of interconnectivity, interdependency, and complexity. An examination of good global governance for the public administrator should offer guidance as to how the public administrator might function effectively within this context.

Ideas about the evolution of governance, involving new hierarchical structures and incorporating new actors, have been brewing within the fields of globalization and public administration since the turn of the century. For instance, Salamon (2002) described what he saw as an emerging trend, "Instead of relying exclusively on government to solve public problems, a host of other actors are being mobilized as well, sometimes on their own initiative, but often in complex partnerships with the state." Governance scholar, Agranoff (2006), suggested that new approaches to governance that involve networks of actors increasingly are not simply an option, but rather a mandatory tool of the trade, arguing that today's public administrator is increasingly aware of the "guarantee" that other governments and NGOs must be engaged. O'Toole and Hanf (2002) reminded us that this phenomenon happens globally, as solving global problems "requires finding ways to gain the cooperation of governments of other countries."

Today's public manager is integrally situated within the swirl of global interconnectivity, interdependence, and complexity, encountering an increasing number of actors. They are attempting to operate effectively within a governance milieu aptly described by O'Toole and Hanf (2002) as "a densely interconnected system in which local decisions and actions may trigger global repercussions—and vice versa—and the fate of communities in one region is bound to choices by decision makers elsewhere." Through their chosen methods and acts of governance, public administrators in turn serve to perpetuate this cycle. Given the tools of good global governance, the potential exists that today's public administrator might leverage the global governance framework to their advantage to advance their mission and improve performance. However, it seems clear that public managers require an expanded perspective and updated skill set if it is to promote good global governance. Moreover, it is increasingly apparent that this must involve more than the traditional government-centric administration approach.

Ideas concerning the evolution of governance in a globalizing world have become so comfortably ensconced within the field of public management that not only theorists, but also those concerned with the practice of public administration are making contributions. "How-to" manuals, such as Gerencser *et al.*'s

(2008) *Megacommunities: How Leaders of Government, Business and Non-Profits Can Tackle Today's Global Challenges Together*, with advice for forming and managing organizations involving public, private, and non-profit entities, are emerging, seeking to describe optimal performance within new global governance systems. Such efforts often emphasize the rapidity of global change and necessity of adaptation in order to respond to the complexity and urgency of problems in the globalizing world. Yet, while there is widespread agreement that global governance—the structure and process of solving shared global problems in a globalizing world—is increasingly critical for public welfare, public managers are still searching for actionable know-how for addressing today's global challenges. They are asking what is good global governance, and what does it require of me? We have begun to recognize the need, and to take steps towards defining governance in a globalizing world, yet work remains to adequately describe the practice of good global governance.

Network governance theory provides an excellent scholarly foundation for re-conceptualizing good global governance. It accepts the shortcomings of conventional approaches to governance that try to develop and implement actions that are effective solutions to global problems. It seeks to identify the potential advantages of government cooperation with business and NGOs to improve the production and delivery of public services. The form of network governance initiatives and the relationships established among participants have been explored for two decades in an effort to discover what type of network governance arrangements work best. The research provides valuable insights to those organizing multisector collaborations that are looking to help improve the lives of underserved global communities.

Types of Network Governance

One form of guidance commonly encountered within the network governance literature is focused on typologies. Agranoff and McGuire (1999) presented a different kind of typology. They argue that networks can be "contracting arrangements, collaborative efforts, multi-actor structures designed to achieve a specific purpose and comprised of any number of organizational actors, or more complex implementation structures." These different ways of describing types of networks suggest that they are to be seen as highly varied and distinguishable with regard to the number of members and the arrangement between them.

Goldsmith and Eggers (2004) also presented a list of types of networks. While cautioning that their list is not exhaustive, they identify six:

- service contract, in which "governments use contractual arrangements as organization tools";
- supply chain, "formed to deliver a complex product to government";
- ad hoc, activated "in response to a specific situation";

- channel partnership, in which non-governmental entities "conduct transactions on behalf of government";
- information dissemination;
- civic switchboard, in which "government uses its broader perspective to connect diverse organizations in a manner in which they augment each other's capacity to produce an important outcome."

The extent of government involvement may vary among these types of networks, as may their size, purpose, and degree of permanence.

Agranoff (2007) studied 14 existing "Public Management Networks" (PMNs) within the United States, interviewing their principals and examining their practices. He identified four broad types of networks:

1. informational;
2. developmental, which adds "education and member service" to the informational function;
3. outreach, which additionally seeks to "enhance access opportunities that lead to new programming avenues";
4. action, in which "partners come together to make interagency adjustments, formally adopt collaborative courses of action, and/or deliver services."

A key distinguishing characteristic in Agranoff's typology is attention to the scope of their work. Some PMNs exist for the relatively limited purpose of exchanging information, while at the opposite end of the spectrum other PMNs may use their collective abilities to produce long-term impact.

These efforts at creativity network typologies share a similar interest. The purpose is to understand the connection between how the partnerships were organized and the implications for what they did. These efforts provide invaluable insights into the form and operations of network governments. The typologies are all very different, reflecting the diversity of networks and the absence of an agreed upon standard for describing network governance. Typical of these examinations of networks is to accept the presumption that "function follows form." That means networks formed in particular ways will have corresponding ways of behaving and operating. A more promising approach is to recognize that networks may decide first what it is they want to do and how they want to do it, and then decide how best to organize and operate the network around that functionality: form follows function.

Network Governance Organization and Management

Other research has delved deeply into the investigation of network governance by exploring characteristics of their organizational and management practices. According to Considine (2005), networks offer a strong model for public management because they can respond more flexibly to local conditions (Giguère, 2003), promote collective action to obtain lower regulatory costs (Ostrom, 1998), decrease transaction costs associated with fragmented goods and service delivery (Sullivan & Skelcher, 2002), and increase legitimacy and accountability through the promotion of participation in decision-making (Rhodes, 1990; Walsh, 2001).

Examining the management of networks without specifying particular types, Salamon suggests that optimal utilization and performance of networks requires three different sets of skills. Networks must first be created, including convincing potential participants to become involved. Salamon (2002) identified the skill set required here as "activation skills." The second essential skill set is that of "orchestration." Referring to the analogous skills of the "good conductor," he explains that the network must be led to perform in a way that produces the desired results, but that this is not achieved through the direct control of all parts. Finally, effective network governance requires "modulation skills," which involve the employment of rewards and penalties applied in proper measure. The unifying theme of these new skill sets is, to Salamon, a transition from "management" skills to "enablement" skills, or "the skills required to engage partners arrayed horizontally in networks."

Networks, to some degree, alter or realign authority and accountability relationships found in traditional government hierarchies. Rhodes (1996) emphasizes that networks likely require a distinctive managerial style based on facilitation, accommodation, and bargaining. In Agranoff's view (2007), PMNs represent a more partnership-oriented management structure in which representatives of the various institutions and organizations comprising the network largely shed the rank or authority associated with their traditional roles. They still, however, maintain some form of organization and "distinct internal power structures along with a set of internal arrangements." To this new model of authority and accountability, he lends the term "collaborarchy." Goldsmith and Eggers (2004), in turn, counsel that network governance involves a balancing of flexibility and accountability that is "more of an art than a science . . . It entails knowing when to be flexible and when to be firm; when to shift risk and when to share it; when to add partners to the network and when to shed them."

Bevir and Richards (2009) describe three broad approaches to the management of networks in their review of network governance literature, "the instrumental, interactive, and institutional." Each approach says something somewhat different about the situation of a government action within networks, but each conceives of networks in a particular way, as an entity that can be managed in a particular way. Networks generally appear to present a model whereby some of the tasks of governance are accomplished using non-governmental actors or less hierarchical or bureaucratic structures. It also appears that under many models, government retains many characteristics of its traditional role.

This observation about different approaches to government roles network governance supports the model developed by Goldsmith and Eggers (2004).

They emphasize the inorganic character of networks for achieving public purposes, arguing, "a network that delivers effective public services doesn't just happen," and in particular that in order for networks to be effective, governments ought to use "the design phase to address up front many of the toughest issues involved in formulating and managing networks." While their analysis of network governance represents a departure from the traditional modes of government approaches to solving public problems, the prescriptions offered for optimal network management and performance contemplate the retention by government of its traditional role in problem identification, solution development, and in determining the optimal means for implementing that solution (even while those means may incorporate actors and actions outside of the traditional mechanisms of government). In other words, the government is to choose which type of network best suits its needs.

The success of network governance depends on applying the right management practices in the right measure at the right time. The proper set of management skills must be employed to encourage partner participation and engagement. Authority and accountability relationships must be established in a way compatible with the goals and functions of the network. Management styles must be attuned to the preferences and expectations of the partners. Most telling, little of what is considered to be good management practices when deployed in hierarchical organizations translate well to managing heterarchical networks.

Goldsmith and Eggers (2004) further develop their conception of network governance by introducing the notion of the "integrator," which serves to connect the components of the network, facilitate interaction, and resolve problems. This integrator may be the government itself, a component entity in the network that is also involved in the provision of services ("prime contractor"), or a third party not involved in the provision of services, but selected specifically to serve as the integrator. Yet, even in cases in which the integrator or "hub" of the network is a third party, or a private or non-governmental agency, the networks in question appear to remain subordinate to the overarching authority of the government agency, which, while delegating some decision-making authority, retains responsibility for the determination of the goals (and even the means) of the network.

Governments and Multisector Collaboration

Even among those researchers and practitioners contemplating various forms of delegation and decentralization of authorities through networked governance, there is resistance to displacing government from the center of governance, or in particular, away from its traditional role as the sole agent to arbitrate what governance action are in the public interest, the determiner of optimal solutions, and the ultimate locus of accountability. Speaking especially emphatically on the importance of the centrality of the state in global governance, Fukuyama

(2004) claimed, "What only states and states alone are able to do is aggregate and purposefully deploy legitimate power. This power is necessary to enforce a rule of law domestically, and it is necessary to preserve world order internationally." This point is echoed by de Senarclens and Kazancigil (2007) when they argued, "statehood is a *conditio sine qua non* for a legitimate global governance." While most observers developing the literature and concept of network governance are not always as emphatic regarding the primacy of the state in global governance, others preserve its central role in their conceptualizations of new models of governance.

Salamon's (2002) observations that networks could operate without government playing a strong leadership role in directing the actions and the priorities of the network was insightful. One inference was that networks would have to govern by, "Markets and civil society play[ing] increasing roles in the identification of public problems and the work to solve them." This key point helps identify the administrative arrangements that link with the more abstract idea of "governance without government." It also stands in opposition to contemporary views about good global governance and the role of government.

There is recognition that global governance, due to the changes brought about by globalization, has evolved in terms of both practice and theory to involve the roles of many non-state actors (Weiss, 2000). Rosenau's (1995) framing of global governance anticipated this critical issue, articulated over 20 years ago, "[It] encompasses the activities of governments, but it also includes the many other channels through which 'commands' flow in the form of goals framed, directives issued, and policies pursued." Presuming that the political legitimacy of a state hinges on it playing a central role in governance is an unnecessarily strict syllogism. In a globalized world, a state's legitimacy is not based on retaining a monopoly on governance, but rather on its capabilities to achieve democratic accountability by governing effectively in a world with a dynamic and unfamiliar global governance landscape (Forrer et al., 2014).

A more expansive view of global governance has not informed research on network governance. As described earlier, the literature on network governance provides three views on the role of governments. Among the common characteristics shared by the types of networks that have been identified is the bringing together of parties of differing experiences and skills, in order to achieve a goal or set of goals which traditional hierarchical government may be less able to achieve. Such arrangements may help to meet the challenges created by the increasing interdependence and interconnectedness generated by globalization. Yet, available descriptions of what networks are and how they may be optimally conceived, organized, or managed so far remain both relatively general, and oriented towards achieving effective management of government-centric networks.

Government faces challenges as it transitions into a networked model of governance. Provan and Milward (1995) view network governance as an asset to governments as they carry out their governance responsibilities. Koliba *et al.*

(2011) argued that governments' organizational, management, and personnel systems were structured to operate within a hierarchical model of government, and not a networked one. Without a realignment of its systems, governments will continue to face inefficacies as public administrators seek guidance in coordinating resources across networks to produce public value. They also pointed out that governments do play a critical role in governance networks as the "democratic anchorage" and by "funneling symbolic power and cultural authority to the network; informing public perceptions of the network, lending it legitimacy; allocating distinctive (tactical) resources and providing sources of information through which interests are pursued."

Some scholars (Peters & Pierre, 1998; Koontz & Johnson, 2004; Pierre & Peters, 2005; Klijin & Skelcher, 2007), have framed government roles in networks in terms of following, encouraging, and leading. Salamon (2002) allowed that neither the activation nor orchestration skills he considered essential to network governance were necessarily "exclusively government functions," yet he suggested it is through modulation that the traditional form of government authority expressed itself in network governance. Under this framing, markets and civil society play increasing roles in the identification of public problems and the work needed to solve them. Nevertheless, government, even while playing the role of "good inspector," and recognizing that "forbearance rather than rigid enforcement best achieves regulatory compliance," is important to the operation of networks, advancing the mission of what is to be accomplished and how it is to be accomplished, and ensuring "regulatory compliance."

Salamon's (2002) observations provide a practical way of operationalizing the idea of "governance without government." It accepts the unconventional idea that multisector collaborations could operate as networks without clear guidance by government and still operate effectively by having the network partners provide that guidance through collaboration. Rather than governments playing essential roles such as anchors of democracy or regulatory compliance, Salamon (2002) has helped liberated multisector collaborations to carry out global governance, relying on the shared interests of partners to adhere to the organizational and management practices that support good global governance. Recognizing that multisector collaborations can perform global governance successfully without a government playing its traditional role is a "tipping point" in understanding what distinguishes GGEs from other forms of global governance (Forrer *et al.*, 2014).

GGEs and Values of Good Global Governance

It should be clear from the literature review on network governance that GGEs use an unconventional approach to helping solve global problems. One implication is that conventional values of good governance should not be expected to be fully applicable. The heterarchical nature of GGEs presents a misfit to the conventional values of good global governance that are grounded in pre-sumptions of hierarchy as the principal organizing concept (Forrer *et al.*, 2014). They are a hybrid organization with management structures and organizational governance that are radically different from traditional bureaucratic models that describe most government entities. What values of good global governance apply to GGE?

> In one essential aspect then, "global governance" is quite distinct from good or bad governance at the national level. A "good" (that is, account-able, efficient, lawful, representative and transparent) government usually leads to good governance, while bad governance is closely correlated with a conspicuously bad government.
>
> *(Weiss, 2000)*

Other values may be added—sustainable, inclusive, resilient, effective, etc.—but there is no one definitive list. Weiss' (2000) point is to recognize that values of good governance based on a notion of state-centric models will not apply to global governance. Several values of good global governance that will matter to partners and may be assigned to GGEs are proposed.

Purposeful

The GGE should have a clear view on what it wants to accomplish and how it will be accomplished. Another way of saying it: the GGE knows what it is doing. This may seem all a more elaborate way of saying, conventionally, it is effective. However, in the context of good governance, effective is doing what a manager or agency is supposed to accomplish. The traditional perspective begs the question of whether government goals and objectives were a good idea in the first place. It may seem to some a slight distinction, but an important one. Good governance for governments is akin to good implementation. It addresses only one side of the issue: was it done? GGEs should be judged on whether their aims are attainable, their actions rational, and linked to specific outcomes, and whether those outcomes are accomplished. All those standards are captured by the value of purposeful.

Impactful

GGEs should make a real difference and create a better world. The effect does not have to be significant in terms of scale and scope, but in terms of changing people's lives—directly or indirectly. GGEs are a time- and resource-intensive approach to governance. To justify the effort and commitment of resources, GGEs should accomplish something important. If the change is for one com-munity, the learnings that come for that effort can be scaled and replicated by others, multiplying the full impact of the original GGE's efforts.

Best-Intentioned

A keystone of traditional good governance is transparency. If a state's legitimacy is founded on being accountable to its citizens, those same citizens must have the information about what their public officials are doing and how they are doing it. As voluntary organizations, the governance value of transparency is not applicable to GGEs. The value of accountability is applicable in only a narrow sense. Typically, GGEs' partners must operate with government approval, even when government officials are not actively involved in the GGE. That authority suggests there is an expectation for the GGE not to exceed any authorities or approvals granted by government officials. However, they are not answerable to the government in the same way government officials are seen as being accountable to their citizens.

Alternatively, GGEs should be expected to be faithful to what they claim to be their mission and aims. Suspicion that a GGE has aims other than those pronounced would undermine their acceptability as global governance actors. Being best-intentioned means they are sincerely attempting to achieve what they have claimed are their aspirations. The merits of those aspirations are subject to debate, the intentionality of GGEs should not be open to question.

Optimize Public Value

Government programs are judged on the extent to which they achieve their program goals and objectives. The benefits associated with these goals and objectives have been identified, so successful execution means the net social benefits will be realized. These goals and objectives are typically linked to a budgeting process, and supported with resources. GGEs select their own aims and whatever goals and objectives they may. In addition, they are free to adjust those aspirations whenever, and as many times, as they choose. As an alternative, GGEs should be expected to optimize the generation of public value.

As semi-autonomous entities, there are concerns that GGEs may use their position filling the global governance gap to advance special interests. Since a key component of GGEs is to engage partners in multiple sectors to work together to advance shared interests and their own interests as well, it is a reasonable concern that GGE partners could exploit their partnership and advance special interests over public interests. Optimizing public value ensures that whatever special interests may be advanced by a GGE, they do not come at the expense of foregone public value.

Value Added Governance

Value added governance seeks to address the question of whether an organization is better able to accomplish its goals through membership in the GGE than through alternative means. This question is an essential component for GGEs because without providing value added to each individual partner, they will not have sufficient incentives for participation. The process by which the value added is determined for each group must be conducted on a case-by-case basis. The value added to each partner is also unique. In a GGE the whole is greater than the sum of the parts, because the network is able to coordinate groups and compile information for optimum effectiveness and efficiency.

The above list of good global governance values seeks to advance the idea that GGEs should be judged in terms of their performance as a global governance actor. The values assigned to GGEs are a hybrid of norms steeped in traditions of democratic accountability and a recasting of conventional standards of conduct to fit their heterarchical, semi-autonomous nature. The description of good global governance values for GGEs is not meant to be definitive. As more GGEs are recognized and built, and people have an opportunity to work in and with them, a better understanding will emerge of what are reasonable expectations for their performance as global governance actors. As described later in Part III, these same good global governance values for GGEs align with organizational and management practices that support well-run and high-performance GGEs. They reinforce how GGEs are organized and managed in particular ways that facilitate and support collaboration among multiple partners to pursue shared interests and shared values to bring about a better world.

Defining GGEs

Four specific criteria are proposed for defining GGEs. The criteria are used to assess two dimensions: standing and deportment. The first is analogous to "standing" in law (locus standi): being entitled to bring a case before a court. GGEs are judged on whether they qualify to take on global governance responsibilities based on the entity's design, mission, and intentions: can they do good and do well? Deportment is associated with how a GGE conducts itself and the implications for its performance and durability. Values associated with deportment are efficacy, sustainability, self-sufficiency, and resilience. The criteria used for assessing GGEs involve both what expectations are reasonable to have for the conduct of GGEs (Held & McGrew, 2002; Rosenau, 2002; Salamon, 2002; Woods, 2002; Kennett, 2008), but also the collaborative arrangements that support and foster such conduct (Forrer et al., 2002, 2010, 2012b, 2014; Goldsmith & Eggers, 2004; Provan & Kenis, 2007; Waddell, 2011).

The combination of these attributes and ambitions places GGEs in the unique role of bridging a global governance gap: the growing ineffectiveness of governments when they act exclusively to address growing global challenges. Moreover, partners in the GGE may differ with regard to their bargaining power, but no partner is subject to the commands of others. GGEs take on governance—sometimes complementing, sometimes substituting—for what has been the traditional prerogative of governments. GGEs are undertaking activities that are generally considered to be within the public sphere and, therefore, they should be held to similar standards of conduct as we would for any government activity. In essence, GGNs are doing what governments would do, but currently are not.

The four characteristics of GGEs by themselves are not precise discriminators, but in combination, they describe a unique set of characteristics that define GGEs. The four criteria for identifying GGEs are:

1. multisector partners;
2. addressing a global problem with a vision for real change;
3. involved in actions and their implementation;
4. self-directed.

Each of the criteria are described in greater detail and rationales are presented on how the four criteria (only in combination) can be used to assess which multisector collaborations qualify as possessing the standing and deportment of GGEs.

Multisector Partners

Partners should represent a properly diverse set of interests relevant to the issue(s) being addressed, and they should be highly regarded within their respective communities. GGEs require diverse perspectives to account for the complexity of issues globalization has engendered and to fuel fresh perspectives for innovative problem solving. Diversity of partners regarding their skills, experiences, and perspectives is a competitive advantage for GGEs as an approach to global governance.

A concern over some multisector collaboration is that they are, in fact, skewed to favor a business or an advocacy position, masquerading as a partnership. No doubt, any number of multisector collaborations use the popularity and support of partnerships as a front to advance special interests. GGEs are motivated for the exact opposite approach. GGEs' partners participate to accrue the benefits true collaboration provides. A partnership that claimed to have diverse representation but only involved narrow interests would not attract those partners that wanted real change and saw the advantages to a collaborative approach. In this way, GGEs are self-selecting. Without a diverse set of partners, GGEs cannot produce the innovative solutions they promise. If they do not have diverse partners, they cannot be GGEs.

The greater the regard in which a GGE participant is held by its peers, the stronger the GGE. GGEs are held accountable—not by the government or citizens—but by themselves. The very same diversity that is an asset to GGE partners brings a wide range of interests and approaches. Since GGE partners self-govern themselves, the reputation value of participants is a strong motivator to ensure that the GGE conducts itself in ways that all the partners find acceptable, and could be represented to their colleague organizations and the public as consistent with that organization's own mission. GGEs with many prestigious partners should assure the public that its activities will be mediated by the participation of multiple perspectives seeking actions that address shared interests.

Addressing a Global Problem with a Vision for Real Change

To qualify as a GGE, it needs to direct its attention to global problems. Identifying what problems are global, as shown in Chapter 2, proves to be more difficult than first imagined. One rationale for supporting GGEs as a form of global governance is their potential to help fill the global governance gap. Justifying that rationale means GGEs need to address those same issues governments would address if they could, but do not have the capacity or will to do so. The SDGs provide one catalog of problems that have been identified as global. However, there is no shortage of global problems for GGEs to set their sights on.

GGEs must also have a vision that presents a realistic chance to bring about change and make a real difference. Just as with any global governance effort, GGEs can offer no guarantees of success. What once was thought of as a great idea can turn into frustration and disillusionment. To be considered suitable as a GGE, it needs to have a credible idea about how it can help solve global problems. One advantage of GGEs is they do not have to follow the public policy preferences of governments. Global policies, or national policies with implications for global problems, are influenced routinely by politics and political ideologies and can side-step rational and systematic justifications for their policy proposals. GGEs have the luxury of developing their own vision for change in an environment uncompromised by advocates who propose change for reasons other than achieving specified outcomes. To be a GGE, the vision for change could be revolutionary, risky, unconventional, or iconoclastic, but it must always be plausible.

Involved in Actions and Their Implementation

The number of groups that advocate for global policies is expansive and grows every day. Social media has reduced dramatically the cost of organizing, messaging, and communicating different ideas for solving problems to a global audience. GGEs take actions that bring about change and make a difference in people's lives. This crucial distinction helps separate those multisector entities that collaborate to develop standards, policies, and proposals from GGEs that develop a plan of action and take steps to see it implemented. Developing and adopting a plan of action by GGEs to help solve a global problem that its part-ners are going to make happen requires a discipline and depth of understanding about problem solving that does not burden many advocacy groups.

GGEs are very different from multisector collaborations that only advo-cate, but the two different entities can be complimentary. Advocacy groups bring attention to global problems. They can raise awareness of problems to government officials and business leaders. The raised awareness can serve as a spark for creating a GGE to address that issue. It could become the mis-sion of the GGE to translate the rhetoric and proposals of advocacy groups into actions that help bring about the change both groups seek. GGEs are guided by a change model on how specific actions will bring about the desired results and where the impacts are clearly defined and measurable. Without such specificity, partners will be reluctant to join, worried that their efforts will not bring about concrete change. Advocates call for change; GGEs make change happen.

Self-Directed

The mission and goal(s) of GGEs are selected by partners, not directed by government authority, or guided by government officials unilaterally. The study of network governance has been positioned largely to see networks of non-state actors involved in governance as a means for helping governments improve their performance. In such a conception, the government still influences what the network does and how it does it, ensuring these multisector collaborations stay on course for achieving policy goals. GGEs act independently of govern-ment direction. They co-create their aims and what actions they choose to bring about real change. Government officials can be partners of GGEs, but no more influential than any other partner.

GGEs are distinctive hybrid entities on the global governance landscape. The definition is intended to distinguish GGEs from other multisector alliances and ascribe to them particular intentions, aspirations, and organizational arrange-ments. The individual characteristics of GGEs themselves may not be unique, but it is their combination that creates a singular type of entity and sets them apart from other multisector collaborations. With a clear definition of what constitutes a GGE, it is now possible to study them and learn how they came to organize themselves and the implications of that approach for their success as a GGE.

PART II

Profiles of Global Governance Enterprises

OVERVIEW

The theoretical justification for global governance enterprises (GGEs) to supplement and supplant conventional global governance approaches leads to the next logical question: which of the countless collaborations that have been formed to address the Sustainable Development Goals (SDGs) issues qualify as GGEs? The purpose of developing a theory of GGEs was to solidify an academic rationale for their acceptance on global governance. However, it is also intended as a practical guide for sorting out which partnerships should be properly encouraged and supported by governments. The enthusiasm for the multisector collaborative approach has encouraged an endorsement of some partnerships on the fact alone that they are governance networks. It is vital for practitioners to move beyond testimonials that praise a set of multisector alliances based on what they are doing and discern which ones are organized and conduct themselves as GGEs.

The seven cases presented in this section are great examples of GGEs in practice. The research and interviews conducted on each of these partnerships revealed that they meet the four criteria set out in Chapter 4. The profiles demonstrate well how the original commitment to be a collaborative effort was deterministic in shaping how they organized themselves, chose their own mission, identified their goals and objectives, and conducted their operations.

Profiled GGEs

Global Network for Neglected Tropical Diseases

Global Network for Neglected Tropical Diseases works with international partners at the highest level of government, business, and society to break down the logistical and financial barriers to delivering existing treatments for the seven most common neglected tropical diseases. Founded in 2006 by six partners—the Liverpool School of Tropical Medicine, the Earth Institute Columbia University, Helen Keller International, International Trachoma Initiative, Schistosomiasis Control Initiative, and the Task Force for Global Health, the Global Network for Neglected Tropical Diseases raises the profile of neglected tropical diseases (NTDs). It builds support for control and elimination activities through their efforts to educate, advocate, catalyze, and convene. They highlight efforts underway in the field, and connect global players and afflicted communities to increase access to vital medicines that can stop these illnesses and lift the world's poorest people out of poverty. NTDs are the most common afflictions of the world's poorest people. These diseases promote poverty, stigmatize, disable, and inhibit individuals from being able to care for themselves or their families. The seven most common diseases are ascariasis, hookworm, lymphatic filariasis, onchocerciasis, schistosomiasis, trachoma, and trichuriasis. As a group, NTDs impose a greater health burden than malaria and tuberculosis, and rival that of HIV/AIDS.

Global Alliance for Improved Nutrition

The Global Alliance for Improved Nutrition (GAIN) is an alliance driven by the vision of a world without malnutrition. Created in 2002 at a Special Session of the UN General Assembly on Children, GAIN supports public–private partnerships to increase access to the missing nutrients in diets necessary for people, communities, and economies to be stronger and healthier. GAIN itself is an alliance of governments, international organizations, the private sector, and civil society. The projects funded and advised are implemented in partnership with government, business, and civil society organizations to ensure that public health objectives are reached. GAIN creates national and regional business alliances of leading companies, which are exploring ways to bring high quality, affordable fortified foods to those most in need, including the "base of the pyramid": the poorest groups.

HERproject

Changing women's lives through workplace programs requires more than one company, one foundation, or one NGO. The HERproject was launched in 2007 by Business for Social Responsibility, a nonprofit that works with business to create a just and sustainable world. HERproject catalyzes global partnerships and local networks in emerging economies to improve female workers' general and reproductive health. Partners include 8 multinational companies, 30 factories, 8 local organizations, and multiple clinics, hospitals, and public-sector population and health departments. HERproject improves the lives of women and creates business value by: (a) promoting investment by international companies in workplace programs that link women's health to business value; (b) creating local networks between health training service providers and supplier factories to create cost-effective, relevant, and sustainable interventions; and (c) engaging female workers in workplace health education and access programs.

Inter-Agency Network For Education in Emergencies

The Inter-Agency Network for Education in Emergencies (INEE) is an open global network of representatives from NGOs, UN agencies, donor agencies, governments, academic institutions, schools, and affected populations working together to ensure all persons the right to quality and safe education in emergencies and post-crisis recovery. INEE serves as an open global network of members working together within a humanitarian and development framework to ensure all people the right to quality and safe education in emergencies and post-crisis recovery. INEE envisions a world where: (a) all people affected by crisis and instability have access to quality, relevant, and safe education opportunities; (b) education services are integrated into all emergency interventions as an essential life-saving and life-sustaining component of humanitarian response; (c) governments and donors provide sustainable funding and develop holistic policies to ensure education preparedness, crisis prevention, mitigation, response, and recovery; and (d) all education programs preparing for and responding to emergencies, chronic crises, and recovery are consistent with the INEE Minimum Standards and accountable for quality and results.

mHealth Alliance

mHealth Alliance works with diverse partners to advance mobile-based or mobile-enhanced solutions that deliver health through research, advocacy, support for the development of interoperable solutions, and sustainable deployment models. mHealth, or the use of mobile devices for health purposes, can revolutionize the ability of governments, corporations, NGOs, and citizens to deliver, access, and use health information to promote well-being, combat disease, and respond to medical emergencies. The mHealth Alliance (mHA) is positioned at the leading edge of the mHealth ecosystem as a convener to unite existing mHealth projects and guide governments, NGOs, and mobile firms to deliver innovative and interoperable solutions in this exploding field. mHA advances mHealth through policy research, advocacy, and support for the development of interoperable solutions and sustainable deployment models. Working with diverse partners, the mHA sponsors events and conferences, leads cross-sector mHealth initiatives, and hosts HUB (Health Unbound), a global online community for resource sharing and collaborative solution generation.

R4 Rural Resilience Initiative

The R4 Rural Resilience Initiative (R4) is a cutting-edge, strategic, large-scale partnership between the public and private sectors to innovate and develop better tools to help the world's most vulnerable people build resilient livelihoods. Around the world, 1.3 billion people live on less than a dollar day and depend on agriculture for their livelihoods. Climate-related shocks pose a constant threat to food security and well-being. There is a need for a mechanism for farmers and rural communities in developing countries to manage their own risk in the face of a changing climate. The partnership promises to leverage the respective strengths of its partners: Oxfam's capacity to build innovative partnerships, the World Food Programme's global reach and extensive capacity to support government-led safety nets for the most vulnerable people, and SwissRe's technical expertise in the field of insurance and reinsurance. R4 will test and develop a new set of integrated tools (that are potentially scalable) to extend risk management benefits of financial services such as insurance and credit to the most vulnerable populations.

The Rainforest Alliance

The Rainforest Alliance is a global nonprofit that focuses on environmental conservation and sustainable development and works through collaborative partnerships with various stakeholders. It believes that the best way to keep forests standing is by ensuring that it is profitable for businesses and communities to do so. That means helping farmers, forest managers, and tourism businesses realize greater economic benefits by ensuring ecosystems within and around their operations are protected, and that their workers are well trained and enjoy safe conditions, proper sanitation, health care, and housing. Once businesses meet certain environmental and social standards, they are linked up to the global marketplace where demand for sustainable goods and services are on the rise.

The seven GGEs are not intended to be an exclusive list of GGEs. There are doubtless scores or hundreds of GGEs operating today that are undocumented. GGEs are forming or disbanding every day. They represent a diverse range of organizations addressing different issues and using very different approaches. Each of these GGEs is singular, organized, and built out of unique circumstances. What they do share is a fidelity to an approach to addressing global problems in a manner that aligns closely with the definition of a GGE.

These profiles of GGEs are intended to be a "bridge" between Parts I and III of this book. The cases provide a tangible description of how the theory of GGEs translates into practice. There is an endless number of alternative ways to build GGEs, so these cases provide concrete examples of manifestations, not limits on possibilities. The descriptions provide inspirations to those who may aspire to build their own GGEs. They serve as examples of the ways GGEs have been built and provide some "lessons learned" for building future GGEs.

5

GLOBAL NETWORK FOR
NEGLECTED TROPICAL DISEASES
Global Governance Enterprise Profile

The Global Network for Neglected Tropical Diseases (Global Network) is an initiative of the Sabin Vaccine Institute. It works with international partners at the highest level of government, business, and society to break down logistical and financial barriers to the delivery of treatments for the seven most common neglected tropical diseases.

Creation and Background

Neglected tropical diseases (NTDs) comprise a group of parasitic and bacterial infections that affect more than 1.4 billion people, vulnerable populations living in extreme poverty (less than US$1.25 per day) mostly in tropical and sub-tropical regions of the world. Treatment and prevention tools exist, yet these disabling diseases flourish where populations have inadequate nutrition, limited access to medical care, poor personal hygiene, and low literacy levels.

They are characterized as neglected because health systems fail to identify and treat them, the political commitment for addressing them is lacking, and there is a dearth of both national and international funding. Poor documentation and under-reporting of NTDs contribute to the lack of funding at both national and international levels. This, in turn, is compounded by health policymakers' current focus on HIV/AIDS, tuberculosis, malaria, and other re-emerging diseases.

Individuals with NTDs suffer disability, are stigmatized, and are often unable to care for themselves, entering them into a cycle of poverty that is impossible to break without outside intervention. Even more, because these diseases frequently cluster and overlap, their impact on developing countries, including lost productivity, aggravation of poverty, and increased long-term healthcare costs, is enormous.

NTDs can be addressed through safe, low-cost technologies that are easily administered and rapidly effective. At one time, treatment efforts were led by non-governmental organizations (NGOs), local governments, and research institutes specializing in a single disease. However, in the early 2000s the World Health Organization (WHO) led an effort to develop rapid-impact packages designed for integrated treatment of the seven most common NTDs: ascariasis, hookworm, trichuriasis, lymphatic filariasis, onchocerciasis, schistosomiasis and trachoma.

Leading experts in the field stressed the importance of advocacy that would bring NTDs collectively to the attention of policymakers, rather than one disease at a time. Those experts included Peter Hotez, President of the Sabin Vaccine Institute; David Molyneux, Director of the Lymphatic Filariasis Support Centre; and Alan Fenwick, Director of the Schistosomiasis Control Initiative.

Neglected Tropical Diseases

1. **Ascariasis (also known as roundworm):** An intestinal infection caused by the worm Ascaris lumbricoides, which is part of a family of parasites known as the soil-transmitted helminthes. It is particularly prevalent in tropical regions of the world, affecting up to 45 percent of the population in parts of Latin America and 95 percent in parts of Africa.

2. **Hookworm:** An intestinal parasite most commonly found in tropical and subtropical areas of Africa and Latin America. An estimated 576 million to 740 million people around the world are infected with hookworm.

3. **Lymphatic Filariasis (also known as elephantiasis):** A disease caused by the Wuchereria bancrofti, Brugia Malaya, and Brugia timori worms. This extremely painful, debilitating, and disfiguring disease affects more than 120 million people in 80 countries.

4. **Onchocerciasis (also known as river blindness):** A parasitic disease caused by the roundworm Onchocerca volvulus. It infects 37 million people living near rivers and fast-moving streams in Sub-Saharan Africa.

5. **Schistosomiasis (also known as bilharzia or snail fever):** A parasitic disease carried by freshwater snails infected with one of the five varieties of the parasite Schistosoma. It is predominantly found in Asia, Africa, and South America.

6. **Trachoma:** An infectious eye disease caused by the bacterium Chlamydia trachomatis and the world's leading cause of preventable

blindness. More than 41 million people currently suffer from active infection, and 8 million people are visually impaired as a result of the disease. It is found in 59 countries.

7. **Trichuriasis:** An infection of the large intestine caused by Trichuris trichiura (also known as human whipworm). The disease is found worldwide but is especially prevalent in Southeast Asia.

The impetus for the Global Network stemmed from this need to address the seven most common NTDs—both with treatment and for advocacy purposes—as a group. The Global Network was formally launched at the Clinton Global Initiative Annual Meeting in 2006 and is headquartered at the Sabin Vaccine Institute in Washington, DC. Its founding partners were the Liverpool School of Tropical Medicine, the Earth Institute at Columbia University, Helen Keller International, International Trachoma Initiative, Schistosomiasis Control Initiative, the Sabin Vaccine Institute, and the Task Force for Global Health.

The Global Network was created through the establishment of platforms for discussion among relevant players in the NTDs arena. At its inception, the network focused on advocacy, resource mobilization for program implementation and dissemination of research and primary data related to the diseases.

In 2008 the Global Network received funding from the Bill & Melinda Gates Foundation (Gates Foundation), allowing it to channel its work through the primary avenues of building awareness, advocacy, and policy. The Gates Foundation grant allowed the network to focus strictly on advocating before the international community for monies to treat NTDs. Later that year, the Global Network received another significant infusion of funding from the Gates Foundation to: support the WHO in its NTD efforts, help launch three regional NTD funding mechanisms, support global and regional fundraising and resource mobilization, and expand advocacy efforts domestically and abroad.

Goals and Objectives

The chief goal of the Global Network is to raise awareness and cultivate the resources necessary to eliminate the seven most common types of NTDs by 2020. The network has already helped mobilize more than US$100 million to directly combat NTDs, as well as US$1 billion in ancillary funds that are used to indirectly combat the diseases through initiatives such as improved nutrition and water and sanitation projects. The Global Network has mobilized resources from the public and private sectors and it has also helped to encourage increased drug contributions from pharmaceutical companies.

The objectives that the organization hopes to accomplish with the funds are:

1. Build awareness of NTDs among key influencers, highlighting both the devastating effects of the diseases and the efficacy of the rapid-impact approach.
2. Strengthen the advocacy and resource mobilization capacity of the network and neglected tropical disease stakeholders.
3. Provide on-going evidence to demonstrate how NTDs contribute to poverty and negatively impact educational and economic development.

An additional, informal way in which success is measured is through policy created around NTDs and related fields. The increase in relevant policy enables the realization of the Global Network goals.

Organizational Structure and Governance

The Global Network is made up of seven member organizations that focus on NTDs: the Sabin Vaccine Institute, the Liverpool School of Tropical Medicine, the Earth Institute at Columbia University, Helen Keller International, the International Trachoma Initiative, the Schistosomiasis Control Initiative and the Task Force for Global Health.

The internal structures of the network are largely established by its grants, which are typically tied to specific indicators, objectives, and reporting and accounting mechanisms.

Global Network Partners

The Albert B. Sabin Vaccine Institute: The organization's mission is to reduce needless human suffering caused by vaccine-preventable and neglected tropical diseases. It does this through innovative vaccine research and development and by advocating for improved global access to vaccines and essential medicines. The Institute was founded in 1993.

The Liverpool School of Tropical Medicine: LSTM was the world's first institution dedicated to tropical disease. A registered charity, LSTM works in more than 60 countries to improve the health of the world's poorest people, taking research, innovation, and scientific breakthroughs from the lab to those most in need.

The Earth Institute at Columbia University: The Earth Institute garners the resources needed to tackle some of the world's most difficult problems, from climate change and environmental degradation to poverty, disease, and the sustainable use of resources.

Helen Keller International: HKI is one of the oldest international NGOs devoted to preventing blindness and reducing malnutrition in the world. Currently the organization is working in Africa, the Asia Pacific region, and the United States.

International Trachoma Initiative: ITI was founded in 1998 in response to the WHO's call to eliminate blinding trachoma by 2020. The organization was founded by Pfizer and the Edna McConnell Clark Foundation. It is dedicated solely to the eradication of blinding trachoma.

Schistosomiasis Control Initiative: This effort aims to control or eliminate the seven most prevalent neglected tropical diseases within Sub-Saharan Africa. SCI has facilitated the delivery of approximately 40 million doses of treatment for schistosomiasis and intestinal worms to sub-Saharan Africans at high risk of serious disease.

The Task Force for Global Health: The Task Force for Global Health has historically focused its work in the areas of disease eradication and control, child well-being, global health collaboration, and public health informatics.

In 2008, the Gates Foundation gave the Global Network a three-year US\$3.8 million grant. Later that year the Global Network received a five-year US\$34 million grant, also from the Gates Foundation. The two grants set a target for the Global Network to mobilize US\$250 million in new funding for treating millions of individuals for NTDs during the five-year grant period.

It is important to note that funds mobilized by the Global Network do not usually flow directly through the organization, but rather are directed by the Global Network to other organizations that implement NTD treatment programs in the field. The Global Network also accomplishes its advocacy goals through participation in and production of events, such as global health conferences, roundtables, regional and disease-specific meetings, and campaigns to raise public awareness of NTDs.

The Sabin Vaccine Institute leads the network, contributing monetarily through its support staff and workspace. Sabin's board of trustees (which includes international leaders in business, civil society, academia, and philanthropy) provides oversight. Initially, the organization attempted a secretariat model, but it was difficult to manage and proved ineffective, and as a result, the decision-making power was transferred to the Sabin Vaccine Institute. While the Global Network does not have a formal process for decision making, staff frequently liaise with the network partners through an approach that allows the Global Network to be more effective and responsive in addressing the needs of the NTD community.

The Global Network's structure embraces the culture of active participation, and its members are aware that the vibrancy of the network depends on the level of their contributions. The concept that a network is only as strong as its members' engagement is one of the Global Network's distinguishing characteristics.

The establishment of a system of transparency and the promotion of a culture of trust among members are mutually reinforcing and can form part of a virtuous cycle. Transparency is also reinforced through tangible results that members can see, including: increased funding for NTD treatment programs, greater potential for NTD treatment implementers to raise money, and the forwarding of science. These are all incentives to continue working together.

A key component of the network's success is its ability to remain an essentially neutral player in the NTD arena. Because it has an independent source of funding, the Global Network is not actively seeking funding for itself in the fiercely competitive development arena, where funds are scarce, particularly as relates to NTDs. If the Global Network were competing with its member organizations for financial support, it could not continue to cultivate the trust it has. Furthermore, the Global Network can advocate for more resources for the field as a whole.

Its role as a neutral and honest broker not only ensures trust between the network and its member organizations, but it also contributes to increased communication and confidence among other stakeholders.

The Global Network's work unfolds at high levels, working with national government bodies, development banks and other influential donor organizations, high-profile individuals and pharmaceutical companies. One of the main mechanisms the network uses to influence governments is the release of white

> *"There was no specific value proposition articulated for each of the members or for being members in the network. I think a lot of people have the perception that a network is supposed to do something for you, as opposed to a network being something you do for . . . And I think that thinking is starting to change now. [Members] understand that a network is as strong as their engagement in it."*
>
> —Dr. Neeraj Mistry
> Managing Director
> Global Network for Neglected
> Tropical Diseases

> *"We have tried to be neutral and honest brokers in the community. This is a key element to building trust. A network CANNOT function without trust. If we can be seen as trusting stewards of the network, the network can encourage organizations to be trusting and work with each other."*
>
> —Dr. Neeraj Mistry
> Managing Director
> Global Network for Neglected
> Tropical Diseases

papers and policy recommendations. They are relayed to governments through partner organizations, either directly or through shared resources and programming. Because of the constraints of a full-time staff of 20, the Global Network generally allows its partners to implement programs and manage relationships with local governments and civil society, although there have been exceptions—such as in Burundi and Rwanda. In those countries, the Global Network fostered relationships directly with in-country partners, and in both cases, the Global Network gave out sub-grants to support national, integrated NTD treatment programs. However, projects of this nature are the exception rather than the rule.

The network has also helped to set up a number of committees. For example, it has helped establish committees of donors and technical experts, which are often housed in partner organizations or the WHO. The Global Network Advisory Committee provides a resource the Global Network can call on for advice and connections regarding important issues. In addition, the network has contracted external consultants to provide feedback on ways to improve internal infrastructure and effectiveness, as well as to assist with effective outreach to donor targets, including public and private sector organizations. As it evolves, the organization has become more interested in finding ways to integrate NTDs into related development activities, e.g., education, nutrition, and water and sanitation efforts, rather than creating new vertical programs that focus exclusively on NTDs.

Distinguishing Characteristics

The Global Network is one of the only organizations in the world promoting the broad use of existing medicines to treat all seven leading NTDs as its core function. Prior to the formation of the Global Network, no mechanisms existed to ensure this work would happen.

One of the network's key contributions has been to move the field from a vertical approach (where organizations worked to combat individual tropical diseases) to a more integrated, horizontal approach. Furthermore, the Global Network is constantly taking stock of how it is operating in the NTDs landscape in order to ensure it is functioning as effectively as possible. Reacting and responding in real time allows for the natural evolution of the organization—and the Global Network is committed to maintaining that ability to evolve.

The Global Network came into being to respond to a specific need; yet, it has a broad mission, allowing evolution without risking mission creep. The Global Network's success can also be traced to its legitimacy within the NTDs community. It is housed in the world-renowned Sabin Vaccine Institute. It includes multi-lateral organizations in the discussion. It has receiving significant funding from the Gates Foundation and, as a result of this funding, has maintained financial independence and a reputation as an honest broker. The structure and role of the Global Network has improved the efficacy of the NTDs' field.

6

GLOBAL ALLIANCE FOR IMPROVED NUTRITION

Global Governance Enterprise Profile

The Global Alliance for Improved Nutrition, working towards a world with stronger and healthier communities, brings together public–private partnerships to improve access to and increase the diversity of affordable nutritious foods which provide targeted populations with the critical dietary nutrients they need to survive

Creation and Background

Malnutrition is a condition that results from taking an unbalanced diet, and can be attributed to a combination of factors, including insufficient or excessive consumption of proteins, energy, fats, and/or micronutrients. It can occur in both developing and developed economies, and the term malnutrition can refer to both undernutrition and overnutrition. Malnutrition is one of the world's most serious problems, accounting for 11 percent of the global burden of disease.[1]

Undernutrition, which is the most common form of malnutrition in developing countries, results from a diet lacking adequate calories and proteins. It is further exacerbated by frequent infections or disease, poor care and feeding practices, inadequate health services, and unsafe water and sanitation.[2]

It is of particular concern in women, children, and the elderly. Women are particularly at risk, because during pregnancy and breastfeeding, they have additional nutritional requirements. For children, the 1,000 day window from conception to two years of age is when nutrition has a significant impact on physical and cognitive development. The 1,000 days represents a sweet spot for nutrition investments. Undernutrition during pregnancy can severely inhibit the health and development of a child. Babies who were malnourished in the womb have a higher risk of infancy death and are more likely to face lifelong cognitive and physical deficits and chronic health problems. Undernutrition during the first two years of life can weaken a child's immune system, leaving the youngster more susceptible to dying from common illnesses such as pneumonia, diarrhea, and malaria.[3]

Overnutrition and the related problem of being overweight or obese are likely to be caused by a diet with excess energy, fats, and refined carbohydrates. Obesity, characterized as an epidemic in developed countries, is beginning to occur in developing countries as well, particularly in peri-urban settings, driven largely by the availability of cheap and high energy based foods. This places a double burden on societies where both forms of malnutrition occur in tandem.[4]

The World Health Organization recognizes malnutrition as the greatest single threat to the world's public health; and improving nutrition is widely considered the most effective form of development assistance.[5] However, despite this, until relatively recently, nutrition interventions largely focused only on treating the acute phase of undernutrition, when people are in famine situations and close to death. While these programs are necessary, they are exorbitantly expensive, consuming the majority of public funding earmarked for nutrition programming and leaving limited resources for preventive measures to address chronic undernutrition.[6]

In 2001, several leading health experts including Dr. Bill Foege (former Director of the U.S. Centers for Disease Control), Dr. Sally Stansfield (former Associate Director for Global Health Strategies at the Bill & Melinda Gates Foundation), and Duff Gillespie (former Senior Deputy Assistant Administrator of the Global Health Bureau at the U.S. Agency for International Development), came together to talk about inefficiencies in the field of nutrition services delivery, and the need for a life cycle approach to malnutrition. They were most interested in ways dominant business practices and funding strategies could be leveraged for more effective prevention of malnutrition.

The majority of the world's population accesses at least some portion of their food through commercial channels either at the farm level, including through the purchase of seeds, or at the post-production level through retail markets. These foods are not necessarily nutritious;

> *"Malnutrition is the basic DNA of most any developmental intervention. Without it, basic development investments will operate ineffectively."*
> —Gautam Ramnath
> Investments & Partnerships
> Global Alliance for Improved Nutrition

GAIN Mission Statement

To reduce malnutrition through sustainable strategies aimed at improving the health and nutrition of populations at risk.

they often lack the right balance of essential fatty acids, proteins, and nutrients. Discussions among the nutrition experts centered on how to integrate the public sector's need for improved nutrition with the private sector's know-how to produce, sell, and distribute large quantities of food. The idea was to create convergence between the public and private sectors in ways that bring to scale the production and availability of healthier food while maintaining sustainability and an exit strategy for continued investment.

One idea looked at ways to improve the level of nutrition by creating public–private partnerships that would, among other things, result in fortifying staples with vitamins and minerals that were already routinely accessed by the poor. It expanded on a concept that was already being done in the developed world with large scale fortification programs.

Historically, the nutrition community has been reluctant to work with the private sector when addressing malnutrition challenges. A neutral platform was needed to foster an environment where both the public and private sectors had a voice and felt comfortable engaging with each other. Global management consulting firm, McKinsey & Company, was hired to analyze whether Global Alliance for Improved Nutrition (GAIN) could be housed by existing organizations. McKinsey's report showed that a new organization was more feasible than reframing an existing one. The Bill & Melinda Gates Foundation, found merit in the proposal and provided $50 million in seed funding for the creation of GAIN. The organization subsequently received additional funding from the Canadian International Development Agency (CIDA) and the United States Agency for International Development (USAID).

In 2002, at a special session of the United Nations General Assembly on Children, GAIN was created to support that goal and provide a platform where public–private partnerships could be created to increase access to essential nutrients that are critical for strong and healthy people, communities, and economies.[7]

GAIN works towards improved nutrition by developing and delivering high quality population-based and targeted programs. The goal is to increase the combined impact and reach of GAIN's investment in a sustainable way, at scale. Although large scale food fortification has been the cornerstone of GAIN programming, recent strategic restructuring has now paved the way for more targeted interventions to ensure that there is further penetration of nutritious foods into a country or regional market. GAIN is currently focused on four main strategic areas of intervention (Figure 6.1):

1. Large scale fortification;
2. Nutritious food for children under two and pregnant/lactating women;
3. Multi-nutrient supplements;
4. Integrated agriculture and nutrition along the value chain.

FIGURE 6.1   GAIN's Strategic Priorities

Source: Global Alliance for Improved Nutrition. http://www.gainhealth.org/.

Population-based programs (such as Initiatives 1 and 4 above) use market approaches to distribute staple foods and condiments, fortified or bio-fortified with vitamins and minerals to large populations.[8] One such population-based effort by GAIN is the National Food Fortification Program. This program encourages projects that fortify foods and condiments—including wheat and maize flour, sugar, vegetable oil, milk, soy sauce, and fish sauce—in 19 countries with high levels of vitamin and mineral deficiencies.[9] Another example is the GAIN-UNICEF Universal Salt Iodization Partnership Project, which aims to provide iodized salt to 90 percent of the population in nations where the project operates. Iodine is essential for human development, yet nearly 2 billion people do not have access to sufficient amounts of the mineral in their diets.[10]

Targeted programs (such as Initiatives 2 and 3 above), meanwhile, deliver fortified food products and agricultural efficiencies to specific populations. These foods and supplements go to targeted populations, including infants and young children, pregnant women and nursing mothers, school children, farmers, people suffering from infectious diseases, remote rural populations, refugees or displaced peoples, and people seriously affected by the economic crisis. Examples of these programs include the Infant and Young Child Nutrition Program and the Nutrition and Infectious Diseases Program.[11]

GAIN utilizes its programming intelligence nimbly to address impediments or market failures to increased investments or programming efficiency. Utilizing the creation of tools such as the GAIN Premix Facility (GPF), a GAIN driven global facility, now also in Kenya, to support its Africa programs, GAIN is able to procure, certify for quality, and finance "premix," a commercially prepared blend of vitamins and minerals used to fortify staple foods to local producers while ensuring quality control.[12]

It has also utilized innovative finance mechanisms and linked itself with specialists such as Root Capital and the Acumen Fund to leverage mutual assets and to create a robust pipeline of investable opportunities.[13] Apart from this, it also established the GAIN Business Alliance in 2005 in order to understand how to better facilitate innovative partnerships between the public and private sectors.[14]

Market-based solutions are a cornerstone of the GAIN network since the private sector dominates the value chains of food accessed by both the rich and poor. And because the public sector is largely responsible for ensuring a strong policy and regulatory environment, participating in GAIN's initiatives gives both the public sector and private companies a competitive advantage by providing a platform for dialog and understanding. Consumers benefit because they have better access to more affordable, more nutritious food. GAIN helps reduce the riskiness of investments made by both sectors.

GAIN Business Alliance

GAIN's Business Alliance is a global partnership to explore new business models, best practices, and sustainable approaches in the fight against malnutrition. Its members include Ajinomoto, AkzoNobel, BASF, Britannia, Cargill, The Coca-Cola Company, DAL Group, Danone, DSM, Essentient, Firmenich, Fortitech, GroupeBel, Hexagon Nutrition, Kemin, Kraft, Mana group, Mars, Nutriset, PepsiCo, Tetra Pak, and Unilever. The alliance meets regularly at the Annual Business Alliance Global Forum as well as at smaller regional events. It brings together a range of business actors, including global and local companies and business associations to discuss ways to engage business in the fight against malnutrition.

Source: GAIN Business Alliance. Global Alliance for Improved Nutrition. http://www.gainhealth.org/partnerships/business-alliance.

Goals and Objectives

GAIN measures success through a rigorous monitoring and evaluation program. The primary goal of the Alliance is to reduce undernutrition, and it takes into consideration a number of sustainability and access indicators. Its end goal is to reach 1.5 billion people by 2015.[15] This is an incredibly important real-time metric since it indicates impact, scale, and sustainability.

GAIN builds a robust performance metric framework into each of its programs that not only tracks health and nutrition-based indicators, but also those that affect business. All with the goal of efficiently managing its own programs and building the evidence base in the nascent yet growing arena for multiple stakeholders to further engage.

The Alliance publishes its progress (showing original targets) as one of its mechanisms for operating as a transparent organization (Table 6.1). GAIN assesses its progress bi-annually in order to accurately judge its effectiveness and success as an organization. The Alliance also monitors and tracks indicators in the following areas: operations, programmatic impact, return on investment, cost effectiveness, and cost benefit.

Organizational Structure and Governance

GAIN's current governance structure is the result of a number of organizational iterations and has evolved drastically over the past few years. Presently, GAIN's leadership is made up of a board of directors—consisting of an executive board, a partnership council, and a secretariat.

The executive board comprises leaders from the donor, United Nations, development, research, business, and civil society communities. The secretariat is a small team of professionals and support staff that manages the organization's day-to-day operations.

TABLE 6.1 Progress against Organizational Targets (FY 2010–11)

Targets	Description	Progress
Target 1	Reach: 1.5 billion individuals consuming fortified foods.	GAIN estimates that over 630 million individuals are consuming fortified foods.
Target 2	Coverage: 500 million target individuals (i.e., women and children) consuming fortified foods.	GAIN estimates that 253 million women and children are consuming fortified foods.
Target 3	Cost-per-target individual reached <US$0.25.	GAIN estimates that it costs US$0.32 to reach each target individual.
Target 4	30 percent reduction in the prevalence of micronutrient deficiencies.	Neural tube defects fell by 30 percent in South Africa after folic acid was added to maize meal and wheat flour. In China, data collected from 21 sentinel sites showed that anemia dropped by approximately one third following the fortification of soy sauce with iron. In rural areas of Western Kenya, iron deficiency dropped by 14 percent, vitamin A deficiency by 10 percent, and anemia by 11 percent.

Source: GAIN Project Results. Global Alliance for Improved Nutrition. http://www.gainhealth. org/performance/project-results.

The partnership council consists of a small group of professionals and secretariat staff members. It serves an advisory role and was formed to allow GAIN still to tap into the expertise of leaders in the nutrition field, who could not be on the executive board due to concerns about potential conflicts of interest.

Executive Director, Marc Van Ameringen, along with the Executive Management Committee and the employees, has been largely responsible for the organization's success. Under his leadership, GAIN has positioned itself as a forward thinker by capitalizing on the latest trends in development and markets, and fosters and encourages thinking outside of the development box to meet the nutritional needs of recipients by capitalizing on public and private interests.

Another skill that GAIN demonstrates is the ability to attract and retain employees with a diverse set of backgrounds. GAIN employees bring a broad range of expertise; they include MBAs, researchers, nutritionists, policy experts, and individuals with years of field experience The organization not only maintains a good balance of specialists, but it keeps its employees engaged and creatively challenged by embracing interesting ideas and projects. This has the added bonus of keeping the organization imaginative and ahead of the curve.

GAIN sees itself as operating on a neutral ground where all sectors can work towards common goals. The challenge is finding out exactly what the shared goals are and how to translate them into real world benefits. To facilitate this process, GAIN has organized into a number of smaller, national-level alliances (as opposed to the broader international alliances that were initially conceptualized). Over time, GAIN is expanding its global reach and creating more regional alliances with relevant partners in each location. GAIN is headquartered in Geneva, Switzerland, with offices in Washington, DC, New Delhi, Johannesburg, Nairobi, Kabul, Shanghai, Abuja, Dhaka, Addis Ababa, and Amsterdam.[16]

To ensure effective cross-pollination between and among these regional alliances, GAIN puts a heavy emphasis on external evaluations and active dissemination of information. GAIN has expanded its senior team to nine people from five and reorganized them in a matrix. Employees' time is spent rotating on projects within GAIN, permitting them quickly to identify redundancies and spread best practices. Captured information is shared among colleagues and partners through gray materials (circulated only within the organization), published data, and individual collaborations.

GAIN encourages staff to reflect on what its constituencies ask of the organization and how GAIN could better respond. Every employee at GAIN understands the importance of shared value. Employees conduct extensive research to determine if other organizations are providing the same services. GAIN does not duplicate the effort and oversaturate the market, but rather looks to link the strengths of these organizations with that of its own. In the same vein, GAIN adopts best practices from all fields to craft its effective internal structure. It is through these qualities that GAIN has been able to continue to work and diversify its donor base beyond the Bill & Melinda Gates Foundation.

Distinguishing Characteristics

In its work to improve nutrition, GAIN bridges the gap between the private and public sectors. Governments, NGOs, research, academia, the UN, and bilateral and multilateral organizations are not necessarily positioned to work comprehensively with the private sector. Building trust is particularly important given the potential disconnects between sectors causing reluctance to work together. Given the diverse nature of its employee base, GAIN is able to create trusted cross-sector partnerships.

To maintain this trust, GAIN manages expectations and clearly defines its scope. Too many organizations are willing to take on any project. GAIN, by contrast, has a very specific objective, vision, and mission statement, and it works hard to combat mission drift. However, since it is a young organization, it sees the importance of re-evaluating its mission regularly to ensure that it operates in the most effective space possible. For this reason, GAIN differentiates between mission shift and mission drift. If the organization purposely changes course to operate more effectively, this is seen as a positive and useful step. In contrast, mission drift is avoided, and employees are willing to reject initiatives that they perceive are out of GAIN's scope.

GAIN's most important success factor may be its marriage between good governance and good management. When GAIN was created, the organization was small enough that there was an almost complete overlap between the governance and the management of the organization. As it has grown, some separation was necessary between the two. However, a complete separation between the organization's management and governance is not currently envisioned. GAIN believes that governance can only be as successful as the organization's management is effective, and skilled management is what sets apart a great organization from a good one.

Notes

1 The big picture. (2003, April 21). Retrieved April 15, 2012, from http://www.unicef.org/nutrition/index_bigpicture.html.
2 Morris, S. S., Cogill, B., & Uauy, R. (2008). Effective international action against undernutrition: Why has it proven so difficult and what can be done to accelerate progress? *The Lancet*, *371*(9612), 608-621. Retrieved May 22, 2012, from http://www.thelancet.com/pdfs/journals/lancet/PIIS0140-6736(07)61695-X.pdf.
3 About 1,000 Days – 1,000 Days. (n.d.). Retrieved June 6, 2012, from http://www.thousanddays.org/about.
4 Malnutrition – Global Alliance for Improved Nutrition. (n.d.). Retrieved May 19, 2012, from http://www.gainhealth.org/about/malnutrition.
5 The starvelings; Malnutrition. (2008, January 26). *The Economist* (US). Retrieved May 20, 2012 from http://www.economist.com/node/10566634.
6 Girerd-Barclay, E. and de Menezes, C. ACF International. (2010) *Taking Action Nutrition for Survival, Growth & Development*. UK: Actions Against Hunger.
7 About Gain – Global Alliance for Improved Nutrition. (n.d.). Retrieved April 29, 2012, from http://www.gainhealth.org/about/gain/.

8 Programs – Global Alliance for Improved Nutrition. (n.d.). Retrieved April 29, 2012, from http://www.gainhealth.org/programs.
9 Large Scale Food Fortification – Global Alliance for Improved Nutrition. (n.d.). Retrieved May 2, 2012, from http://www.gainhealth.org/programs/initiatives.
10 Universal Salt Iodization – Global Alliance for Improved Nutrition. (n.d.). Retrieved May 2, 2012, from http://www.gainhealth.org/knowledge-centre/universal-salt-iodization/.
11 Nutrition for Women and Children – Global Alliance for Improved Nutrition. (n.d.). Retrieved May 2, 2012, from http://www.gainhealth.org/programs/maternal-infant-and-young-child-nutrition/.
12 GAIN Premix Facility – Global Alliance for Improved Nutrition. (n.d.). Retrieved May 2, 2012, from http://www.gainhealth.org/knowledge-centre/project/gain-premix-facility/.
13 Innovative Finance Program – Global Alliance for Improved Nutrition. (n.d.). Retrieved May 2, 2012, from http://www.gainhealth.org/knowledge-centre/project/innovative-finance-program/.
14 Alliances – Global Alliance for Improved Nutrition. (n.d.). Retrieved May 2, 2012, from http://www.gainhealth.org/about/alliances/#business.
15 GAIN Project Results. Global Alliance for Improved Nutrition. (n.d.). Retrieved May 2, 2012, from http://www.gainhealth.org/performance/project-results.
16 About Gain – Global Alliance for Improved Nutrition. (n.d.). Retrieved April 29, 2012, from http://www.gainhealth.org/about/gain/.

7

HERproject

Global Governance Enterprise Profile

BSR's HERproject catalyzes global partnerships and local networks to improve female workers' general and reproductive health in eight emerging economies: Bangladesh, China, Egypt, India, Indonesia, Mexico, Pakistan, and Vietnam.

Creation and Background

Young, uneducated, low-income female migrants moving from rural areas to cities for work represent a vulnerable population. Many of them are employed in factories and live either with their husbands and children or in dormitories with other young, single women.

In 2001, the David and Lucille Packard Foundation approached Business for Social Responsibility (BSR), a nonprofit membership organization that helps business advance sustainable models, with concerns about the reproductive health risks that result from the urban migration of young women. The foundation is a long-time BSR supporter, and at their request, BSR conducted preliminary research into the health landscape for female factory workers.

BSR's findings showed that these women face risks such as anemia, poor nutrition, reproductive tract infections, poor maternal health, sexually transmitted infections, and diabetes. They also have poor access to family planning. Not only do these risks lower women's quality of life and their ability to provide for their families, they have serious implications to employers in that they lead to increased absenteeism, employee attrition, reduced concentration, exhaustion, and decreased productivity in the work place. The majority of these diseases or health conditions are preventable with proper care and behavior. However, this low-income demographic has limited health knowledge and poor access to health care services. Furthermore, diseases and infections, as well as dangerous misinformation about health problems, can spread quickly in a closed factory environment.

Follow-up research conducted by BSR in 2005 reinforced this message as it showed that the number of women migrating to cities was increasing, and their health needs were still not being met by the inadequate civil society networks in place. The report from that investigation also shed light on why this demographic had such poor knowledge and awareness of health issues. Many women leave their villages too young to benefit from outreach from local nonprofits and community health workers providing services in rural areas. After they migrate to the city, they remain isolated from health awareness campaigns, which are more traditionally targeted at the poorest of the poor.

In addition, cultural biases and gender-based power structures play a key role in health decision-making. Biases run the range from the belief that worker training interferes with factory production to women's own reticence about discussing hygiene and reproductive health issues. Against this backdrop, the global economy is increasingly dependent on the participation of female workers, and healthy workers promise a more stable workforce.

How does HERproject work?

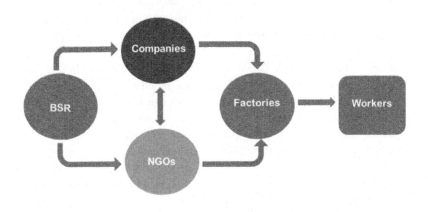

FIGURE 7.1 Cooperation between HERproject Partners

Source: Schappert, J. & Yeager, R. *"HERproject Overview Presentation: Healthy Workers, Healthy Business"* BSR, February 2012.

This 2005 report highlighted an opportunity for BSR to intervene and leverage its network of international corporate members to improve the reproductive health of female workers. With the continued support of the David and Lucille Packard Foundation, which provided initial grant funding, the HERproject concept was born in 2007. HERproject is a factory-based women's health education program. The project aims to show that investing in women workers' health is good business. As the creator of HERproject, BSR leads a coalition of partners, including international companies, their supplier factories, and locally based NGOs, that seeks to promote women's health awareness and access to services (Figure 7.1).

BSR undertook advocacy with its member companies in the first year to raise awareness around the issue and to garner support for the new program. Interestingly, a key appeal for most companies was not only the reputational benefit that could be gained from participating, but the potential to work closely with their suppliers to make a social investment at the factory level. Early in the creation phase of HERproject, the Packard Foundation introduced BSR to the Extending Service Development Project, a USAID undertaking, which had completed a study in a Bangladesh factory that found a 3:1 return on investment from support of women's health programs that provide education and basic health services.[1]

HERproject's first corporate partner was U.S. apparel retailer, Nordstrom, which piloted the project in four of its factories in China in 2007. Other early starters included Levi Strauss, Hewlett-Packard, Abercrombie & Fitch, Columbia Sportswear, and Timberland. BSR's involvement for early starters was critical: with trust already built with companies, BSR acted as a go-between with less known local NGOs and the experience of addressing a new, atypical compliance issue of women's health. Additionally, since the initial investment required was small and scale was not a prerequisite for success, the companies viewed HERproject as a low-risk undertaking. They could test the waters with just one or two factories.

To this day, BSR remains directly responsible for overseeing HERproject, including finding a satisfactory local NGO partner to provide quality health programming and services to female factory workers and helping those partners build their capacity and improve their organizations' over time. At companies, BSR works directly with the corporate responsibility team, which monitors compliance in the supply chain and ensures ethical manufacturing practices.

Local NGOs receive very limited funding—mostly they receive non-financial technical assistance and support from BSR. Still, they see value in having a relationship with BSR. Among other things, HERproject gives them an opportunity to work with a population to which they traditionally would not have access. Most factories view NGOs with suspicion and are unlikely to open their doors to them. In addition, HERproject enables local NGOs to access the larger global network of other NGOs, multinational companies, factories, and suppliers.

Not only does HERproject help NGOs establish direct relationships with large multinational companies, it helps them build their capacity through mutual sharing of best case practices with other NGOs across the world.

Some NGOs see HERproject as an opportunity to grow their capacity in a different area. In Kenya, BSR's local NGO partner was better known for its expertise in HIV/AIDS training than its work with maternal and reproductive health. That NGO sees HERproject as a platform to broaden their skill base and build internal capacity. Similarly, in Bangladesh, one of the local NGO partners had more expertise in advocacy and interventions around workers' rights. HERproject offered an opportunity to broaden its reputation and expand its capacity to implement new types of programs within the industry where it was already working. BSR embraces these opportunities to work with NGOs that want to grow their capabilities, since they see them as important contributions to their collective ability to deliver HERproject in different markets, and therefore reach more women in need.

> *"Trust [at the factories] isn't necessarily needed on Day One, which is really good because it is near impossible to build trust on Day One. What we find in most of our programs is that [during] the first couple of visits, the factory is very skeptical with a perspective like: 'Ok, ok. I am letting you in because my buyers want me to, but I am not sure what you doing here and I am not particularly interested. I just want you to get it done and go away.'*
>
> *That is what we are dealing with in the first couple of months of the project. But once the factory management starts to see the results on the workers, and once they realize that the workers aren't going on strike and that the NGO isn't telling the workers anything that they are uncomfortable with, then that trust really starts to build and it's absolutely incredible."*
>
> —Racheal Yeager
> Manager, HERproject
> BSR

Additionally, HERproject provides NGOs with stable funding and a model for growth—and as much work as each NGO's capacity allows. For example, if an NGO has the capacity to work with 15 factories, BSR likely can connect that NGO with enough participating companies so that it can continue to work at full capacity.

Thus far, the most challenging partnerships within the HERproject have been those of BSR with local suppliers and factories. These groups are traditionally quite reticent to change, and they are suspicious of NGOs and other external partners, which they fear will foster dissension among factory workers. In many cases, their prejudices are formed in previous negative experiences. Building trust between the factory leadership and the NGO partner is crucial for the success of any workplace empowerment program. However, this is often a long and complicated process.

TABLE 7.1 Overview of HERproject Partners

Country	No. of Factories	No. of Women Served	Company Participant	Local Partner
Mexico*	2	2,000	Hewlett-Packard	Health and Community development, Ciudad Juarez (SADEC)
Egypt	3	4,045	Levi Strauss & Co.	Center for Development Services
Pakistan	3	1,450	Li & Fung, Levi Strauss & Co.	Aga Khan University
India	9	7,491	Li & Fung, Levi Strauss & Co. Columbia Sportswear Talbots Abercrombie & Fitch	St John's Medical College Dept. of Community Health, Division of Workplace Programs
Bangladesh	12	9,979	Li & Fung, Primark Marks & Spencer Talbots	Awaj Foundation Phulki Momota
Vietnam	11	14,690	Li & Fung, Clarks Columbia Sportswear, Talbots Timberland Abercrombie & Fitch Marks & Spencer	Aga Khan University, Faculty of Health Services
Indonesia	2	3,602	Columbia Sportswear Talbots	YBS
China	19	50,400	Nordstrom, Columbia Sportswear Timberland Hewlett-Packard Marks & Spencer J. Crew, Microsoft Talbots, Li & Fung	Quining Marie Stopes International

*Project Closed

Source: Where HERproject works, HERproject. http://herproject.org/our-work/where-we-work.

HERproject is able to speed the process by leveraging the support of the inter-national company involved in the initiative. BSR's involvement also provides an added buffer "guarantee" that local NGOs will be collaborative rather than combative. Seeing that their buyers are keen on implementing HERproject, the local factory owners allow into their facilities the NGOs who they otherwise likely would not invite. Once program implementation begins and factory man-agers begin to see positive results and improvements in worker productivity, the trust builds automatically (Table 7.1).

Since its inception, HERproject has grown from 4 to approximately 50 active factory programs. As of December 2011, HERproject has been completed in 82 factories, reaching more than 120,000 female factory workers and over 25,000 male factory workers. HERprojects spans across eight countries: Bangladesh, China, Egypt, India, Indonesia, Kenya, Pakistan, and Vietnam. It works with 13 companies and 10 local organizations, and multiple clinics, hospitals, public sector population, and health departments.[2]

Goals and Objectives

As an initiative of BSR, HERproject represents one approach at realizing BSR's mission to build a just and sustainable world through collaboration with business. HERproject was founded on the premise that healthy workers lead to a healthy business—in other words, that investing in the health of a workforce leads to returns and, therefore, that supporting women's health in particular should be an objective of businesses in global supply chains. The program model centers on the identified health needs in a particular factory. That means HERproject in each factory has its own unique goals and targets.

HERproject results so far look quite promising. Participating workers have improved awareness about personal hygiene, nutrition, family planning, pre- and post-natal care, and prevention of sexually transmitted infections such as HIV/AIDS and Hepatitis B and C. These women also adopt healthier behaviors and are more likely to consult factory nurses and other health services when they need support or services.

Apart from the health benefits, HERproject has also resulted in improved relationships between managers and workers. In addition, the female factory workers are now more willing to discuss sensitive subjects with peers and family. Through their involvement in peer education activities and by assuming a leadership role in the factory and in the community, female workers become empowered, displaying new confidence thanks to their improved communication skills and knowledge.

Furthermore, HERproject has also gathered data on its effect on the bottom-line benefits from the program's investments in women workers' health. An in-depth return-on-investment analysis is conducted in each of the factories in which HERproject works. For example, in one of the factory programs in Egypt, in partnership with Levi Strauss & Co. and the Center for Development Services, women's absenteeism rates show a significant decline, falling to 10.7 percent from 19 percent and making women less likely to miss work than their male counterparts. Turnover also declined by around six percentage points. These productivity results yielded a 4:1 return on investment and saved that Egyptian factory an estimated $48,000.[3]

> ## BSR Mission Statement
>
> *We work with business to create a just and sustainable world.*

It is important to underscore that the HERproject is fundamentally a women's health and empowerment project, and not a cost-saving project for the private sector. This is an important distinction to make. Its main priority is to have a positive impact on the health of female factory workers, but it also seeks to prove business benefits (such as better worker relations and cost savings) so as to encourage more and more companies to invest in women's health.

Organizational Structure and Governance

HERproject benefits from multisectoral support and is funded from a number of sources, with both private and public contributions (Figure 7.2). Each of its multiple stakeholders has a clearly defined role and motivation for participating.

BSR is the owner and manager of HERproject, providing general oversight. BSR conducts private sector outreach, promotes women's health as a critical supply chain and sustainability issue, ensures quality control of workplace programs, develops tools and processes for more efficacious implementation, builds the capacity of local NGO implementing partners, supports M&E and

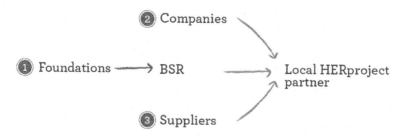

FIGURE 7.2 Funding Model for HERproject

Source: BSR. *"Investing in Women for a Better World"* BSR, March 2010.

project reporting, and builds partnerships to support long-term sustainability of workplace women's health programs.

A key role of BSR is to foster partnerships with stakeholders internal and external to the project, in particular between the private sector and local NGOs. BSR scopes out potential local partners and interviews them to see if they meet the initiative's criteria; it then vets them with company partners. These criteria include whether or not the organization has a strong gender focus, its training capacity, its health expertise, its experiences in implementing workforce training programs, and the organization's reputation within the country. Since each local participant is considered a partner of HERproject *first*, rather than the partner of any specific company, it is critical that BSR finds an NGO that meets all these criteria. The BSR team makes the final decision on whether to work with a certain local organization. HERproject is a multi-buyer program, and so one NGO might work with many factories.

To operate the initiative, BSR receives core funding from the Swedish International Development Cooperation Agency and area-specific funding from the Levi Strauss Foundation. As noted, the David and Lucille Packard Foundation was a founding funder of HERproject. Foundation and government funding are used to support BSR's oversight of HERproject and roles as described above. Funding is also used for local NGO capacity building, through small investment sub-grants and annual capacity-building partner workshops.

For international companies, the key motivation is subsidized participation in a quality-controlled program. The partnership requires these companies to ensure access to factories, cover the workplace implementation costs, and enable program replication and expansion. International companies usually provide their individual suppliers with funding to cover the cost of program activities. These costs can range from $5,000 to $7,000 per factory per year. The funds go directly to the local NGO partner.

USAID's Extending Service Delivery Project (2005–11) also supported HERproject by providing expertise on women's health and ROI data for the initiative in select countries.

Local NGOs implement the workplace training programs locally and build partnerships to support women's access to health services near the workplace and their living areas. All local HERproject partners form a direct relationship with BSR by signing a non-binding, non-financial memorandum of understanding. By joining HERproject, local NGOs gain BSR's support and access to an international network of peer organizations and multinational companies.

For monitoring and evaluation, local HERproject partners are required to provide three types of reports. Prior to the program's start, a local NGO must conduct a pre-implementation Health Needs Assessment within the factory. This determines a baseline for the factory workers' health landscape and identifies

Program Timeline

Activity	Timeline by Month													
	Mo 1	Mo 2	Mo 3	Mo 4	Mo 5	Mo 6	Mo 7	Mo 8	Mo 9	Mo 10	Mo 11	Mo 12	Mo 13	Mo 14
Supplier recruitment	→													
Kick-off meeting		→												
Health needs assessment & peer health educator selection			→											
HNA report			→											
Peer health educator trainings				→		→		→		→		→		
Refresher trainings					→		→		→		→	→		
Impact assessment and analysis														→
Sustainability discussion													→	→
Final Report														→

 = On-site Activity

 BSR

FIGURE 7.3 HERproject Implementation Timeline

Source: Schappert, J. & Yeager, R. *"HERproject Overview Presentation: Healthy Workers, Healthy Business"* BSR, February 2012.

which training topics and health services are most needed. The local NGO also provides BSR with monthly reports for the duration of the program. Once the program has been completed, the local NGO is required to prepare a final Impact Assessment report that draws comparisons with baseline data in order to determine how health behavior and attitudes have changed. BSR provides a report template and support with editing and translation services, but the local HERproject partner produces the final report. Figure 7.3 shows an implementation timeline for HERproject.

Implementing HERproject

The HERproject workplace program lasts 12 months and uses a peer-education training model. By clarifying roles, responsibilities, and expectations among project partners, project buy-in is solidified and alignment is ensured.

(continued)

(continued)

1. **Organize kick-off meeting and establish project team:** An on-site meeting takes place with the NGO partners, brand representatives and suppliers' upper management to discuss roles and responsibilities, key activities, and the project timeline. By clarifying roles, duties, and expectations among project partners, project buy-in is solidified and alignment is ensured.

2. **Organize on-site meeting with middle management and line supervisors:** The NGO partner conducts an on-site workshop for middle management to introduce the HERproject, explain the activities it will conduct, and explore the role of supervisors and clinic staff. Not only does this help supervisors understand the importance and the benefits of focusing on women's health, it builds factory-based support for HERproject activities and ensures support throughout the duration of the program.

3. **Conduct on-site health needs assessment and select peer educators:** The NGO partner conducts an on-site assessment to understand health needs for curriculum development and to establish a baseline upon which to measure project impact via interviews with female workers, management, and clinic staff.

4. **Develop health curriculum based on outcome of health needs assessment:** The NGO partner tailors the standard curriculum provided by BSR to develop six to ten training modules that address specific needs identified in the Health Needs Assessment.

5. **Facilitate training and follow-up of Peer Health Educators (PHEs):** Roughly 2–5 percent of all female workers, as well as on-site factory clinic staff, are targeted for Peer Health Educator training in women's health in general and, more specifically, reproductive health. The local NGO partner provides six two-hour trainings and six one-hour follow-up refresher trainings in peer-to-peer outreach. Random checks are also conducted to determine whether non-PHEs are aware of the program and health material. PHEs pass on information in many ways, including during worker orientation meetings, informally at lunch, and during travel to and from the factory.

6. **Conduct impact assessment:** At the end of the 12-month factory program, the local NGO partner conducts an impact assessment to measure progress on reproductive health education among women workers. It conducts on-site interviews with female workers, middle and upper management, clinic staff, and brand representatives. It then analyzes those findings to prepare a final Impact Assessment report for the multinational corporate partner.

7. **Facilitate sustainability discussion:** The program concludes with a discussion between factory management and the local NGO partner, facilitated by BSR, on ways to maintain the established investment in female workers' health.

Source: Schappert, J. & Yeager, R. *"HERproject Overview Presentation: Healthy Workers, Healthy Business"* BSR, February 2012.

HERproject works with doctors and nurses from local public and private hospitals to map locally available health services for women reached through the training programs. A key motivation for local health facilities to participate in HERproject is the increased demand for health services that results from educating a previously underserved population about health risks and needs.

By participating in HERproject, local suppliers and factories are able to increase the productivity of their workers. They play a pivotal role by providing access to workers, supporting worker participation, and implementing clinic improvements. These local suppliers and factories absorb the costs associated with program implementation, such as staff time and meeting space for training activities. In some cases, these suppliers enter cost-sharing programs with their international buyers in order to continue a second phase of HERproject; more frequently, suppliers undertake costs to maintain women's health investments independently.

The most important stakeholders are also the most immediate benefactors of the HERproject: the female factory workers. Their motivation for participating is clear. HERproject works towards directly improving their health. These women are encouraged to be proactive and support peer educator activities by spreading health information to their co-workers and communities.

Distinguishing Characteristics

Trust is crucial to the success of HERproject. One of the core competencies of the HERproject team at BSR is its ability to create and leverage trust on multiple levels. By building and maintaining trusted partnerships with international companies, BSR can reach out to a stakeholder group (that is likely to be uncooperative) and encourage behavior changes within the ranks of factory owners and local suppliers. One lasting impact of the HERproject may be that it breaks down the fear of NGOs within a factory and creates an environment in which NGOs and factory management can become trusted partners. Such a shift in mindset opens factories to other workplace improvement programs.

> *"Our mission is actually quite broad. We are always looking at ways that we can work with the same HERproject members to continue to impact women's health."*
>
> —Jennifer Schappert
> Associate, Advisory Services
> BSR

The strong emphasis on trust highlights the need for a central actor or key broker around which the network is created. In HERproject, BSR plays this central role. As a neutral broker, BSR is able to understand and take into account varying stakeholder perspectives while still making decisions that are focused on achieving the desired program outcomes for the female workers.

From its central vantage point, BSR is also able to sustain stakeholders' engagement within HERproject. This explains the project's concentrated effort to demonstrate the business benefits of workplace health programs for women. BSR has conducted return-on-investment studies in Egypt, Pakistan, and Vietnam with the aim of providing quantitative evidence and helping suppliers (and their international buyers) assess the return from their social investments.

Like many of the other governance networks studied, HERproject too has a broad vision—to improve women workers' health awareness and behavior, and to illustrate the business benefits from those improvements so that investments in workplace women's health are sustained and replicated throughout global supply chains. While this vision provides a clear picture of what the HERproject team hopes to accomplish, it is broad enough to allow them to remain agile and opportunistic while focusing on the creation of resilient and relevant local partnerships.

Notes

1 Frequently Asked Questions. (n.d.). Retrieved May 15, 2012, from http://herproject. org/about/faq
2 Where HERproject Works. (n.d.). Retrieved May 15, 2012, from http://herproject. org/our-work/where-we-work
3 Yeager, R. & Goldenberg, E. (2011). HERproject women's health program delivers real business returns. *Global Business and Organizational Excellence Glob. Bus. Org. Exc.*, *31*(2), 24–36.

8

INTER-AGENCY NETWORK FOR EDUCATION IN EMERGENCIES

Global Governance Enterprise Profile

The Inter-Agency Network for Education in Emergencies is a global nexus of individuals and representatives from non-governmental organizations, United Nations' agencies, donor agencies, governments, academic institutions, schools, and affected populations working to ensure that all persons have the right to a safe, quality education during emergencies and post-crisis recovery.

Creation and Background

In 2000, United Nations member nations committed to a series of time-bound targets around economic and social development, better known as the Millennium Development Goals (MDGs). Among these commitments, education was identified as a key focus area. MDG2 charges the global community to "ensure that, by 2015, children everywhere, boys and girls alike, will be able to complete a full course of primary schooling."[1]

However, it is difficult to reach this target given that almost half of the out-of-school children living in the world live in conflict or crisis zones—and education has traditionally not been viewed as a necessary intervention in emergency response (limited to the provision of food, shelter, water and sanitation, and healthcare as illustrated by the Sphere Project). However, waiting for stability to be restored can render entire generations uneducated, disadvantaged, and unprepared to contribute to their society's recovery—especially since, on average, conflicts last for 10 years and populations remain in refugee camps for an average of 17 years.[2]

The Inter-Agency Network for Education in Emergencies (INEE) was conceptualized in April 2000 at the World Education Forum in Dakar. During the forum's Strategy Session on Education, it was proposed that a process be

The Sphere Project

The Sphere Project (a voluntary initiative of humanitarian organizations) created the Humanitarian Charter and identified minimum standards for humanitarian response. Those standards cover four life-saving areas of humanitarian aid:

1. water supply, sanitation and hygiene promotion;
2. food security and nutrition;
3. shelter, settlement and non-food items; and
4. health action.

Education—traditionally viewed as a development, rather than humanitarian, goal—was excluded from the standards because it was not seen as life saving.

Source: The Sphere Project in Brief. The Sphere Project. http://www.spherepro ject.org/about/.

INEE Mission Statement

INEE is an open, global network of practitioners and policy makers working together to ensure all persons the right to quality education and a safe learning environment in emergencies and post-crisis recovery.

developed to improve inter-agency communication and collaboration regarding education in emergencies (EiE). Not only does INEE's work support progress towards MDG2, it also aligns with the World Bank's Education for All initiative, designed "to bring the benefits of education to every citizen in every society." INEE was launched in Geneva in November 2000.

INEE maintained that education also required a fundamental humanitarian response and that the response needed standardization; the result was the INEE Minimum Standards on Education in Emergencies, Chronic Crises and Early Reconstruction. This has since been updated and is now titled INEE Minimum Standards for Education: Preparedness, Response, Recovery (Figure 7.1). INEE Minimum Standards are Companion Standards to the Sphere Standards.

Organizational Structure and Governance

With more than 7,500 members, INEE communicates principally through its website, bi-weekly information updates, and a listserv. Additionally, members self-organize through working groups, task teams, language communities, and individual member initiatives and organizations. A core secretariat staff is based in the New York offices of UNICEF and the International Rescue Committee (IRC), the Paris offices of UNESCO, the Geneva office of UNHCR, and the Nairobi office of IRC.

FOUNDATIONAL DOMAINS

Community Participation	
Standard 1: Participation	Community members participate actively, transparently and without discrimination in analysis, planning, design, implementation, monitoring and evaluation of education responses.
Standard 2: Resources	Community resources are identified, mobilized and used to implement age-appropriate learning opportunities.
Coordination	
Standard 1: Coordination	Coordination mechanisms for education are in place and support stakeholders working to ensure access to and continuity of quality education.
Analysis	
Standard 1: Assessment	Timely education assessments of the emergency situation are conducted in a holistic, transparent and participatory manner.
Standard 2: Response Strategies	Inclusive education response strategies include a clear description of the context, barriers to the right to education and strategies to overcome those barriers.
Standard 3: Monitoring	Regular monitoring of education response activities and the evolving learning needs of the affected population is carried out.
Standard 4: Evaluation	Systematic and impartial evaluations improve education response activities and enhance accountability.

DOMAINS

Access and Learning Environment	
Standard 1: Equal Access	All individuals have access to quality and relevant education opportunities.
Standard 2: Protection and Well-being	Learning environments are secure and safe, and promote the psychosocial well-being of learners, teachers and other education personnel.
Standard 3: Facilities and Services	Education facilities promote the safety and well-being of learners, teachers and other education personnel and are linked to health, nutrition, psychosocial and protection services.
Teaching and Learning	
Standard 1: Curricula	Culturally, socially and linguistically relevant curricula are used to provide formal and non-formal education, appropriate to the particular context and needs of learners.
Standard 2: Training, Professional Development and Support	Teachers and other education personnel receive periodic, relevant and structured training according to needs and circumstances.
Standard 3: Instruction and Learning Processes	Instruction and learning processes are learner-centered, participatory and inclusive.
Standard 4: Assessment and Learning Outcomes	Appropriate methods are used to evaluate and validate learning outcomes.
Teachers and Other Education Personnel	
Standard 1: Recruitment and Selection	A sufficient number of appropriately qualified teachers and other education personnel are recruited through a participatory and transparent process, based on selection criteria reflecting diversity and equity.
Standard 2: Conditions of Work	Teachers and other education personnel have clearly defined conditions of work and are appropriately compensated.
Standard 3: Support and Supervision	Support and supervision mechanisms for teachers and other education personnel function effectively.
Education Policy	
Standard 1: Law and Policy Formulation	Education authorities prioritize continuity and recovery of quality education, including free and inclusive access to schooling.
Standard 2: Planning and Implementation	Education activities take into account international and national education policies, laws, standards and plans and the learning needs of affected populations.

FIGURE 8.1 Foundational Domains

Source: Inter-Agency Network for Education in Emergencies. "*Minimum Standards for Education: Preparedness, Response, Recovery*" INEE, 2010.

INEE's membership is individually based; however, both INEE Working Groups require organizational/institutional membership. The interaction among INEE members takes many forms. The work on the INEE Minimum Standards, for example, is driven to a disproportionate degree by the humanitarian community and service delivery groups, while policy making is the focus of donors and policy experts in the Working Group on Education and Fragility.

Collaboration among members unfolds in many forms, including through task teams. These teams allow members to work collectively on specific areas of interest, advocate for key cross-cutting issues, and develop tools and resources to enable practitioners to provide inclusive, safe, and quality education for persons affected by crisis.

INEE is designed as a flexible and responsive mechanism that brings organizations and individuals together to facilitate collaboration, share experiences and resources, establish standards for the field, and advocate for the right to education. The network has put particular emphasis on avoidance of duplication, and at the same time promoting a diversity of ideas, approaches, and gender sensitivity. INEE does not implement projects or provide coordination for agencies. Rather, it works to enable members to be more effective.

INEE members benefit from access to information and each other. They are also given the opportunity to participate in and work on something bigger than their own organizations. Since the field of EiE is relatively new, members are able to see how their work is making a difference. For example, members created the INEE Minimum Standards Handbook and the INEE Pocket Guide to Gender, among many other tools, which set the stage for changes that were greeted with enthusiasm throughout the INEE network.

The member-driven INEE prides itself on crafting strategies based on member input. Its strategic plan has been developed through surveys and interviews with members. The strength of its leadership, especially that of former INEE Director, Allison Anderson, and the Secretariat, created the space for the organization to be successful. The drive of the members to communicate their message and their dedication to the field have been pivotal in the organization's ability to excel.

Form has followed function in the evolution of INEE's operational procedures. With growth, internal processes have begun to formalize and become more centralized and less diffused. In most cases, the INEE Secretariat takes members' feedback into account before establishing procedures such as, for example, when determining which version of English to use for handbooks and published materials.

Membership support is maintained through electronic communications and list serve messages providing new and relevant publications, job bulletins, and other information. In addition, the INEE assigns one point person to each task team and working group; this provides support for member organizations working to fill gaps in the field, such as producing guidebooks.

Oversight for INEE's activities comes from a nine-person Steering Group, with each person representing one member organization. The Steering Group provides overall guidance through input on the strategic plan. Decisions are made by consensus, which usually eliminates the need for formal voting. INEE hopes to step-up communication among its Steering Group member organizations so that their on-the-ground work may come together more effectively.

All Steering Group members have specified terms of office, as do the Chair and Co-chairs. Once their terms are completed, these members must step down and new members are voted in.

The vast majority of INEE funding comes from grants, and funds are directed to INEE through the IRC and the Norwegian Refugee Council. Individual and organizations also provide a great deal of in-kind resources (office space, printing, travel to meetings, etc.). This results in a complex financial system, since money runs through various organizations and employees who are administratively responsible to both their hiring agency and INEE.

Recognition of the value and work of INEE is growing rapidly. The network is included at key international-level meetings, conferences, and policy discussions. Recognition at a national government level is not universal, although some countries have invited INEE to assist in the design of disaster risk-reduction planning. In South Sudan, the Ministry of Education invited INEE to work with Ministry of Education staff to identify conflict mitigation factors in education policy planning. Since INEE has a signficant focus on policy, local community buy-in is the responsibility of individual and organization members working on the ground. However, it should be noted that the community participation elements in the INEE Minimum Standards Handbook are often cited as their most relevant and useful component.

INEE has worked very hard to gain acceptance for its role as a policy resource, and it has made great progress on that front over the last ten years. The next step is to push for wider acceptance of EiE as an essential component of humanitarian assistance. Currently, the proportion of humanitarian funding for EiE stands at 2 percent.

Objectives and Goals

The provision of a safe, relevant, and quality education for all during a crisis and in crisis-prone contexts is strengthened through prevention, preparedness, response, and recovery. To that end, INEE seeks three strategic outcomes:

1. to strengthen members' and stakeholders' capacity and knowledge regarding the contextualization, application, and institutionalization of all INEE tools, including the INEE Minimum Standards;
2. to enhance knowledge and capacity within and beyond the INEE network;
3. to enable an environment that promotes strengthened education in crisis and crisis-prone contexts and that influences policy makers and other stakeholders.[3]

Quantifying INEE's outputs is challenging since it is not in its purview to measure the impacts on or the number of children receiving education based on the INEE tools. What INEE can measure is the creation, distribution, and use/

implementation of its tools, as well as its membership numbers, which continue to grow.

Success is also measured by increasing recognition of the importance of EiE. Creation of the Education Cluster at the United Nations' Office for the Coordination of Humanitarian Affairs, for example, can be seen as a result of INEE efforts to bring EiE to a broader audience. Another landmark moment occured on July 9, 2010, when the United Nations General Assembly adopted a resolution on EiE.[4]

Perhaps the most important step in building recognition of the value of EiE is INEE's Companionship Agreement with the Sphere Project. Under this agreement, the Sphere Project adopted the INEE Minimum Standards as a companion to Sphere Project standards. In January 2012, the two organizations announced that they had renewed that agreement, strengthening their collaboration.[5]

Distinguishing Characteristics

INEE does not co-ordinate agencies, but works to enable members to be more effective. The result of this approach is a variety of choices, behaviors, and characteristics that have come to define the "culture" of INEE. Specifically, members share a clear vision and collective determination to ensure that education becomes a priority humanitarian response. Individual members are willing to take off their organizational hats and work towards a common goal. Having a membership that is so committed and mission driven is a truly distinguishing characteristic of INEE.

INEE has been able to generate trust among its members, to a large degree, because it does not implement programs. In other words, it does not work in the competitive atmosphere that is found when organizations are vying for the same funding. Additionally, INEE has built its members' confidence by successfully meeting its short-term objectives, allowing members to feel pride in their accomplishments while keeping enthusiasm and momentum high.

Notes

1 *Goal 2: Achieve Universal Primary Education Factsheet* [PDF]. (2010, September). United Nations Department of Public Information.
2 Education in Emergencies. (n.d.). Retrieved May 30, 2012, from http://www.ineesite.org/en/education-in-emergencies
3 About INEE. (n.d.). Retrieved June 1, 2012, from http://www.ineesite.org/en/about
4 Advocacy Achievements and Updates. (n.d.). Retrieved June 1, 2012, from http://www.ineesite.org/en/advocacy/achievements
5 Advocacy Achievements and Updates. (n.d.). Retrieved June 1, 2012, from http://www.ineesite.org/en/advocacy/achievements

9

mHEALTH ALLIANCE

Global Governance Enterprise Profile

The mHealth Alliance works with diverse partners to advance mobile-based or mobile-enhanced solutions that deliver health through research, advocacy, support for the development of interoperable solutions, and sustainable deployment models.

Creation and Background

Arguably, the most significant barrier to sustainable global development remains challenges related to public health. Disease and the lack of adequate preventative care can take a significant toll on developing populations and economies. These problems are further exacerbated by a global shortage of health workers, and the resource constraints on health systems in the developing world.

Government, businesses, non-governmental organizations (NGOs), foundations, and multilateral organizations all recognize the importance of leveraging new tools and solutions to address these challenges. Mobile technology is one such tool that offers an effective means of bringing health-related services and information to low-resource areas. The mobile phone is ubiquitous, with global penetration now at 87 percent, and 79 percent in developing countries.

In July 2008, the Rockefeller Foundation hosted a series of consultations in Bellagio, Italy on the future of eHealth. One of the four themes of the consultation series was mobile health (mHealth) and telemedicine. At the time, mHealth was still a nascent field and this was the first time experts were convened to discuss the issue. Vital Wave Consulting Group facilitated the week-long consultation with a diverse group—25 individuals representing academia, the private sector, the public sector, and the NGO community. One of the outcomes of this meeting was a commitment to form an organization to maximize the impact of mHealth, specifically in developing countries, by ensuring better coordination among key stakeholders within the mHealth ecosystem.

About mHealth

Mobile Health (mHealth) can be defined as "medical and public health practice supported by mobile devices, such as mobile phones, patient monitoring devices, tablets, personal digital assistants (PDAs), and other wireless devices." Some of its applications include education and awareness campaigns, diagnostic and treatment support, disease and epidemic outbreak tracking, supply chain management, collect data remotely and remote monitoring, and health-care worker communications and training.

Source: FAQ. mHealth Alliance. http://mhealthalliance.org/about/faq.

This commitment was realized the following year at the GSM Mobile World Congress in Barcelona, where the mHealth Alliance was launched by the Rockefeller Foundation, the United Nations Foundation (UNF)-Vodafone Foundation (VF) Technology Partnership.

The mHealth Alliance is often compared to one of its own Founding Partners—the Global System for Mobile Communications (GSM) Association, a global association of mobile operators, which also has an mHealth program. There is a difference in aims and goals between the two organizations—a natural distinction considering the different constituencies. Furthermore, the mHealth Alliance is housed within the UN Foundation, which is considered a more neutral organization.

UNF-VF Technology Partnership

Established in 2005, the UNF-VF Technology Partnership was an innovative public–private alliance which focused on issues surrounding the use of technology for development. It was a five-year $30 million commitment towards strategic technology programs to strengthen the United Nations' global humanitarian efforts. The partnership had two primary areas of investment—mHealth, and the use of technology in emergency and disaster relief. It served as the platform from which the mHealth Alliance was created.

Source: UN Foundation – Technology Partnership. UN Foundation. http://www.unfoundation.org/what-we-do/campaigns-and-initiatives/mobile-technology/technology-partnership.html.

As a result of these distinctions, many private sector partners are increasingly being drawn to it. Companies view the mHealth Alliance as a connection to the larger ecosystem—which makes it easier for them to broker relationships independently and tap into a network that would otherwise be closed to them. In order to facilitate this connection, the mHealth Alliance hosts Health Unbound (HUB), a global online community for resource sharing and collaborative solution generation.

Apart from this, the mHealth Alliance also focused on convening stakeholders around the specific issue areas, and began hosting regular conferences and events. The largest of these is the annual mHealth Summit, which has been held annually since 2008. At the most recent mHealth Summit in Washington DC, the conversation shifted to a new level of maturity, where instead of treating mHealth as a panacea for the world's health woes, it is now being discussed as a strategic tool to help stakeholders understand where mHealth can have the most impact.

Furthermore, in recent years, there has been an emergence of leadership from developing countries, who have limited resources to spend and large populations who lack access to healthcare services. These governments want to make good investments that are sustainable. Given that mHealth is a relatively new field, all the stakeholders need evidence of the efficacy and effectiveness of mHealth. However, each stakeholder requires different types of evidence and information for their decision-making, and so it is important to have a neutral organization with adequate representation of the different stakeholder groups, in order for it to provide independent, technical guidance for the diverse groups.

As a result of these developments, the leadership of the Alliance wanted to conduct a strategic realignment—mostly to set boundaries and determine priority areas for the Alliance's work. The mHealth Alliance contracted Dalberg Global Development Advisors to provide an overview of the mHealth landscape to help inform the new strategic direction for the Alliance.

Findings from Dalberg's report highlighted that the Alliance should not be involved in any sort of mHealth implementation, but rather serve as a neutral broker and convener—bringing together key experts and stakeholders to address critical issue areas related to health systems' strengthening using mobile technology.

Goals and Objectives

The mission of the mHealth Alliance is to catalyze the power of mobile technologies to advance health and well-being throughout the world, with a focus on low-income countries. The Alliance seeks to advance the integration of mHealth into global health practices, programs, and policies. It acts as the global convener in the mHealth community, working with governments, NGOs, academic institutions, and mobile firms to deliver innovative, interoperable solutions in the evolving mHealth field.

**mHealth Alliance
Mission Statement**

Catalyze the power of mobile technologies to advance health and well-being throughout the world, with a focus on low-income countries.

The mHealth Alliance is focused on the following five strategic priorities. Each of the issues has a working group and a Community of Practice established around it on HUB, Alliance's online portal.

1. **Building the evidence base** with links between mHealth, improved health outcomes, and operational benefits.

2. **Supporting technology integration** and interoperability among mHealth players, including increased connection with mServices and eHealth. The mHealth Alliance is working on furthering the creation of standards and the reuse of technology.

3. **Identifying sustainable sources of financing** for mHealth, with the right funders at the right times. The mHealth Alliance also seeks to understand the different business models emerging out of developing countries and what different groups are willing to pay for certain services.

4. **Championing global and national policies** that support the use of mobile for health. The introduction of mHealth is introducing a whole range of policy issues that governments are not familiar with, such as data security, confidentiality, and managing personal health information on distributed devices. As mHealth interventions move past the pilot stage serving only a few hundred people and scale up to the country level, governments need to determine appropriate regulations to govern this process.

5. **Strengthening the health community** with capacity to design and deploy mHealth initiatives. There is a gap within the curricula of local academic institutions within country, resulting in a next generation of health care professionals that is woefully underprepared to use mobile health technology within their communities.

Apart from these five strategic priorities, the mHealth Alliance is also continually expanding its reach into specific health topics and organizes its work along health focus areas. These topics are determined by the Alliance's strategic partnerships, and together, the Alliance and its partners consider ways to maximize the impact of mHealth solutions for these issues. The current list of health focus areas includes maternal, newborn and child health, HIV/AIDS, tuberculosis, and smoking cessation, and so on.

To measure progress, the mHealth Alliance's newly revised business plan has a detailed results framework that lays out its specific objectives and targets, including everything from a basic output level, i.e. how many members do we have, how active they are as a result of the Alliance, and what type of new research is being funded and so on.

"Our ultimate goal is to see mHealth get mainstreamed into global health. Are the major global health initiatives actually systematically implementing mobile health? Do countries have national mHealth policies? These are all measures that, for me, are the true indicators of success.

So for example, we have a conversation later this week with the Stop TB partnership of WHO and they have done a huge review of mHealth for TB. They now want to do a joint advocacy campaign to reach out to their partners to systematically leverage mobile health. Those are the types of things that are really success factors—when you have a pull from the health sector and then very proactive take on leveraging mobile in a systematic way, and more intelligent discussions around it, like at the mHealth Summit."

—Dr. Patricia Mechael
Executive Director
mHealth Alliance

At the highest level, the Alliance is looking to mainstream mHealth across global health policies, programs, and campaigns. Its approach is to leverage the collective wisdom of the community to start building "the 'mHealth Commons,' which can be defined as public goods that would accelerate the impact and mainstreaming of mHealth, which do not disproportionately benefit any one player, and are unlikely—and often impossible—to be undertaken by any individual stakeholder."

Organizational Structure and Governance

The mHealth Alliance is hosted by the United Nations Foundation, but it is governed by a Partnership Board that is made up of industry leaders from health, technology, and business, as well as representatives from government and leading NGOs. Its purpose is to provide general guidance, including strategic decisions related to its mission, programmatic focus, growth, and development.

The mHealth Alliance has six Founding Partners:

1. 1 UN Foundation
2. Rockefeller Foundation
3. Vodafone Foundation
4. Global Systems for Mobile Communication Association (GSMA)
5. Norwegian Agency for International Development (NORAD)
6. Hewlett-Packard.

Founding Partners provide leadership by serving on mHealth Alliance's Partnership Board and providing significant financial support for the Alliance's core operations. The Partnership Board takes most decisions by consensus, but on occasion, they vote on specific issues.

As part of its revised strategy, the mHealth Alliance recently revamped its membership offerings as well as its approach to strategic partnerships. The new process is an open membership, where groups have to agree to the Principles of the mHealth Alliance in order to participate in the Alliance's activities.

The Alliance is also re-evaluating its existing partnerships and re-scoping these agreements based on its new strategy—in order to find ways to engage these partners on an in-country level.

Distinguishing Characteristics

The Alliance is unique in that it serves two roles—*a neutral broker* that can convene together the appropriate stakeholders to have constructive discussions around mHealth, and *a technical expert institution* that can provide advice and expertise to practitioners and donors alike.

In order to balance these two roles, the mHealth Alliance is engaged in leveraging collective action to build the mHealth commons—public goods (action and collateral) that would benefit the advancement of mHealth, which no individual stakeholder is incentivized to undertake, and which do not disproportionately benefit any one player.

In fact, this is one key aspect that emerged from the mHealth Alliance's strategic planning process; the Alliance will not invest in any program that will benefit only a single organization. In other words, activities have to be in the interests of many if the Alliance were to take them up.

As a result of this approach, no one member is more prominent than another. The mHealth Alliance follows a horizontal network structure, wherein members organize themselves around specific groups and Communities of Practice on HUB. These groups are small enough to ensure that each member can still have a voice and represent its own interests independently, while still being effective.

This collaborative approach explains why the mHealth Alliance's mission has evolved in the way it has. Within three years of its existence, it

> *"The Alliance is now repositioning itself—and a lot of this is because the environment has changed and the needs have changed. I don't think anybody would have anticipated that the connectivity would be where it is today or that the technology would be nearly as advanced and the networks as capable of as much data flow as they are right now. And so, we went back to the community to reassess the Alliance's niche and where we could provide the most value."*
>
> —Dr. Patricia Mechael
> Executive Director
> mHealth Alliance

had already re-evaluated its strategy and goals because its members' needs had changed. Alignment of the members' individual goals and the group's shared vision is paramount. This also explains why the collaborative approach doesn't work when working with partners who joined with a fixed idea of what they hope to gain from their participation in the Alliance. Groups that are unwilling to engage in a broader conversation with stakeholders and participate in activities that further the shared vision as opposed to their individual goals are not a good fit. Partners that are willing to listen and contribute to the shared vision will ultimately see a benefit come back to their work.

10

R4 RURAL RESILIENCE INITIATIVE
Global Governance Enterprise Profile

A cutting-edge partnership between the public and private sectors, the R4 Rural Resilience Initiative is a strategic large-scale initiative to innovate and develop better tools to help the world's most vulnerable people build resilient livelihoods.

Creation and Background

About 1.3 billion people around the world live on less than a dollar a day and 70 percent of this population depends on agriculture to survive.[1] A dearth of investment in agricultural production by governments of underdeveloped countries, donor countries, and inter-governmental institutions has resulted in declining harvests and severely degraded land. In the coming years, climate change is expected to exacerbate the already high risk of weather shocks faced by these populations. More than 40 percent of farmers in developing countries contend with weather-related threats to their crops.[2]

When harvests fail, farmers suffer immediately. They also suffer in the long term, often forced to sell off productive assets to survive, thereby entering a vicious cycle of impoverishment. Given their precarious existence and lack of access to financial services, poor rural farmers adopt extremely conservative risk-taking strategies. A number of informal self-insurance mechanisms exist, such as community-based savings and lending groups, but they are inadequate. Shocks such as droughts or floods affect whole villages or regions and quickly overwhelm these traditional strategies. To address the enduring problems of global poverty, it is critical to build rural resilience against climate-related risk.

In response to this challenge, the United Nations World Food Programme and Oxfam America launched the R4 Rural Resilience Initiative (R4) in 2010. Its mission is to promote rural resilience, enable adaptation to climate risk, and help the most vulnerable populations avoid poverty and food insecurity. Started in Ethiopia, R4 will expand in the next few years to Senegal and two countries in the developing world.

The origins of R4 can be traced to the creation of the Private Sector Engagement team at Oxfam America in the early 2000s. Behind a shift in mindset, Oxfam America's executive leadership established the team to reshape its private sector interactions—fundraising, advocacy, and programmatic support—in order to foster opportunities for constructive collaboration. One of the first examples of innovative private sector engagement to emerge was the Horn of Africa Risk Transfer for Adoption (HARITA) project, the immediate predecessor to R4.

The impetus for HARITA came from a conversation between Marjory Victor, an erstwhile member of Oxfam America's private sector team, and Mark Way of SwissRe Insurance. They spoke at a conference on climate change in New York City in the spring of 2007 and realized that they had a number of shared interests. SwissRe wanted to build commercially viable micro-insurance markets but had neither access to those markets nor the trust of the local communities. Oxfam, meanwhile, had a large local network and the trust of the community, but it did not have expertise in micro-insurance. It was on the lookout for a private sector partner.

Exploratory conversations began, with Victor and Way serving as internal champions for collaboration within their respective organizations. At the Clinton Global Initiative meeting in New York in September 2008, Oxfam America and SwissRe formally announced a joint risk management initiative for farmers in Tigray, Ethiopia. In the year that followed, both partners conducted preliminary field visits and worked to engage local partners and refine local relationships. Finally, in the spring of 2009, HARITA was launched as a three-year pilot project. HARITA emphasized two strategies: (1) reducing on-the-ground risk at the community level through infrastructure improvements, and (2) transferring community risk through micro-insurance, micro-savings and micro-credit. HARITA broke ground in the field of risk management by creating the innovative "insurance-for-work" model, enabling Ethiopia's poorest farmers to use their own labor to pay for insurance on community-level infrastructure-enhancement projects.

At about the same time, the World Food Programme was exploring the potential of weather index insurance as a tool to make donor aid more effective. Most pilot programs in the field were cash only, but there was much skepticism regarding their sustainability. The time seemed ripe for an innovation to address the cash constraints faced by farmers seeking such services. It was at this point, in 2010, that David Satterthwaite, Oxfam's senior global micro-insurance officer, met Richard Choularton, senior policy officer at the Climate Change and Disaster Risk Reduction Office at the World Food Programme. The "insurance-for-work" model caught Choularton's attention.

A number of follow-up conversations took place between Oxfam America and the World Food Programme to scope out a potential collaboration. Buy-in from both sides proved a challenge because the envisioned scale-up, which was to be rapid, called for a dramatic increase in the project budget. However, both Satterthwaite and Choularton successfully championed the projects within their respective organizations.

The Story of HARITA

The Horn of Africa Risk Transfer for Adoption (HARITA) project was the immediate predecessor to R4. Teams at headquarters at Oxfam America and SwissRe began working on conceptualizing the project in 2008.

At first, the project's center of gravity was Boston. It then shifted to Zurich, but the project team knew that getting strong local buy-in was necessary for success. HARITA team members from Oxfam America and SwissRe began traveling frequently to Ethiopia. With the help of the then director of Oxfam America's Horn of Africa office, Abera Tola, the team began to build relationships with local NGOs and private sector partners. Tola's approval and support was crucial for HARITA's success.

One of the key players in the launch of HARITA was a powerful local NGO, the Relief Society of Tigray (REST). Oxfam America's Horn of Africa office had a longstanding relationship with REST, having worked with it on issues related to water and irrigation. This trusted relationship opened doors for Oxfam America's Private Sector Team, bringing in support from other community-level organizations. REST facilitated local partnerships with entities such as Nyala Insurance Share Company, Africa Insurance Company, Dedebit Credit and Savings Institution (DECSI), Mekelle University, the Tigray Regional Food Security Coordination Office, the Tigray Cooperative Promotion Office, and Adi-ha Multipurpose Cooperative.

All the partners wanted to take a demand-driven, community-driven approach to designing the risk-reduction activities and the insurance products. Local design teams were set up with representatives from the community, including local leaders, women, and farmers. These teams enabled an interactive, iterative process for local stakeholders to share ideas with technical experts and local insurance managers. In fact, the idea for HARITA's most critical innovation—"insurance-for-work" (see Figure 10.1)—came from a local farmer at a community meeting. Although proposals were vetted at broader community meetings, it was helpful to have core local leadership so engaged in the project.

The HARITA project was launched in the village of Adi Ha in Tigray province in 2009. Two hundred households purchased insurance in its first season. By 2011, HARITA had scaled up to serve 13,000 households across 43 villages, and the project experienced its first year of insurance payouts. At present, HARITA is managed and coordinated by two full-time staff members at Oxfam America's Horn of Africa office in Addis Ababa. Early results demonstrate that the model can effectively reach vulnerable families that were once considered uninsurable. HARITA will continue to scale up in Ethiopia as one of the four countries in the R4 Rural Resilience Initiative.

R4 collaboration between Oxfam America and the World Food Programme was first announced publicly at the 16th Conference of Parties (COP-16) in Cancun, Mexico, on December 7, 2010. R4's mission is "achieving rural resilience by enabling adaptation to climate risk through a community-oriented, risk-management focused, and market-based approach that supports the most vulnerable people to graduate from food insecurity and escape the poverty trap."

In providing a new model for building resilience, R4 uses existing government-owned—and led—safety nets to reduce disaster risk and as a delivery mechanism. The idea is to expand insurance and other financial services to create an enabling environment for pro-poor market growth. From a private sector perspective, R4 allows insurance companies to diversify risk and open up new markets in developing countries. Farmers, in turn, benefit from an increasingly

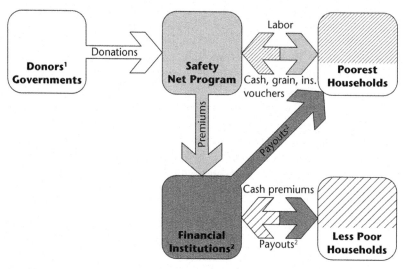

[1]new donors
[2]payouts occur when weather index is triggered

FIGURE 10.1 R4 "Insurance-for-Work" Model

broad array of insurance options as well as competitive pricing that should bring down premium rates over time. For donors, the R4 model doubles their investment value. Unlike "traditional" development programs where funds could be used either to pay insurance premiums or to carry out risk reduction measures, this project does both with the same amount of money.

Goals and Objectives

The primary goal of R4 is to improve the effectiveness of efforts to build resilience among food-insecure communities affected by recurrent climate hazards. The R4 model is based around the provision of holistic risk management for farmers, and it focuses on mechanisms that can be integrated into national social protection systems. R4 constitutes a first step towards developing a sustainable insurance market for poor people.

> ### R4 Mission Statement
>
> *Achieving rural resilience by enabling adaptation to climate risk through a community-oriented, risk-management focused, and market-based approach that supports the most vulnerable people to graduate from food insecurity and escape the poverty trap.*

Its conceptual framework (see Figure 10.2) incorporates four risk management strategies:

1. **Risk Transfer:** This key innovation of R4 gives cash-poor farmers the option to work for their insurance premiums by engaging in community-identified projects—such as improved irrigation or soil management—aimed at reducing risk and building climate resilience.
2. **Community Risk Reduction:** R4 can promote climate resilience and reduce overall risk for the community by encouraging food-for-work and cash-for-work programs.
3. **Prudent Risk Taking:** By providing farmers with access to micro-credit, R4 helps diversify their income and create disposable assets that increase their productivity and reduce their risk.
4. **Risk Reserves:** R4 provides farmers with access to savings products that help build community capital and smooth farmers' incomes amid adverse climate change.

Over the next five years, R4 will replicate this program across Ethiopia and expand to Senegal and two other developing countries. The aim is to cover 72,000 households—or 18,000 households in each country (representing a population between 100,000 and 120,000 people)—by 2016. As depicted in the phased rollout schedule in Figure 10.3, each pilot program will be implemented

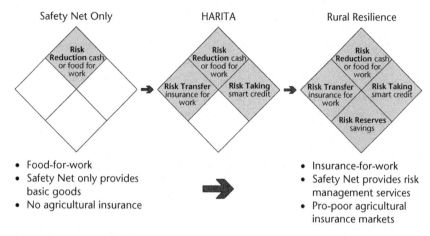

FIGURE 10.2   R4 Risk Management Framework

	2011	2012	2013	2014	2015	2016
Ethiopia	Program Implementation					
Senegal	Assessment		Program Implementation			
Country 3		Assessment	Program Implementation			
Country 4			Assessment	Program Implementation		

FIGURE 10.3   Five Year Implementation Plan

Source: (Satterthwaite & Choularton, 2011)

within a three- to four-year period to allow for program sustainability to be assessed. The immediate plan is to scale up HARITA in Ethiopia to reach 18,000 households across 50 villages in 2012.

Organizational Structure and Governance

R4 is a strategic collaboration between two primary partners: the World Food Programme and Oxfam America. Although the exact breakdown of responsibility and operations is still being finalized in each country, it is clear that R4 will be implemented in a decentralized manner. Regional offices from both organizations will be offered a program, which they must accept for implementation to advance.

R4 aims to leverage the respective strengths of its partners even as it recognizes that the participation of each will be motivated by different factors. As the creator of the HARITA pilot in Ethiopia, Oxfam America's responsibilities include program design, project management, policy and advocacy expertise, and private sector engagement. The World Food Programme, with its vast experience of implementing large-scale community-based disaster risk reduction programs and global safety nets, will play a critical role—along with local partners—in bringing the project to scale. In each country, R4 will partner with national and local government agencies, local non-governmental organizations (NGOs), local insurers, and micro-finance institutions (MFIs), as well as other partners from the local community. For local insurers, the key motivation is finding cost-effective and profitable ways to reach vulnerable and underserved populations. Lenders benefit as R4 helps them manage the risk of a default within the community. For reinsurers such as SwissRe, R4's real value comes from its experience in identifying extremely large risk pools.

R4 relies on three "technical partners" for expertise in insurance provisions, climate change, and rural finance. SwissRe, one of the world's largest reinsurance companies, will provide technical know-how and funding, while the Weather Risk Management Facility will provide expertise in risk transfer and rural finance. The International Research Institute for Climate and Society is responsible for research and technical knowledge in climate data and weather index insurance design for rural farmers.

The primary partnership will raise approximately $28.5 million for anticipated expenses over the five-year term—just under $1.5 million per year to administer each country. Each partner is responsible for raising funds to support its activities within the partnership, and there is no co-mingling of funds. This arrangement results from stringent guidelines on appropriate funding sources at Oxfam America. The World Food Programme is responsible for raising $19.5 million; of that, it has already received $8 million from USAID for the full term of the project in Senegal. Oxfam America is responsible for $9 million, of which it has received $1.25 million from SwissRe and $450,000 from the Rockefeller Foundation.

At both the global and country levels, R4 is structured similarly (Figure 10.4). The Global Coordination Team is responsible for project implementation, learning and policy support, technical support to country pilots and resource mobilization, and project reporting. The team is composed of staff from both the World Food Programme and Oxfam America.

A similarly staffed R4 Country Team is envisioned as managing the pilot program's national-level coordination, planning, and implementation. R4 Country Team leads from both organizations report to and coordinate with their respective country offices to ensure integration of R4 activities in other relevant activities. A key objective of the R4 Country Team is to garner support, legitimacy, and recognition for the project with local government and community-level organizations. This requires a lot of soft engagement upfront to inform key stakeholders within the government and NGO communities. The expected result is positive cross-pollination where R4 experts contribute to national policy discussions around social safety nets and micro-insurance. The R4 Country Teams will take technical direction from the R4 Global

Coordination Team. Both global and country-level teams meet every week among themselves and together with each other.

Thus far, Satterthwaite at Oxfam America and Choularton at the World Food Programme have handled day-to-day decision-making. Moving forward, the partnership will rely on a detailed Memorandum of Understanding (MOU) that is currently being finalized. This MOU explicitly identifies the oversight structures and puts in place various safety valves for decision-making. To tackle decisions related to global governance, a six-member management committee has been proposed, with three members from the World Food Programme and three from Oxfam America, including Satterthwaite, Choularton, and their superiors.

"We need to be able to advocate against companies when the time is right—we need to be able to apply that sort of pressure, and we need to be able to harness the power of the private sector when the time is right. And, we really need to be willing to improve our ability as an organization to engage flexibly. What situations call for constructive collaboration? What situations call for advocacy? What are the different steps involved?

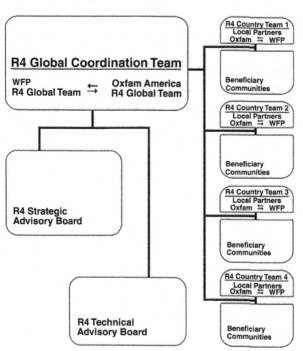

FIGURE 10.4 R4 Management and Coordination Structure

(continued)

(continued)

We definitely don't have a pro-market or anti-market focus. It's more about understanding that markets really matter for poor people and we need to insure that they work well for poor people, and don't run contrary to their interests.

It's neither a pro-private sector, nor an anti-private sector approach. Our objective should be to engage flexibly and use the right tool for the right moment."

—Stéphane de Messières
Micro-Insurance Advisor
Private Sector Department
Oxfam America

Apart from the Global Coordination Team, two other groups exist at the global level: the R4 Strategic Advisory Board and the R4 Technical Advisory Board. The R4 Strategic Advisory Board is composed of eight to ten members, including leading policy advisors (from the public and private sectors) who have made a commitment to support R4. This board's mandate is to provide high-level policy guidance and support to R4. The R4 Technical Advisory Board, meanwhile, will provide specialized technical input and review and will support dissemination of the results of the initiative to the practitioner community. It will consist of 10 to 12 members with expertise in areas such as climate change adaptation, disaster risk reduction, social protection, insurance and risk transfer, and other relevant technical areas. Both boards will meet one to two times per year.

Distinguishing Characteristics

One of the most striking features of R4 is its strong community-based approach. The local design teams were instrumental in creating R4's innovative approach; in fact, it was a local farmer who first proposed the idea of an "insurance-for-work" model. R4 partners work closely with the local community to conduct vulnerability assessments and identify infrastructure-enhancing, climate-resilience projects for the community.

Intensive and productive multisectoral collaboration at both global and regional levels will contribute to R4's success. Oxfam America, SwissRe and the World Food Programme are working closely together on program design and implementation, and not just funding each other. It is rare to find this level of fluid partnership on a global and regional scale. Such organizational agility—representing a huge cultural transition for Oxfam America—has not come overnight. It has come through creation of Oxfam America's Private Sector Department, with a central mandate to address the traditional tension surrounding private sector engagement in international development. For Oxfam America, the leap to engage with the private sector in a constructive and collaborative way has been challenging, but also highly rewarding.

Looking retrospectively, both R4 and its predecessor, HARITA, were conceived in an opportunistic environment. Oxfam America was on the lookout for private sector partners, and SwissRe proved a good fit. The partnership determined the mission of the project: to develop a commercially viable weather index insurance market that serves the interests and needs of farmers. As the partnership evolved and needed to be scaled, the approach shifted to accommodate the World Food Programme's primary interest: to improve the effectiveness and efficiency of a massive government-led safety net program. Although providing farmers with micro-insurance makes the aid more effective, creating a commercially viable insurance market is not a necessary prerequisite to improving public safety nets. Only Oxfam America was in the position to see the value in both approaches.

R4 emerged as a result of this evolution and now stands out as the only initiative working on climate mitigation that focuses on integrated risk management through micro-insurance as well as existing social protection policies.

Notes

1 Oxfam America and the World Food Programme, *"R4 Rural Resilience Initiative: Five Year Plan."* August 2011.
2 World Bank, *"Commodity and Weather Risk Management Programs to be Expanded,"* The World Bank News & Broadcast, May 24, 2005. http://go.worldbank.org/06TQDNH750

11

RAINFOREST ALLIANCE
Global Governance Enterprise Profile

The Rainforest Alliance is a global nonprofit that focuses on environmental conservation and sustainable development across 70 countries around the world, and works through a number of collaborative partnerships with various stakeholders.

Creation and Background

Forests are essential to the survival of life on Earth. They provide a number of goods such as food, fuel, fiber, medicine, and building materials, as well as ecosystems services such as shelter for wildlife, erosion prevention, water filtration, coral reef protection, pest control, carbon sequestration, and so on.

They are also the planet's fastest-disappearing natural resource—over the past 400 years, the planet has lost more than half of its forest canopy. The world's remaining forests are often concentrated in the most biologically diverse and sensitive areas, typically in countries with few protections or forest preserves in place, making them as vulnerable as they are valuable.

There are many reasons for the rapid degradation of this precious resource. By 2050, the human population is expected to have grown from roughly 7 billion at the start of the twenty-first century to more than 9 billion. And population growth has led to rampant global consumption to meet this burgeoning demand. Agricultural expansion alone, is responsible for 70 percent of global deforestation, and is the single greatest threat to tropical forests. Tourism, another one of the world's largest industries, also plays a role in increasing deforestation, pollution, inefficient energy use, and cultural exploitation.

Widespread awareness about the rainforest crisis only came about in 1986 when a major environmentalist conference in New York City resulted in the first feature on rainforest devastation in the *New York Times*. By the April 1987, the organizers of this conference had joined together to incorporate the New York Rainforest Alliance (NYRA) (Joswig & Perez, 2011).[1]

The founders of the Rainforest Alliance were a diverse group, ranging from several different professional backgrounds including a masseuse, a toxicologist, a theater worker, and a returned Peace Corps volunteer. These individuals shared a common belief that the loss of tropical biodiversity would be devastating for the planet, and wanted to act as a voice for the unrepresented peoples, plants, and animals of the tropical rainforest.

> *"People aren't cutting down trees because they are bad people—we didn't want to penalize people who are trying to make a living. And so, we concluded that we need standards to sustainably manage the resources we have such as sustainable forestry standards, etc. In order to create responsible standards, we need to have all the players in the room and work together with everybody to create transformational change."*
>
> —Tensie Whelan
> President
> Rainforest Alliance

Initially, the group did not want start a new organization, but as they spoke to other national groups, they learned that these groups were not interested in establishing a volunteer contingent to raise awareness about the issue. One of the key players in the founding of the Rainforest Alliance was Daniel Katz, a young China expert, who served as the Executive Director for 13 years, and then took up the position as Chairman of the Board of Directors. He was particularly adept at networking and his way of engaging with a broad group of stakeholders in the early stages set a precedent for the Rainforest Alliance's current approach.[2]

Underlying the Alliance's mission is the ideology that the best way to prevent environmental destruction and keep forests standing is by ensuring that it is profitable for businesses and communities to arrest the major drivers of deforestation and environmental destruction—timber extraction, agricultural expansion, cattle ranching, and tourism.

The Rainforest Alliance takes a systems view of problem solving, and considers the farm or business as a system. In order to have a system-wide impact, many changes need to take place along each step of the value chain, and multi-stakeholder representation is important to generate buy-in from all the key players. It works with a number of partners along every step of a particular supply chain—businesses (buyers and producers), nonprofits, consumers, scientific experts, educators, and students—each with their own motivation to participate but who are willing to work together to achieve a shared vision.

The Rainforest Alliance strives to redesign the agricultural and forestry supply chain by adopting a dual approach. First, it helps farmers, forest managers, and tourism businesses ensure that ecosystems within and around their operations are protected and that their workers are well-trained and enjoy safe conditions, proper sanitation, healthcare, and housing. Once businesses meet certain environmental and social standards, the Rainforest Alliance certifies them and helps link them up to the global marketplace where the demand for sustainable goods and services is on the rise. The key is to use these certifications to help drive consumer demand for sustainably managed resources along the supply chains.

The process of establishing the standard advances the goal of engaging the different stakeholders. The non-governmental organizations (NGOs) own the standard and ensure that individual farms and businesses adhere to these standards. The Rainforest Alliance merely serves as a neutral broker that convenes the network, but relies on the network to put in place the mechanisms of checks and balances.

Within two years of its formation, the Alliance had set up its first office abroad, in Costa Rica, and its first forest certification program. By 1992, Rainforest Alliance helped establish the Forest Stewardship Council (an international sustainable forestry management accreditation body), its first agriculture

FIGURE 11.1 Rainforest Alliance's Global Reach

Source: Rainforest Alliance. *"Rainforest Alliance: Twenty-five Years and Still Growing 2011 Annual Report"* Rainforest Alliance 2011.

certification program and sustainable tourism project. Since then, the Alliance has expanded its work to over 70 countries around the world (see Figure 11.1).

It offers the following certification, verification, and validation services for the following sectors:

1. **Agriculture:** Rainforest Alliance Certification to the Sustainable Agriculture Network standards is a way for farms to distinguish their products as being socially, economically, and environmentally sustainable. Crops certified include tea, coffee, cocoa, bananas, and so on.
2. **Forestry:** Services include Forest Stewardship Council (FSC) forest certification; legality, logging, and forest carbon verification and validation; and forest products chain-of-custody certification (wood, paper, furniture, etc.).
3. **Tourism:** Certifications are offered to hotels, restaurants, and inbound tour operators interested in improving their environmental, social, and economic practices.
4. **Forest Carbon:** These are offered under a variety of credible standards, including the Chicago Climate Exchange, Plan Vivo, and the Verified Carbon Standard.

Goals and Objectives

The Rainforest Alliance envisions a world where people and the environment prosper together. Its mission is to conserve biodiversity and ensure sustainable livelihoods by transforming land-use practices, business practices, and consumer behavior. Listed below are the five broad aspirational goals of the Rainforest Alliance, with no specific targets related to them:

1. **Keeping Forests Standing:** The Rainforest Alliance seeks to provide forest managers, farmers and tourism entrepreneurs with the tools to manage their land responsibly. Since 1997, the Rainforest Alliance has certified over 157 million acres (63.6 million hectares) of forestland around the world according to FSC standards. In some cases, FSC certification can protect forests even better than governments can; in the Maya Biosphere Reserve, the rate of deforestation in government protected areas is 20 times greater than in certified communities.[3]
2. **Protecting Wildlife:** Forests are home to some two-thirds of the world's plants and animals. Deforestation and degradation of these ecosystems endangers these species. Rainforest Alliance Certification evaluates if forestry, agricultural, and tourism businesses are monitoring wildlife populations, protecting migratory pathways, and prohibiting the hunting and trafficking of wild animals. In Spain, Portugal, and Morocco, Rainforest Alliance has helped to preserve the habitats of several endangered species, including the Imperial eagle, the Iberian lynx, and the Barbary deer.[4]

Rainforest Alliance Mission Statement

The Rainforest Alliance works to conserve biodiversity and ensure sustainable livelihoods by transforming land-use practices, business practices and consumer behavior.

3. **Curbing Climate Change:** Farmers seeking Rainforest Alliance Certification are prohibited from deforesting their land and must maintain healthy soils, protect native ecosystems, and decrease their use of energy, water, and agrochemicals—thereby increasing carbon sequestration and reducing greenhouse gas emissions into the atmosphere. In 2011, an additional Climate Module was added to the criteria for certification that highlights those activities that have demonstrated the greatest climate change mitigation and adaptation benefits.[5]

4. **Transforming Businesses:** The Rainforest Alliance seeks to help diverse businesses—ranging from forest managers and farmers to large retail stores and supermarkets to develop and implement sustainable alternatives to forest destruction and unsafe, unethical labor practices. Five percent of all Fortune 500 companies purchase Rainforest Alliance Certified products that are sold to consumers for billions of dollars every year by retail giants such as Wal-Mart, Costco, Safeway, Home Depot, Sam's Club, Staples, and Lowe's (Figure 11.2).[6]

5. **Alleviating Poverty:** To enable vulnerable communities to break free from the vicious circle of impoverishment and pollution, Rainforest Alliance seeks to provide them with alternative means of livelihood. It works with farmers and forest managers to provide them with the tools and know-how to manage their natural resources, and certification helps them differentiate their projects and reach new markets. On Rainforest Alliance Certified™ farms and in sustainable tourism businesses, employees receive decent wages, respectable housing, healthcare, and education for their families (Figure 11.3).[7]

The Alliance measures its progress by setting annual targets, which are specific, timely, and measurable. These targets are disclosed publicly on its website and through various communication channels such as its newsletter and blog. For example, some of the Rainforest Alliance's annual targets for 2012 included helping to increase the availability of new Rainforest Alliance Certified™ products; ensure sustainable management of more than 177 million acres (71 million hectares) of forestland; train 1,000 farmers to implement climate-friendly agricultural practices; and so on.[8]

Apart from goals and targets, however, there is also a need for the Rainforest Alliance to have metrics and data on its progress. This is particularly important, given the emergence of competitors within the sustainability certification

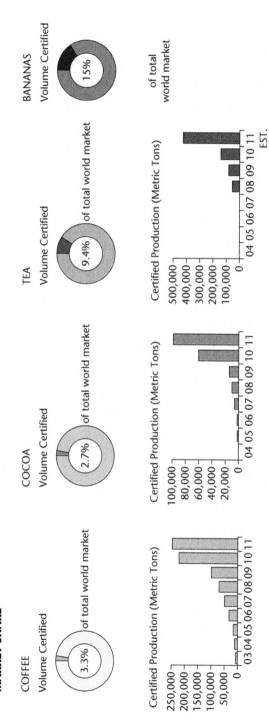

FIGURE 11.2 Market Share of Rainforest Alliance Certified Products

Source: Transforming Business Practices. Rainforest Alliance. http://www.rainforest-alliance.org/about/business-practices.

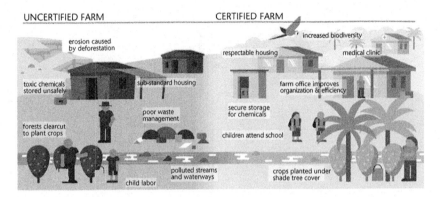

FIGURE 11.3 Alleviating Poverty through Certification

Source: Alleviating Poverty. Rainforest Alliance. http://www.rainforest-alliance.org/about/poverty.

space. There is an ever-growing need for the Rainforest Alliance to differentiate its brand by demonstrating the impact its activities have on the land and the people. This can be challenging, which is why standardized information, also known as "global indicators," is being collected from the farms, forests, and tourism enterprises that work with the Rainforest Alliance to examine its performance.[9]

The Rainforest Alliance strives to determine its impact by conducting rigorous scientific research in the following areas—water, biodiversity, environmental degradation, threatened and endangered species, treatment of workers, community health, competitiveness of community-based operations, and overall benefits of certification of sustainability practices. The Alliance also works with universities and research institutes to investigate particular project aspects and then communicates these findings to the stakeholders involved.[10]

Organizational Structure and Governance

Since the start of the twenty-first century, Rainforest Alliance's activities have grown from $4 million to $50 million—with diverse sources of funding. As a result of the Rainforest Alliance's successful growth, it faces an issue that is common to other rapidly growing organizations—a lack of funding for organizational capacity enhancement. Generally, funders are willing to provide support for specific projects in specific countries and not invest in training or new technologies for the managers. Nearly half of the Alliance's funding comes from institutional donors such as multilateral organizations and foundations, and one-sixth comes from individual donations.[11]

The Rainforest Alliance conducts two types of activities—certification and technical assistance—and is very careful to separate these within its

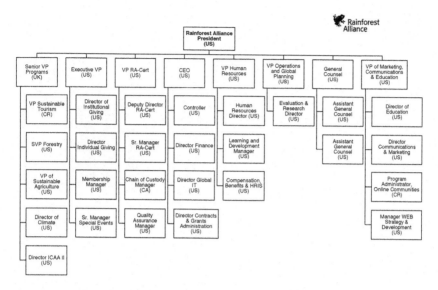

FIGURE 11.4 Rainforest Alliance Organization Chart

Source: Rainforest Alliance. December 2012.

organizational structure. Technical assistance activities are conducted globally by a network of managers and overseen by the Senior Vice President
for Programs, while the certification activities are managed separated and
overseen by the Director of the Rainforest Alliance Certification Division
(RACERT) (see Figure 11.4).[12]

Maintaining financial independence from Rainforest Alliance Certified and
verified farms and forestlands is a critical element for maintaining its ability to
provide technical assistance, certification, and verification services. The Alliance
has adopted a policy to accept contributions (monetary or in-kind) from entities
that use the certification or verification services, only in the following ways—as
fees for certification, verification, and related services, as sponsorships or other
support of public events, or as funding for educational, training, or outreach
activities. Only one-third of the Alliance's total funding comes from fees for
certification services (Figure 11.5).[13]

A Board of Directors provides fiduciary oversight of the Alliance's activities,
as well as ensures the independence of the Alliance. The Board receives recommendations from the Rainforest Alliance Audit and Risk Committee, a
committee of the Board which meets on a quarterly basis and is charged with
conducting an annual review of the Alliance's performance in retaining its
independence and neutrality.[14]

The certification and verification process of the Rainforest Alliance are
known as "audits." They are conducted by program staff and consultants

SUPPORT & REVENUE

- Fee-for-Service (36%)
- Government (27.4%)
- Foundation (18.3%)
- Contributions/Membership (11.7%)
- Other (3.3%)
- Special Events (3.3%)

FIGURE 11.5   Sources of Funding

Source: Rainforest Alliance. *"Rainforest Alliance: Twenty-five Years and Still Growing 2011 Annual Report"* Rainforest Alliance 2011.

specially selected for this job, who have not provided consulting services or technical assistance to the business being audited for at least the past two years.

Audit decisions are based upon review of audit reports, comments from the audited business owners and managers, and the input of stakeholders and peer review comments. Decision reviews are done by staff members who also have previously made written declarations of independence, which include the requirement that they have not participated in the audit being reviewed or provided technical assistance or consulting services to the business being certified for at least a two-year period prior to auditing.[15]

Sustainable Agriculture Network

Founded in 1997, the Sustainable Agriculture Network is a coalition of leading conservation groups that promotes efficient and productive agriculture, biodiversity conservation, and sustainable community development by creating social and environmental standards and linking responsible farmers with conscientious consumers.

Source: About Us/History. Sustainable Agriculture Network. http://www.sanstandards.org/sitio/subsections/display/2.

Sustainable Tourism Certification Network of the Americas

In 2003, Rainforest Alliance launched the Sustainable Tourism Certification Network of the Americas to accredit tourism certification programs, with support from the Inter-American Development Bank. Its mission is to promote sustainable tourism in the region through strengthening tourism initiatives based on mutual respect and recognition; joint efforts; harmonizing systems; and sharing information and experience.

Source: About Us. Sustainable Tourism Certification Network of the Americas. http://www.certificationnetwork.org/about.html.

Apart from these activities, the Rainforest Alliance serves as the international secretariat of the Sustainable Agriculture Network (SAN), as well as the technical secretariat of the Sustainable Tourism Certification Network of the Americas, which brings together certification programs, public and private entities that promote tourism certification and related organizations, all aiming to share information, identify training needs, and define a progressive market strategy.

Distinguishing Characteristics

Since the start of the twenty-first century, the Rainforest Alliance has focused all its efforts in three areas—developing standards, addressing supply chain issues, and auditing and certification—in which it has developed concrete tools that are effective and impactful. This focused approach, coupled with the culture of dynamic problem solving makes the Rainforest Alliance a place where people are always looking for out-of-the-box, innovative solutions.

For businesses, the reputational value of meeting Rainforest Alliance standards is an important sign of their commitment to being a good corporate citizen. However, the motivation to participate goes deeper than just traditional corporate social responsibility (CSR), which is perceived as a list of activities and projects that provide public relations benefits. In a world where tangible, demonstrable, financial projections and business cases dominate conversations for what firms should do, strategic CSR sounds very ephemeral and is not a strong foundation for private sector engagement. Increasingly, businesses are recognizing that the benefits associated with participating in the Rainforest Alliance come through its ability to improve its risk management throughout the entire supply chain. Companies greatly value the Rainforest Alliance's ability to work along every step of their supply chains, and engage with these individual stakeholders on a tactical level to create the capacity for system-wide efficiency. Other

> *"Once Unilever, which is the market leader, began purchasing all its tea from Rainforest Alliance Certified plantations, the other players—Lipton, Twinings, etc. all followed suit soon after. Today, one-half of all the tea in the United Kingdom is Rainforest Alliance Certified. And there are similar examples from the cocoa industry with Mars Company and Kraft."*
>
> —Tensie Whelan
> President
> Rainforest Alliance

benefits measured include increased productivity, improved communications, improved worker safety, and greater energy and water efficiency.

Interestingly enough, the approach of certifying products and marketing them as high-end brands for boutique markets has not really worked, as globalization has made the world a riskier place in which to do business. Instead, Rainforest Alliance has been adopted by large multinational companies who own the big, household name brands. They have the sheer market power to sell any product they want to the average consumer. With these firms, the concept of product authenticity is becoming increasingly popular. They are interested in communicating to their customers that what they sell can be relied upon, is authentic, and is responsibly manufactured.

In many ways, the biggest challenges that Rainforest Alliance will face in the future are a direct result of its success. Its efforts have proved the effectiveness of the concept of certification, and it is being adopted in the mainstream. As other certifiers move into this space, the standards are less rigorous and less impactful than those put forward by Rainforest Alliance. This may result in a dilution of the positive effects of Rainforest Alliance's work in these communities.

Hopefully, the Rainforest Alliance's unique approach will help it overcome these challenges. Whereas a number of environmental nonprofit organizations are focused merely on advocacy, the Alliance has adopted a pro-market, collaborative approach. Not only does this allow for more sustainable programs with a wider range of stakeholders, it also nurtures solutions that address multiple problems simultaneously.

However, this can be challenging at times for a number of reasons. During these collaborations, businesses can at times be quite aggressive, making partnering difficult. Meanwhile, NGOs that have a specific focus only work towards achieving their individual goal, rather than looking for ways that they can advance more than one goal. Additionally, some NGOs are brought in for political reasons as they bring a necessary legitimacy to the discussion. Government, too, can sometimes be difficult to work with when they are not directly driving the change. For this reason, it is important to balance all the different interests and keep the partners involved in the collaboration—working towards a shared goal and a shared vision of change, while also helping them address their particular issues. The Rainforest Alliance strives to maintain its position of independence and neutrality, and this is one of its key success factors.

Notes

1 25 Years of Conservation. (n.d.). Retrieved Rainforest Alliance. http://www.rainfor est-alliance.org/history
2 25 Years of Conservation. (n.d.). Retrieved Rainforest Alliance. http://www.rainfor est-alliance.org/history
3 Keeping Forests Standing. (n.d.). Retrieved Rainforest Alliance. http://www.rainfor est-alliance.org/about/forests
4 Protecting Wildlife. (n.d.). Retrieved Rainforest Alliance. http://www.rainforest-alli ance.org/about/wildlife
5 Curbing Climate Change. (n.d.). Retrieved Rainforest Alliance. http://www.rainfor est-alliance.org/about/climate
6 Transforming Business Practices. (n.d.). Retrieved Rainforest Alliance. http://www. rainforest-alliance.org/about/business-practices
7 Alleviating Poverty. (n.d.). Retrieved Rainforest Alliance. http://www.rainforest-alli ance.org/about/poverty
8 Happy New Year from the Rainforest Alliance. The Frog Blog. (n.d.). Retrieved http://rafrogblogus.wordpress.com/2012/01/05/happy-new-year-from-the-rainfor est-alliance/
9 Measuring Our Impact. (n.d.). Retrieved Rainforest Alliance. http://www.rainforest-alliance.org/work/impact
10 Measuring Our Impact. (n.d.). Retrieved Rainforest Alliance. http://www.rainforest-alliance.org/work/impact
11 Rainforest Alliance. *"Rainforest Alliance: Twenty-five Years and Still Growing 2011 Annual Report"* Rainforest Alliance 2011.
12 Ensuring our Integrity. (n.d.). Retrieved Rainforest Alliance. http://www.rainforest-alliance.org/about/integrity
13 Ensuring our Integrity. (n.d.). Retrieved Rainforest Alliance. http://www.rainforest-alliance.org/about/integrity
14 Ensuring our Integrity. (n.d.). Retrieved Rainforest Alliance. http://www.rainforest-alliance.org/about/integrity
15 Ensuring our Integrity. (n.d.). Retrieved Rainforest Alliance. http://www.rainforest-alliance.org/about/integrity

12

ISSUES OF ORGANIZATION AND LEADERSHIP

Although research in this field is growing, many questions about what global governance enterprises (GGEs) are, what they do, and how they do it remain unaddressed. The case studies provide valuable descriptive information on GGEs and introduce this emergent form of global governance to many who may not be familiar with them, or may not even be aware that they exist (Forrer et al., 2012b). The organizational and leadership issues of GGEs are a key factor in their formation and their development of their operations. A summary of these issues is presented below, drawing from the interviews conducted with the seven profiled GGEs.

Unflagging Leadership

Two specific GGE leadership roles stand out more distinctly than others—the Catalyst and the Synergist. Sometimes these roles are played by the same person, and other times they have been played by partners at different times.

Catalysts play a key role in the initial stages, as they are responsible for brokering many of the partnerships that serve as the foundation for the GGE. Often the Catalysts are renowned international leaders such as CEOs, Heads of State, etc., who command a great deal of political influence and support, and can leverage their extensive personal networks. Other times they are simply individuals (or groups of individuals)—usually practitioners who have worked in the area—whose passion for wanting to make the world a better place has an infectious enthusiasm on others to join together to do something different and to affect change.

Synergists, on the other hand, are typically not as well-known, although celebrated and respected experts within their own fields, who ensure the credibility of the GGE's actions. They help build the organizational framework for the GGE by finding ways to keep the different partners regularly engaged. Synergists must not only demonstrate the leadership qualities that "inspire the heart," but must attend to the crucial, although sometimes mundane, organizational requirements of managing, guiding, and securing funds.

One of the case studies illustrates the difference between these roles quite clearly—wherein a renowned business tycoon and a Head of State served as the Catalysts, and facilitated the launch of the GGE by helping to unite the different stakeholders. Once the GGE had been established, an expert in the topic area of the GGE was brought in to serve as the chairman of the GGE's international board, i.e., as a Synergist. He was the key negotiator in securing the commitment of various groups as partners and was responsible for cultivating a strong leadership role for the GGE early on.

Practical Visioning

All of the GGEs profiled had clearly articulated visions and/or mission statements. These visions are usually broad, open-ended statements and are determined by the interests, abilities, and expectations of the individual GGE members. A vision on how the world could be made a better place is what brings people together to form a GGE. But the final version of that vision is negotiated at the time the GGE is formed.

As the GGEs gain experience implementing their activities, membership begins to evolve and grow and the group starts to learn together. The vision continues to be the "inspirational glue" that gives the GGE its focus and rationale for existing. However, insights and understanding that come from practice lead the GGEs to adapt and modify their activities. And so the vision remains central to the GGE's purpose, but the GGE's success and its ability to partner and bring about change is grounded in the impacts and results it can demonstrate.

In some GGEs, the transition and adaptation is formally re-examined and the GGE redrafts its vision. In other cases, the original vision remains intact, although the activities of the GGE are modified and changed in response to a changing world and changing partners.

Flexibility and agility are the key for GGEs to stay relevant and to successfully pursue new opportunities and mitigate new risks as they arise. The approach of practical visioning makes GGEs seem to some as slightly opportunistic in nature, moving away from some original efforts and adopting new approaches. For some GGE partners, the attraction was the clear identification of supporting and taking specific actions to bring about change.

As one interviewee, with a background in the non-profit sector, declared:

> *The partnership determined the mission of the project . . . As the partnership evolved and needed to be scaled, the approach shifted to accommodate a new partner's primary interest. It's neither a pro-private sector, nor an anti-private sector approach. Our objective should be to engage flexibly and use the right tool for the right moment.*

Trust

Even though each member has their own motive for participating within the GGE and therefore has a stake in its success, it is rare for there to be a formal established framework to hold each member accountable and ensure that commitments are met.

For all their good intentions and earnestness, the impacts and outcomes sought from collaborating with a GGE can never be guaranteed. Unlike in an organization with a clear hierarchical structure where there are rules of engagement, in a GGE, participation is voluntary.

Trust is a key element that makes GGE members willing to participate. Initially, the GGE relies on personal trust within the small circle of Governance Entrepreneurs. The Governance Entrepreneur is an internal champion responsible for driving the GGE's agenda within their own organization.

This is emphasized by an example from one of the case studies in which buy-in for the GGE from the member organizations was proving a challenge because the envisioned scale-up, which was to be rapid, called for a dramatic increase in the project budget. The Governance Entrepreneurs at each of these organizations successfully managed the expectations of their management teams and championed the GGE project within their respective organizations.

GGE members believe that more can be accomplished through a GGE than some other effort. But members have to believe that the goals of the GGE will be accomplished, and as a new entity on the governance landscape, that means members have to trust that the GGE Synergist and Catalyst will be successful. And members have to trust that the other members will play their roles and stick to their commitments.

In the earliest stages of the formation of GGEs, establishing trust among members is crucial. As many initial decisions are made about the form and activities of the GGE, the diverse interests of members can strain relations and bring into question whether all members are committed to the common cause. Gradually, as the GGE matures in scale and scope, trust among members begins to be institutionalized.

Often the ability to leverage trust on multiple levels to create institutional confidence is crucial to the success of a GGE.

As explained by one of the GGE Project Managers, by building and maintaining trust with other partners with international companies, her organization was able to reach out to other stakeholder groups that depended on these companies. In some instances, there had been poor relationships between the international company and these other stakeholders. But the Project Manager leveraged relationships with one partner to attract other partners. In addition, her organization developed the skills and competency to create an environment in which previously unaffiliated stakeholder groups, through their relationship with the GGE, built trust with each other.

Standing and Legitimacy

The case studies revealed that standing and legitimacy are two critical factors in claiming the support of potential members and partners. The Catalyst's expertise and achievements are important bases for gaining establishing legitimacy. Reputation as an honest and neutral broker is another crucial factor. Members of GGEs have their own organizational goals and objectives. And sometimes prospective members of a GGE have had unfavorable interactions before, differences over policy or competing in the same policy space. A GGE cannot survive for long if it were to be perceived as favoring one member's interests over another. Quite often, a GGE's legitimacy is personality-driven, which is why it helps when the Catalysts are renowned and influential international leaders.

Once the GGE is established, it has to attract support and endorsement from others on the governance landscape, including government officials, well-known non-governmental organizations, and foundations. The need to have standing—acknowledgement that the GGE has a role to play in global governance—is one pressure that compels GGEs to have diverse and representative members. If the GGE membership is too narrow or seen as sectarian, other important global governance players will shy away from being partners.

In one of our case studies, the specific GGE is housed within an institute that is widely recognized as the thought leader in its field. Furthermore, this particular GGE has attracted substantial funding and has been able to maintain financial independence. This fortunate position enhances the GGE's role as an honest broker. With financial independence, it no longer needs to satisfy the specific outcome requirements that are inconsistent with its mission and goals that might otherwise be imposed by various donors.

Confederation Structure

The organizational arrangement is horizontal and networked. This ensures a leveling of individual power and influence among the GGE members. Each GGE member becomes aware of the implications of its role in the loose confederation structure. It is typical that some members are more influential in the GGE than others, but the confederated structure allows each member to participate and represent its perspective and, in some cases, its constituency.

The unifying goals of the GGE are to make some change and make the world a better place. The actions of the GGE are judged on the extent to which this is accomplished. Some members may have strong opinions about how to achieve that change. Or some members may have strongly held believes about why the problems have been created in the first place. But it is the GGE's impact that provides the "bottom-line" for what the GGE should do.

The confederation structure allows members to retain a sense of their own "sovereignty" while searching for common interests and a common cause. As the GGE matures, members become more flexible and more willing to cross boundaries in search of solutions to the global problems they are trying to solve. This structure creates a de-siloization effect within the governance space, which in turn results in the gradual evolution of more effective solutions.

This effect is recognized as the key contribution of one of the GGEs profiled. It was able to alter the approach taken to solve the global problem and move its field operations from a vertical approach (where individual organizations worked on specific solutions to one part of the problem) to a more integrated horizontal approach. As a result, it is better able to constantly evaluate its progress and respond in real-time to potential challenges.

An interviewee from another case study also spoke about the impact of having a horizontal structure:

> *Any change of [the GGE objectives] will have to go through all of our stakeholders. The revision of [GGE] Rules last year was quite an extensive process and it is likely that the [GGE] will be different in a few years' time, but the changes are evolutionary and gradual by learning from experiences in country, rather than revolutionary.*

Conclusions

The global governance landscape is crowded and chaotic, with no signs that the phenomena of governance networks forming to fill a global governance gap is abating. Therefore, it is important to understand how the different models of collaboration function and their relative effectiveness.

GGEs are a relatively unexplored territory in the space of multisectoral collaboration, and many questions are yet to be answered. Future research in this space should include questions on what makes certain GGEs more effective than others, what are appropriate measures of success, how to create resilient and effective global governance that is replicable across issues, time, and space.

PART III
Building Global Governance Enterprises

OVERVIEW

The unfortunate persistence of the global governance gap presents significant challenges to those who seek to help achieve the Sustainable Development Goals (SDGs) by 2030. Global governance enterprises (GGEs) offer a realistic prospect for contributing to these efforts in a meaningful and tangible way. Part III describes a process in five stages for building GGEs as a guide for those who seek to make the world a better place. The stages presented here are drawn from research on GGEs, the experiences of governance entrepreneurs, and others creating GGEs (such as those presented in Part II). They are introduced to be addressed sequentially, but they are refined and completed through an iterative process. Each stage makes a contribution in persuading potential partners of the benefits of joining the GGE.

Chapter 13 describes the role of the vision in attracting initial interest of potential partners to a GGE and distinguishes it from the roles and processes global policy plays in building a consensus around solutions to global problems. A description of the importance of the role a credible change model plays, relating in detail the actions that would bring about the change articulated by the vision, is presented in Chapter 14. A discussion of the reasons why different organizations—businesses, NGOs, government—might be interested in participating in a GGE is provided in Chapter 15. A specific focus is given to the motivations behind business interests in being a GGE partner. The importance for GGEs to create value that their partners can capture is presented in Chapter 16. An emphasis is made on the different techniques GGEs can use to generate both public and private value from the same GGE activity. Chapter 17 proposes organizing principles to use when building a GGE: four addressing issues of GGE design and four addressing issues of GGE collaboration.

Each of the five stages is like a rung on a ladder: each one provides solid footing for advancing and completing the next stage. However, changes and modifications made in one stage in the process of building a GGE have implications for other stages, which need to be adjusted and modified as well.

Perhaps the most important thing to recognize about GGEs is that they invent themselves. They do make recommendations on what others should do to solve global problems. They are not constituted to implement a policy chosen by others. Through their collaborative deliberations, they determine what they believe they can and want to accomplish as a GGE. The final purpose of the GGE is not known until it is assembled, as described in Chapter 17. The process that results from employing the five stages is used to take people on a unique journey that is the building of a GGE: convince people that they could join together with others (some they have never worked with before), co-create a solution that needs to be invented for a global problem that is difficult to understand and has not yet been identified, and, in the end, achieve success.

Finally, Chapter 18 argues that the global governance approach used by GGEs is largely incompatible, and sometimes at odds, with conventional global governance. New ways of thinking about good global governance are needed if GGEs are to flourish and make important contributions to helping make the world a better place.

13

ENVISIONING A BETTER WORLD

The goal for stage one is to inspire others to join together to do something different, something impactful, something good. That means articulating very clearly what it is that should be different. The vision appeals to both the heart and the head. It is something that captures people's imaginations and convinces them both about the importance of what is proposed and its plausibility. The appeal does not need to be made to some ideal world. In fact, the more grandiose the vision, the less useful it is to building a Global Governance Enterprise (GGE). It can focus on the most common and mundane global problems facing people: disease, poverty, insecurity, lack of water, poor education, etc. These most basic of human needs still have appeal to people's sense of compassion and/or duty. Alternatively, it can target broader global issues: such as global warming, human rights, sustainable supply chains, poaching, deforestation, etc.

At the same time, for all of its ambition, the vision for change has to persuade potential collaborators that real change that makes a difference is in fact plausible. The question of plausibility is not a matter of scale or scope, but whether it would actually be worth people's dedication of time and effort and resources to bring about the articulated change through the proposed GGE. The scale of global problems is staggering and provides their own justification for taking action. The GGE does not need to persuade potential partners that something needs to be done. The first question will be about what specifically it is proposing to do that will bring about real change.

Since GGEs are voluntary organizations, along with inspiring people to join a collaborative effort, it has to persuade potential participants there is enough likelihood of success to make it worthwhile for any partner. It is about "doing good," but it is also a matter of being successful: doing well. The decision to participate in a GGE creates an opportunity cost for potential partners. Today, given the proliferation of multisector collaborations, businesses, non–governmental organizations (NGOs), social entrepreneurs, investors, governments, and local communities have a wide array of choices of initiatives in which they might participate. There are so many initiatives addressing global problems to choose from that GGEs should see themselves in competition with other organizations and opportunities to address global problems. Therefore it is critical that GGEs articulate a vison that will be attractive to potential partners.

The vision sets out the focal point of the GGE and affects all other aspects of its design, collaboration, and funding. Initially, it informs who are likely to be potential partners (based on their interests or missions), the scope and scale of its efforts, expectations for its impact, determinants of success, and the resources and skills that will be required. Visions evolve over time as partners join and contribute to it. It also sets the expectations for how the partners in the GGE can themselves benefit by their participation. Articulating the change is the central organizing principle for any GGE. This first stage is the most difficult task to get right when building a GGE.

Crafting the Vision

The focus of the vision is to present to an unknown audience what the GGE would make better in the world. In one way, the potential partners may be known from their reputation working on global problems. However, working on similar global problems does not ensure collaboration. In fact, a GGE starting a new initiative is just as likely, if not more so, to be seen as a competitor than as a possible partner. In the first stage of building a GGE, some obvious potential partners may never join and other organizations, never thought of, could be future partners.

Of course, the vision has to start with identifying the general global problem(s) it is going to address. One easy place to start is with the Sustainable Development Goals (SDGs) (Figure 13.1). They are comprehensive and easily recognized as global problems. They have been selected due to their significance. The fact that they made the list of 17 goals demonstrates the global appeal to making progress in these areas. A GGE addressing one of the SDGs will have a built-in audience that could be interested in a new initiative.

Countless other organizations are looking at how their efforts can advance the SDGs. Many are looking to work on these global problems in partnership with others. Yet the SDGs are too general to serve as a useful vision. By themselves, they do not convey nearly enough specificity to those trying to discern what the GGE may do. Of course, the goals describe clearly and precisely what global problem they are addressing: "End poverty in all its forms everywhere" (SDG 1); "Ensure availability and sustainable management of water and sanitation for all" (SDG 6). However, a GGE is unlikely to select actions that end poverty or ensure water and sanitation "for all." What a GGE could do is address

FIGURE 13.1 United Nations Sustainable Development Goals

Source: http://www.un.org/sustainabledevelopment/sustainable-development-goals/.

an aspect of the complex dimensions that affect poverty or water, sanitation, and health (WASH) issues, The vison needs to make clear on which aspect the GGE should focus. A vision for a GGE needs to be more explicit than sweeping ambitions. Words like "end" and "all" should be avoided when describing what change a GGE wants to bring about.

One source that could help GGEs be specific in their aims is to take on one of the targets associated with each of the SDGs. The SDGs are accompanied by more specific statements of the issues that should be targeted in order to achieve the goal. They are more specific and identify aspects of the global problems that need to be given attention. Table 13.1 provides the targets associated with SDGs 1 and 6.

After examining what the targets say, that is still not nearly enough information for a fully delineated vision for a GGE. The SDG targets are excellent at articulating what improvements are sought in people's economic, social, and environmental circumstances. However, the vision needs to inspire: potential partners need indications that the GGE might be capable of doing something great, something profound, and something new. There needs to be more than saying we are going to work on SDG 1, Target 1. Working to reduce "extreme poverty for all people everywhere, currently measured as people living on less than $1.25 a day" is an admirable aim. No one would deny the merit of it. However, the question is: what does the GGE propose to do about it? The inspiration of the vision is not rooted in the righteousness of the cause, but in the specific change the GGE proposes to bring about.

Even SDG targets that seem very concrete and quantified need further refinement to be a vision for a GGE. SDG Target 3.1 states, "By 2030, reduce the global maternal mortality ratio to less than 70 per 100,000 live births."

TABLE 13.1 Targets for Sustainable Development Goals 1 and 6

Sustainable Development Goals 1 and 6 Targets

Goal	Targets
Goal 1: **End poverty in all its forms everywhere**	• By 2030, eradicate extreme poverty for all people everywhere, currently measured as people living on less than $1.25 a day • By 2030, reduce at least by half the proportion of men, women, and children of all ages living in poverty in all its dimensions according to national definitions • Implement nationally appropriate social protection systems and measures for all, including floors, and by 2030 achieve substantial coverage of the poor and the vulnerable • By 2030, ensure that all men and women, in particular the poor and the vulnerable, have equal rights to economic resources, as well as access to basic services, ownership and control over land and other forms of 13 property, inheritance, natural resources, appropriate new technology, and financial services, including micro-finance • By 2030, build the resilience of the poor and those in vulnerable situations and reduce their exposure and vulnerability to climate-related extreme events and other economic, social, and environmental shocks and disasters • Ensure significant mobilization of resources from a variety of sources, including through enhanced development cooperation, in order to provide adequate and predictable means for developing countries, in particular least developed countries, to implement programs and policies to end poverty in all its dimensions • Create sound policy frameworks at the national, regional, and international levels, based on pro-poor and gender-sensitive development strategies, to support accelerated investment in poverty eradication actions
Goal 6: **Ensure access to water and sanitation for all**	• By 2030, achieve universal and equitable access to safe and affordable drinking water for all • By 2030, achieve access to adequate and equitable sanitation and hygiene for all and end open defecation, paying special attention to the needs of women and girls and those in vulnerable situations • By 2030, improve water quality by reducing pollution, eliminating dumping, and minimizing release of hazardous chemicals and materials, halving the proportion of untreated wastewater and substantially increasing recycling and safe reuse globally • By 2030, substantially increase water-use efficiency across all sectors and ensure sustainable withdrawals and supply of freshwater to address water scarcity and substantially reduce the number of people suffering from water scarcity

- By 2030, implement integrated water resources management at all levels, including through transboundary cooperation as appropriate
- By 2020, protect and restore water-related ecosystems, including mountains, forests, wetlands, rivers, aquifers, and lake
- By 2030, expand international cooperation and capacity-building support to developing countries in water- and sanitation-related activities and programs, including water harvesting, desalination, water efficiency, wastewater treatment, recycling, and reuse technologies
- Support and strengthen the participation of local communities in improving water and sanitation management

What could be more specific than that? As a statement of global policy it is very precise, but for a GGE it leaves open many questions to potential partners. Will the GGE focus its efforts on one country were maternal mortality is above 70 per 100,000 births? If so, should the aim be to reduce maternal deaths to 70 per 100,000 live births in that country? Alternatively, is the target to go below 70? How much lower? Since the SDG addresses maternal mortality as a global target, lower rates in one country would offset higher rates in another country, so what is the right level in any given country for the GGE? Reducing maternal mortality can be more expensive and more difficult in one country than in another. Will the GGE focus its attentions on countries where maternal mortality rates can drop quickly? Alternatively, will it focus on countries where reducing maternal mortality rates are a stubborn and difficult problem?

In addition, maternal mortality has numerous different causes. Between 2003 and 2009, hemorrhaging, hypertensive disorders, and sepsis were responsible for more than half of maternal deaths worldwide. More than a quarter of maternal mortality deaths were attributable to other indirect causes such as malnutrition or disease. Sometimes these causes present themselves alone and other times they are found together (Say *et al.*, 2014). Which will the GGE focus on—just one of them? All of them? However, how do we account for the fact that these causes are found to have different incidences in different countries; and different incidences in women of different ages? Any contribution a GGE might make to reducing maternal mortality anywhere in the world contributes to achieving the SDG. A GGE's vision must move beyond what is important to do and articulate specifically and in great detail about how the GGE plans to make the world a better place.

There is any number of possibilities for describing what the GGE is proposing to accomplish as long as it inspires others to consider joining in a collaborative effort. The vision that is first presented to potential partners will not be the same as the final vision agreed to by the GGE partners. It is a living document that grows and changes over time. At a minimum, it needs to be interesting and intriguing enough to make potential partners want to learn more. The vision may start out modestly and be further refined as interest is piqued.

For example, the Ford Motor Company partnered with the U.S. Department of State, Hand in Hand, and other participating organizations to create the Sustainable Urban Mobility with Uncompromised Rural Reach (SUMURR) Pilot in Chennai, India (Figure 13.2).

Building on their successful SUMURR partnership, the Ford Motor Company decided to expand their partnering efforts to multisector collaborations in Africa. The new project was named the X-Car (later renamed to Better World Learning Community [BWLC]) and aimed to deploy the mobility and connectivity capabilities of their Ford vehicles to improve services made available to

SUMURR Pilot Summary

In early 2011, the Ford Motor Company launched an innovative concept called Sustainable Urban Mobility with Uncompromised Rural Reach (SUMURR). SUMURR seeks to examine how Ford could use its vehicles and its technology platforms to bridge the mobility gap for isolated, rural communities by providing them with sustainable access to key services such as healthcare, clean water, and education. Ford is not planning to enter any of these spaces, but rather is interested in exploring the commercial opportunities, both new and traditional that might arise from supporting these new markets. Ford envisions SUMURR as "wheels on the ground and apps in the cloud", empowering underserved communities around the world.

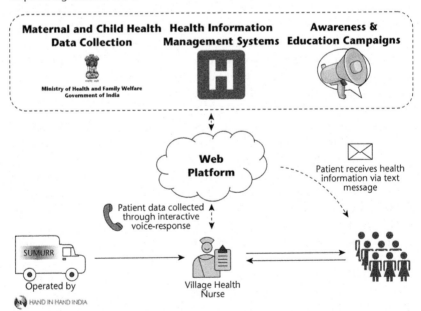

FIGURE 13.2 Sustainable Urban Mobility with Uncompromised Rural Reach Partners

Source: Author created.

communities in need. Figure 13.3 shows the illustration that conveyed Ford's early vision for the BWLC project. With one graphic, it conveyed to executives within Ford Motor Company that a solid business case was behind the project, consistent with Ford's core business interests and their values. To potential partners, it showed Ford's commitment to improving the "human condition," the importance of partnerships, the focus on impact, and the possibilities for originality and innovation. Of course, after this initial effort, Ford Motor Company continued to expand and elaborate on its vision for future pilots with other partners, including World Vision and Riders for Health. However, the example demonstrates the power of new ideas about how to make a difference and inspire others to be engaged—or at least enough to make them interested in learning more. As the project has evolved and partnerships developed, the vision has been expanded and described in much greater detail. Yet, the core idea of this GGE collaborating to use mobility and connectivity to improve the human condition has remained as the key touchstone that is the shared interests of all the partners.

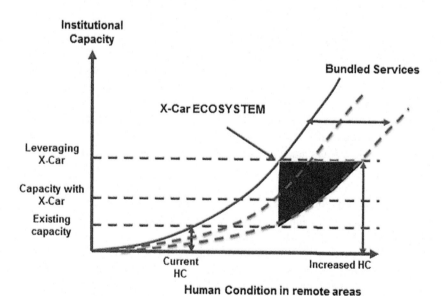

X-Car shifts the curve out and when the X-Car provides bundled services (creating an ecosystem), it shifts the curve even farther

FIGURE 13.3   Vision for Project Better World

Source: Author created.

The claim that neither the SDGs nor their targets are precise enough to inform potential partners of the GGE's vision is not a criticism of how they have been conceived or written. Of course, they were not crafted to serve the role of a vision for a future GGE. As statements of global policy, they were parsed and honed in reaction to the various constituencies, interests, and stakeholders who needed to fashion language reflecting their shared ambitions and ideals. Such descriptions of global policy goals reflect a fine art of stating the goals in enough detail so people understand the basic aims, but not making them so particular as to exclude support from important constituencies. However, visions for GGEs have a very different role. They need to be written with a different result in mind, and so the articulation and the process used to development these ideas need to be different as well.

The Vision is Not Global Policy

Building support to advance a global policy that addresses a global problem follows a well-worn pathway. Once the problem has been identified, a problem statement is sorted out, a solution is formulated and described, interests and supporters are recruited, and then success is found in legislation, frameworks, treaties, proclamations, declarations, and accords being approved that adopt the proposed solution. This approach is built around a series of actions, including: calling attention to a problem to solve, building support around its importance, identifying alternative approaches for a course of action to take, and then securing a coalition to support approval of a specific policy approach. Those who work on such problem statements typically anticipate they are not the only ones putting forward ideas that they are advocating to be taken. Advancing global policies is a competitive sport. Different ideas about the nature of the global problem, the causes behind it, what actions will be effective (and ineffective), and how quickly change can be achieved all compete with each other.

From one point of view, this is a healthy way to pressure those who are putting forward global policies to make clear that their ideas are rational, supported by evidence, and cost-effective. It is a "market-place" of ideas, and those who assemble the best ideas and make the most persuasive case flourish. On the other hand, the competition over whose global policy is adopted tends to push advocates to overstate their claims about policy benefits and impact, and narrow the focus to more simple formulations and catchy phrases in order to counteract doubts about the policy's efficacy. They also redirect attention away from ambiguities in the theories and research that are invoked to justify it.

Nothing in the above discussion is intended as a criticism or a shortcoming of any of these advocates of global policies. Building successful GGEs requires a very different approach to articulating a concise vision that describes the "global problem" the GGE will address fully and adequately. First, the language that is used to build political coalitions around global policies is different from the language that articulates the vision for the GGEs. The language of making global policy is the language of advocacy and persuasion. The language is used to create or secure coalitions that will endorse and support the policy. That means the inclination is to make statements about the global problem in broad and more generalized terms in order to attract and accommodate as many supporters as possible.

A good example is the global problem of human trafficking. The definition now used by the United Nations, brings together a composite of problems that have been recognized for some time: women and child prostitution, human rights violations with migrant workers, child labor, and slave trafficking, among others. The global policy perspective of human trafficking amalgamates all these issues together and puts them all under one "policy umbrella" and claims they are common and related aspects of the "human trafficking" problem. By bringing all these separate issues together as one global problem, the issue becomes bigger in size, more far reaching, and affecting many more people and stakeholders. Therefore, the aggregation has been successful in bringing greater attention to the problem, building a coalition that agrees more action must be taken, getting needed funding, and developing policies to deter human trafficking.

The drive to build a broad coalition also means that the statement of the global problem and the ambitions to solve it become extravagant. The first seven SDGs state their aims in absolute terms: poverty and

---

Protocol to Prevent, Suppress and Punish Trafficking in Persons, Especially Women and Children, Supplementing the United Nations Convention against Transnational Organized Crime

"Trafficking in persons" shall mean the recruitment, transportation, transfer, harbouring or receipt of persons, by means of the threat or use of force or other forms of coercion, of abduction, of fraud, of deception, of the abuse of power or of a position of vulnerability or of the giving or receiving of payments or benefits to achieve the consent of a person having control over another person, for the purpose of exploitation. Exploitation shall include, at a minimum, the exploitation of the prostitution of others or other forms of sexual exploitation, forced labour or services, slavery or practices similar to slavery, servitude or the removal of organs.

Source: https://www.unodc.org/documents/treaties/UNTOC/Publications/TOC%20Convention/TOCebook-e.pdf.

hunger should end for all; biodiversity losses and land degradation should halt, and; healthy lives, education, gender equity, access to water and hygiene, and energy should be provided to all. Other goals are written using more relative terms like conserve use of oceans, urgent action on climate change, reduce inequality, and promote inclusive development. Making such absolute targets such as ending poverty for all is an inspiration for some: if you aim high, you will reach farther. However, in fairness, solving any global problem "for all" is improbable.

The point of setting out the SDGs in terms of helping and providing opportunity and access to all is less about the extent of the intended outcomes and more about avoiding debates and arguments over more precise descriptions. If the ambition in the SDGs is not to end problems and provide for "all," then what is less than "all" needs to be described. If the challenge for developing global policies is to articulate them in a way that attracts broad approval, such discussions are counterproductive. Better to make a broad sweeping claim that sustains broad appeal and the actual details will have to be worked out later.

The drive to build strong and broad support around the description of what constitutes global problems make sense for those whose job it is to develop global policies and get them approved. However, for GGEs, this approach is antithetical to what makes for a good vision. The language used for a vision is more grounded, circumspect, measured, particular, and specific. The broader the definition of the global problem, the less clear it is what actions a GGE could take to make a difference. In GGEs, solutions are not touted and sold, they are co-created and discovered. In the first stage of building a GGE, partners agree to participate with only a general idea of what actions they might take together. Rather than claiming that the GGE can solve a problem, it first finds it niche that suits the ambitions, interests, access to resources, and skills of the partners themselves.

GGEs: A Different Approach

Understanding the differences between what leads to success in developing and gaining support for global policy and what it takes to have a successful first stage in building GGEs is critical. It is a different approach than most people have encountered, as shown in Table 13.2.

The differences between developing global policy and GGEs are not intuitive and can be difficult for some to grasp. This is especially true when developing a vision for a GGE that people have never participated in or heard of. It is this difference that inspires and attracts people to think about joining a GGE. The conventional approach to developing and implementing global policies can be frustrating. People who have worked on global problems as employees on international organizations, NGOs, government agencies, contractors, corporate agencies, volunteer organizations, impact investors, foundations, etc., can see

TABLE 13.2 Difference in Approaches

Global Policies	Global Governance Enterprises
Global policies are grounded in generalizations as they secure support and move to implementation	GGEs are formed around specifics as it attracts partners
Global policy is about selling broad ideas about what works and then trying to apply these ideas (most often problematically) into local conditions	GGEs are about understanding local norms, institutions, and practices well enough to fully anticipate success in making a better world
Global policy needs to make a case for inclusiveness and comprehensiveness under the name of equity	GGEs are selective and coherent
Global policy is about what people believe should be done	GGEs are about what a specific group of people, working collaboratively, are convinced is possible to do

so clearly the gaps between the rhetoric around program goal and their actual effects. They know first-hand the frustrations behind not being able to get the types of policy changes that better reflect the realities in the field and that could improve program performance. They have seen money that is spent on development and humanitarian efforts and which is too often wasted or even makes conditions worse than before. GGEs offer a fresh opportunity to do things differently, make a difference in people's lives, and make the world a better place.

Visions are Impactful and Purposeful

The purpose for articulating in the vision the change the GGE seeks to accomplish is to state clearly to possible partners what the scope and remit of a future GGE would entail. To be useful in that role, the nature of the change needs to be very focused and clear-cut. It is difficult to find that proper balance between invoking big global problems and calling on people and organizations to join together to solve some aspect of it, and specifying in detail what a future GGE will do. Getting it right is an art.

SDG targets are too imprecise to be the basis of a vision, in part because they only address one aspect of the equation regarding what a GGE will do. Like the SDGs and their targets, the vision needs to identify what problems should be addressed. However, unlike the targets, it has to explain what changes specifically are sought to make it a better world. Potential partners need to see in the vision clarity of purpose and an understanding of the issues being addressed. To that end, visions need to address with precision: (a) what change they want, and (b) why making that change will make for a better world. The first issue is about understanding the problem so the change can be explained. The second issue is about not confusing means and ends.

The Vision Is Impactful

Successful GGEs need to demonstrate enough expertise and understanding of the nature of the problem and the issues that will have to be considered. The aim of SDG 7 is to "Ensure access to affordable, reliable, sustainable, and modern energy for all." If the aim of an emergent GGE were to address this global problem and identify a way to bring about change that would result in an increase in the amount of electricity provided to communities, the questions to be considered and addressed would include by how much will it increase (hours, output, accessibility)? Will it be 24/7 or a few hours a day? Is it available at any time, during peak hours for cooking, and/or only at night for reading? These questions quickly demonstrate the complexity of the issue: energy yes, but in what form? Electricity? Gas? In addition, it does not make sense to answer that question if you have not decided what uses the power would go towards: household uses for cooking, lighting, and heating? Alternatively, commercial uses such as run water pumps or light machines like sewing machines? Will people be charged for the electricity or is it free to users? If it is free, how do we determine who the users are? If people are going to be charged, how much? Will provision of the electricity (or gas) be linked to their payment?

The different possible combination of answers to these questions—and countless other questions—are the ones that need to be considered and sorted out in a vision for the GGE. The answers have profound implications for the sets of actions that could be taken by the GGE. Each of these actions—separate or in combination—will be of interest to different government agencies, NGOs, and businesses. Most organizations have set out their mission and goals and have established the activities they believe will help them to be realized. Does the vision align with their values and organizational goals? Will the GGE vision be aiding organizations taking a similar approach or will it be in competition, offering an alternative approach?

Potential partners will look at the GGE's vison and see if there is a possible role for them that could advance their own organizations' missions and goals. How these details are described in a vision determines which partners might find sufficient inspiration to think of themselves as participating in a future GGE. Whether a vision for a GGE is impactful is not a standalone assessment. Impact is answered through the perspective of potential partners. If a combination of organizations is interested in exploring partnership possibilities, that suggests by itself the vision being impactful. That is what matters to GGEs.

The balance between having enough answers to the questions to persuade people that the proposed GGE may be worth supporting, and recognizing that there will be further questions to answer as the GGE takes shape and develops it mission and goals, is the "sweet spot" during this stage. There has to be confidence that what is being proposed will work in the communities where it is being applied. That means having a deep understanding of the realities and conditions in specific communities across the span of the globe. Remember, the actions of the GGE are not targeting all, just a set cohort (large or small). Which means, in turn, that the vision has to fit specific situations.

The Vision is Purposeful

The vision needs to explain why making that change will make for a better world. On the one hand, the answers are straightforward: to relieve the misery and suffering of people; to create opportunities and fulfillment; to allow for freedoms, liberties, and security in people's lives who currently do not have them. These certainly are a motivation for people to work together to bring about these changes. On the other, the vision needs to represent very clearly whether the change the GGE proposes to bring about is prized because of its positive impacts.

It is a matter of proposing change for reasons that are either practical and/or moral. When proposing global policy, the two are typically linked. The SDG 1 states "End poverty in all its forms everywhere." The practical rationale is ending poverty allows people to have more productive, meaningful, and satisfied lives. The moral rationale is no one should endure the scourge and suffering of poverty. Either rationale can be supported and justified, so advocates of global policies that end global poverty are happy to have the support of those no matter which rationale is more persuasive.

Alternatively, GGEs have to make this distinction clear and concise. Anticipating future partners working together and achieving consensus on what should be done will always be built on what the expectations are for the results of the GGE's efforts. In addition, making explicit in the GGE vision any distinction between a practical or moral rationale for the aims of the GGE is critical to avoiding confusion among GGE partners over whether their actions to address a global problem are focused on "the means or the ends." Making explicit in the vision the logical linkages that exist between what the GGE will do and why it should be done can expose important differences of opinion between partners. As mentioned before, when building a coalition in support of a global policy, the reasoning behind why one group or another supports it is not so important: the goal is securing support for a global policy, no matter why it is supported.

Participants in a GGE collaborate and co-create social innovations that help solve global problems. They cannot be successful in such a collaboration if they are unclear among themselves what results should be expected from the GGE's actions. Visions for GGEs do not need to choose between pragmatism and morality—they are certainly compatible. Partners need to have a shared understanding of what the GGE will consider as success: making a change for its own sake (moral rationale) or for the results it will bring (practical rationale).

Illustration: A Vision for Child Labor?

Making this articulation of a better world is not as easy as it might seem to some. The issue of child labor is a good example. What if someone wanted to build a GGE to address the abuses of child labor? How might such a vision be articulated? First, it is one of the SDGs, so it is easy to consider it a global problem.

Searching for more precision could be found with SDG 8.7, which states: "Take immediate and effective measures to eradicate forced labour, end modern slavery and human trafficking and secure the prohibition and elimination of the worst forms of child labour, including recruitment and use of child soldiers, and by 2025 end child labour in all its forms." End child labor in all its forms by 2025 seems to be a very clear and measurable vision.

Definition of Child Labor

The term "child labour" is often defined as work that deprives children of their childhood, their potential and their dignity, and that is harmful to physical and mental development.

It refers to work that:

- is mentally, physically, socially or morally dangerous and harmful to children; and
- interferes with their schooling by:

    o   depriving them of the opportunity to attend school;
    o   obliging them to leave school prematurely; or
    o   requiring them to attempt to combine school attendance with excessively long and heavy work.

In its most extreme forms, child labour involves children being enslaved, separated from their families, exposed to serious hazards and illnesses and/or left to fend for themselves on the streets of large cities – often at a very early age. Whether or not particular forms of "work" can be called "child labour" depends on the child's age, the type and hours of work performed, the conditions under which it is performed and the objectives pursued by individual countries. The answer varies from country to country, as well as among sectors within countries.

Source: http://www.ilo.org/ipec/facts/lang--en/index.htm.

Naturally, the next focus is on what constitutes "child labor"? As to a definition of child labor, the UN International Labour Organization (ILO) recognizes that some work by children—such as helping parents or a family business and working outside school—can be a positive experience. Already, it is apparent that the overarching language used for describing child labor presents immediate ambiguities for a GGE vision. The SDG calls for child labor in all its forms to be ended, but at the same time, the ILO recognizes that not all forms of child labor are pernicious. Even adopting the language of the SDG would be confusing to potential partners about the prospective efforts of the GGE.

When the SDGs cite "child labor," it really means the worst situations, those involving enslavement, separation from their families, and exposure to serious hazards and illnesses; they are all clear targets of elimination (ILO, n.d.).

> Hazardous child labour is the largest category of the worst forms of child labour with an estimated 115 million children, aged 5–17, working in dangerous conditions in sectors as diverse as agriculture, mining, construction, manufacturing, service industries, hotels, bars, restaurants, fast food establishments, and domestic service. It is found in both industrialized and developing countries. Girls and boys often start carrying out hazardous work at very early ages. Worldwide, the ILO estimates that some 22,000 children are killed at work every year. The numbers of those injured or made ill because of their work are not known.
>
> *(Say et al., 2014)*

However, it is not always so clear what type of working conditions for children qualifies as unacceptable. For example, according to the ILO's definition of child labor, some situations where parents bring their children to farms or factories to live and/or work are to be eliminated. The SDG may not explicitly endorse children to be separated from their parents, but some family living situations are highly dangerous and harmful to children. To be consistent, should these practices end? What about the cases where parents arrange to send their children away for their own safety and security when they live in dangerous settings and protections cannot be provided from their own community? Should the goal of ending child labor mean discouraging parents from protecting their children by sending them to other locales that are safer than their own homes?

The ILO also flags homeless children living on their own on streets in large cities—a terrible condition—but stretching what we think of as "working conditions." Other definitional clarification by the ILO offered around the idea of child labor adds new layers of ambiguity around the operational definition of child labor. It refers to work that is "mentally, physically, socially or morally dangerous and harmful to children" (ILO, n.d.). Again, the ILO acknowledges that deciding what type of work qualifies as child labor regarding these characteristics is far more subject to opinion, interpretation, and community norms. Child labor is a real and serious global problem. It has infiltrated deep into modern global supply chains (Lee, 2016). However, the meaning of the term itself becomes more abstruse the more the specific and/or local conditions are taken into account.

As opposed to eliminating child labor for moral reasons, because it is considered by some to be wrong, a practical concern is that child labor affects schooling negatively, whether that means not attending at all, or interfering with time in class. Such concerns provide even more difficulties in using the term "child labor" as a foundation for developing a clear vision. When objections to child labor are based on its implications for schooling and learning, a completely new level of complexity and ambiguity is added to the discussion. If working prevents or deters a child from attending school and learning, the trade-off between earning money for a family and gaining an education arises. Is there no common ground between the economic needs of families and the educational needs of children? What if the communities where there are high incidences of child labor have poor or no schools? What good would ending child labor do if there were no schools or distance learning opportunities? What if the schools that are in place are run by extremist groups or militias that radicalize children at an early age? In such cases and others, the whole logic of banning child labor in favor of schooling is undermined. If the goal of banning child labor is to allow them to get an education, it makes little sense to assume that quality schooling exists everywhere.

Finally, the ILO acknowledges that labelling particular forms of work as "child labor":

> [d]epends on the child's age, the type and hours of work performed, the conditions under which it is performed and the objectives pursued by individual countries. The answer varies from country to country, as well as among sectors within countries.
>
> *(ILO, n.d.)*

This last clarification of the definition of child labor takes the final step to the opposite end of the spectrum of definitional precision from the statement of the SDG target. It starts with the unequivocal ban of child labor by 2025. However, bit by bit, conditions and contingencies are introduced until we are left with the ultimate in definitional ambiguity of what is meant by "child labor": it depends!

Seeking to build a vision on the conceptual foundations of the SDG target on child labor illustrates the difficulties and discontinuities that arise. Attempting to translate the concepts and language of global policy into a GGE vision does not typically work. Starting at broad generalizations about global problems and recoding it into a vision that attracts potential partners to a GGE leaves one stumbling through a swamp of imprecise concepts and ambiguous language. Rather than attempting a top-down approach that starts with the SDG goals and targets and tries to forge a vision based on the broad policy areas, it is better to employ a bottom-up approach. A GGE could easily set its sights on reducing the worse cases of child labor in a given country or community, focusing on a specific industry and job type that everyone agrees is harmful; or against child labor that involves slavery, prostitution, or illegal drugs, but not all of them, as that would be too much. A GGE does not carry out global policy so it is at liberty to pick and choose what it wants to change to make a better world, not by eliminating child labor, but by taking aim at a specific condition involving children and work—it is very important and a valuable distinction to make when forging a vision for a GGE.

One of the advantages of using a vision to launch a global governance initiative is that it is unencumbered by the political and institutional constraints that development of any global policy must contend. A vision does not have to be "politically correct" or conform to the way global problems have been conceptualized, analyzed, and discussed. It is free to present and bring about change in any manner the GGE and its members see fit to adopt. GGEs need to follow their hearts and keep their heads close at hand. They need to change what they feel is the right thing to do and the right way to do it. The vision empowers new beginnings and is a vehicle for risk-takers and innovators to make a difference.

It is possible that the change the GGE wants to achieve could be in conflict with the way the global problem is discussed by other organizations, funders, and experts in the field. This is why articulating the change the GGE seeks with great precision and exactitude is critical to what makes for a successful vision. At the end of the day, most people care about results. Where there are shared interests, clearly articulating what a GGE wants to accomplish can attract partners even when it is unconventional or challenges conventional assumptions and claims. Making the world a better place is the great equalizer.

The search for a clear articulation of what should be different to make the world a better place could seemingly never end. Some potential partners will get frustrated with the fine slicing of issues and their permutations and possibilities. It is one reason why many well-intentioned collaboration starts off with so much enthusiasm and then fades. Too many initiatives are founded on ideas about problems and solutions that are very abstract. Their descriptions do a much better job of conforming to political ideologies and conventional policy narratives than describing purposeful and impactful initiatives that will change people's lives for the better. But that is the core strength of a really good vision. It sets out from the very beginning what it will try to change with enough specificity and context to make it both inspiring and plausible to potential partners.

Scale and Scope of the Vision

Crafting visions for GGEs are a tricky business. The author needs a great breadth and depth of understanding of the issues at play and an appreciation for the different ways in which local conditions influence the global problem in question. And yet the vision itself must be reserved and humble enough to allow that what is to be done to bring about a better world must be left to the partners to debate and finalize for themselves. When building a GGE, vision is not about being "right," and it is not about winning; it is the first step in a discovery of how to bring about a desired change that has been agreed upon together by the collaborators. There are two specific issues that arise when formulating the vision.

Smaller vs. Bigger

It will always be a challenge when deciding how ambitious a GGE should be in demarking the boundaries of its vision. There is no reason to focus on a nation—in many instances, the scope of a global issue in a nation will be beyond the reach and likely resources of a new GGE. A specific rural or urban community may present needs and challenges that are more than a sufficient objective for a GGE. Yet, if the scale and scope of the GGE's aims seem too limited, it can be unattractive to partners, because it may seem underwhelming and will not have sufficient impact to warrant the effort partners will have to make. Over ambitious visions can be equally unattractive to partners due to worries about an inability to deliver on big projects.

A good middle ground is to "talk big" and "act small." The vision needs to have an energy and vitality that captures people's imagination, but the focus of the initial activities should look plausible and doable with very specific metrics on what change will happen. For GGEs, notable successes are much easier to build upon and grow. Any success that makes the world a better place for a community will be important to those that benefit. As the GGE evolves, partners will bring to the collaboration their own program and service delivery capabilities that might be leveraged by the GGE.

Subject Area vs. Cross-Cutting

The SDGs are framed as both subject matter and cross-cutting issues. The topics themselves are cast in both ways. Selecting a subject matter topic has the advantage for the GGE of having a history of experience, understanding of the problem(s), lessons learned about success and failure, and accepted best practices. However, it also means that there will be considerable policy-baggage that will come with discussions of the global problem.

Focusing on cross-cutting issues is consistent with the recognition that globalization has made the world more interconnected and interdependent. A cross-cutting issue like *Girl Effect* by Nike Foundation takes a more comprehensive perspective. It looks to enhance the safety, security, and well-being of young women across country and region. At the same time, such an approach means having to address numerous factors at one time in order to achieve success. The approach is laudable, but it adds layers of complexity to a GGE's future organization and operations.

A case could be made that in a globalized world, the distinction between subject matter topics and cross-cutting are less viable and useful. Given the levels of complexity and interdependencies in our world, it is increasingly unreasonable to think that global problems can be solved by thinking about them in isolation of other forces. Poverty, clean water and sanitation, health, education, and hunger each have their own SDGs. However, the interconnections between these different issues and the need to take account of many, if not all of them, when devising actions that will bring about change are increasingly apparent.

The Vision: First Step, Long Journey

GGEs are fragile in their early days. For those interested in the ideas, inspired by the vision, or impressed with their potential, their first engagement with potential partners and the governance entrepreneur building the GGE is the articulation of the aspiration. The initial phases of collaboration require confidence building in potential partners—not only the initial ideas but also that such a collaboration could turn out to be impactful and purposeful.

The articulation of the aspiration needs to find a balance of not promising too much so partners can see the opportunities for them to put their own stamp on the GGE's mission. However, it cannot be too reserved or general without risking a loss of confidence in the opportunities of the proposed GGE to take on and deliver innovative solutions to important and pressing global problems.

It may seem paradoxical to advocate for the benefits of a well-crafted vision only to turn around and underscore how essential it is that such articulations remain flexible and iterative throughout the GGE building process. Yet there is logic to it. The initial articulation creates enough credibility for partners to be willing to be engaged in a process of discovery on how a GGE would be designed, how it will collaborate, and how it will be funded. Partners understand that the GGE's vision provides a starting point of shared interests in which they find a common cause. That initial vision has to be modified, changed, and adapted to the specific ideas and priorities of the partners themselves. GGEs cannot get started without a vision as it provides a foundation for co-creating the aims and activities of the future GGE.

In public policy, the more typical approach is to line up sponsors and supporters around alternative approaches and then contest and debate to see who perseveres. Politics is no stranger to compromise, and some may argue that it is the very lack of compromise that has led to our current governance gridlock that has spawn the formations of GGEs in the first place. But the compromises that happen more often are at the expense of a policy's particulars and lead to either a dilution of impact or elevate the policy to such generalities so that more people can sign on: in these instances, the more generalized and noncommittal the language, the easier to gain supporters.

For GGEs, the opposite case holds true. Compromise and change in the ambitions and dimensions of a GGE make it more specific and detailed. Modifications to original articulation are made to clarify the actual impact, the costs, the commitments needed as partners determine the options, the possibilities, and what they are willing to commit.

Making the focus on outcomes—not rhetoric or generalities—provides greater understanding to potential partners of what the GGE might accomplish and gives these same partners a better understanding of the advantages of joining and promoting such an arrangement.

As GGEs develop and collaboration grows, understanding of possibilities, barriers, and innovative approaches grow as well, allowing for an effort of "continual improvement" of the core mission of the GGE, as shaped by those partners who will be the ones to carry out that same mission.

In political debates, it is often the case to bury real conflicts and contractions under the rug in the name of making progress and getting something done. It is left to those experts in the government and their contractors and associations to shape the details for implementation. In GGEs, it is the experts who are building the GGE, as they constantly work on making the most impactful and purposeful entity they can.

14

THE CHANGE MODEL

With the articulation of the vision of what will be the focus of the Global Governance Enterprise's (GGE's) efforts, next is stage two: a formulation of the change model that sets out what changes are needed to realize the vision. The change model shares with the vision a mixture of inspiration and practicality. It is a companion piece that complements the vision. Where the vision sets out what change(s) will be sought and the impact of those changes, the change model provides the reasoning and the logic that supports the belief that such change(s), in fact, could be realized. Where the vision sets out to engage and inspire others to join together to make a difference, the change model makes the case that such an effort is a feasible and reasonable venture.

Setting out a change model that perpetuates the inspiration of the vision and presents with exactitude how that change can happen is not an easy task. If the change model is too reliant on generalities and platitudes as it makes its case, it leaves many unanswered questions about the future prospects for the GGE. Even though there will always be a lot of future consultation among the GGE partners on the details of design, collaboration, and funding, the partners will look for the basic direction and types of activities envisioned in the change model. If the change model is too detailed and sets out the agenda of the GGE too specifically, it will suggest that many decisions have already been made and there will be limited opportunities to co-create an agenda for the GGE.

A change model is like a first audition. It gives potential partners enough sense of the ideas and approach to decide if they want to engage in the building of the GGE. Potential partners also know they have only seen a limited portion of what the GGE's full potential could be. The change model must instill confidence that what is being proposed is important, feasible, and impactful. The thoroughness of the change model, taking into account the complexities that are often at the root of global problems, and the particulars of local conditions, is a powerful way to create a favorable impression on potential partners.

There can never be a guarantee that the aims of a GGE will be attained—any potential partner recognizes this fact. Persuading potential partners to join the GGE means that doubts about its possible success need to be addressed. What are the real prospects for affecting the sought after change? What are the risks involved? What are the costs involved? Do we understand the nature of the problem fully enough to know what to do? What are the obstacles and the opportunities? What will be attempted that others have tried but failed? Why did they fail? What will the GGE do that is different? Change models need to have good answers. All these questions and dozens more could be described as providing the assessments partners need in order to do their preliminary due diligence on the GGE.

The sequencing of the vision and the change model presented here for building a GGE might appear to be out of order. Would it not be more logical to start with the change model that articulates what actions taken by the GGE could bring about the changes and the outcomes it wants to accomplish? Should not the solution to the problem be presented first so potential partners can judge whether they are excited about the idea? Is it not better to explain to potential partners what a GGE would be doing first, and then, once partners understand the proposed approach to move on next to the implementation and some of the specifics now in the vision? Maybe. However, that ordering does not work well when building a GGE. GGEs need to start with a vision that inspires partners that its aims are plausible. What comes next is working with partners to articulate the change model that demonstrates the changes sought by the GGE is feasible.

At their core, GGEs are collaborative, which means the potential partners co-create the GGE in an iterative process. The vision and the change model are just the starting points for building the GGE. There are plenty of groups that advocate for making the world a better place. There are plenty of groups who have solutions to those problems they want to implement. A GGE offers a unique opportunity to develop a social innovation that makes success more likely. The more the change model is refined by partners, the more stylized it becomes to the interests of the partners. The more the partners can express their own goals and ideas through the GGE, the better partners they will be; the better the partners, the better the GGE.

Making a Better World

The change model should describe: (a) information about the conditions affecting the global problem, (b) a Root Cause Analysis (RCA) on how those conditions promote or inhibit the better world, and (c) particulars about relevant local conditions. Combined, the vision and the change model give the GGE partners the guidance they need to make informed decisions about what actions will bring about the change they seek. The change model used to build a GGE does not have to start from scratch. Numerous change models have been designed to help people conceptualize the factors that need to be taken into account. See Figure 14.1 for one example.

The actual decisions about what the GGE would do evolve over time as the GGE evolves. Once there is a comprehensive and coherent understanding of the forces and conditions affecting the global problem to be addressed, GGE members have the necessary insights to select the types of actions that will be purposeful and impactful and suit the interests, ambitions, convictions, and resources of the partners. Often, groups form partnerships to carry out some policy or agenda that has been set and members are recruited to help execute the program. GGEs recruit partners to make a decision on what actions the GGE should take.

The change model will not be of much use to the GGE partners if it is too simplistic or too theoretical. In a globalized world, "wicked problems" come about because there are many factors involved, some obvious and others more subtle. For example, in India (as in many other developing countries), maternal mortality rates are high. Many women die in childbirth due to a lack of access to medical facilities. The World Bank estimates in 2015 there were 174 maternal deaths in India (per 100,000 live births), compared to 3 maternal deaths for

FIGURE 14.1 Pennington Change Model

Source: http://www.penningtongroup.com/leading-change-isnt-about-the-model/.

Finland, Greece, Iceland, and Poland. India remains one of the most high-risk places in the world to give birth. A study ranked India as the fourth worst country among 80 less developed nations in its survey, with nearly half of all births taking place without a trained health professional (Save the Children, 2015). It should be clear that pregnant women in India need better pre- and post-natal care and access to health care facilities for delivering babies.

While that is a rational inference, advocating more births in hospitals in India may not be a good way to reduce maternal mortality rates and make a better world. Particularly, public hospitals in India are notable for unsanitary conditions. In public hospitals, doctors and nurses do not wash their hands, surface tops are not cleaned or wiped in between patients' use, medicines are in short supply, and they are dirty. Women giving birth in hospitals are at high risk of infectious diseases. Bribes are a common requirement to receive basic medical care and service (Gale & Gokhale, 2014). Ironically, poor women in India may be less at risk giving birth at home or local clinics with midwives than in public hospitals (Tiwari, 2015).

Of course, it should be assumed the authors of the Save the Children (2015) report understood well that the health care they are recommending is expected (or assumed) to be safe and sanitary. The example demonstrates the importance of being precise in the description of the change model. Maternal deaths may not decrease with expanded access to health care facilities—at least in India; it depends. If a GGE were only to focus on access to health care services, it would not necessarily bring about the vision. The example also illustrates the importance of understanding local conditions as a critical component of a GGE change model.

In 2013, UNICEF procured 2.8 billion vaccine doses for children for use in 100 countries, including vaccines for polio, measles, pertussis, Hepatitis B, diphtheria, etc. (UN International Children's Emergency Fund, n.d.). A GGE could have a vision to improve child health through making vaccines available to remote communities, where it is most expensive to provide them due to transit costs. The change model then might be persuasive in convincing pharmaceutical companies to expand the number of donated vaccines. But expanded donations of vaccines may have minimal effects on reducing the incidence of diseases among children in remote communities.

Vaccines need to be refrigerated at a specific temperature from the time they are manufactured until the time the dose is given. The equipment and processes used to maintain vaccines at a proper temperature is called the cold chain. The maintenance of quality cold chains is crucial to the effectiveness of vaccine supply chains and the efficacy of the vaccines. Despite availability of refrigeration and other cooling technologies, maintaining proper vaccine temperature when being delivered to remote locations is notoriously difficult, and vaccines frequently become too warm or are frozen during their transportation. As a result, their efficacy is compromised. Without effective cold chains, all the donated vaccines in the world may not improve the health of children living in distant communities. These are the types of issues and understandings change models need to capture and address if they are to be useful in informing partners what course of actions a GGE could choose.

Given the complexity and interdependencies of many global problems, it is useful to assess which factors are the most important determinants of the global problem the GGE is addressing. A root cause analysis (RCA) is a good way to sort out this question. A RCA is a tool to help identify the underlying cause or causes behind some condition or phenomenon. The RCA searches for the factor that is most useful in explaining why the problem exists at all. It helps clarify the cause-and-effect dimensions of the global problem. If done properly, it sets out a rich description of the "what, how, and why" around a given global problem. The purpose is not to solve a riddle, but to identify the conditions that inform a GGE what actions it needs to take to accomplish the vision.

It should not be assumed that a GGE would try to alter the root cause of the global problem being addressed. In fact, it might be a misguided step to do so. For example, the problem of "conflict minerals" gained attention with the passage of the Dodd-Frank bill in 2010 (The Dodd–Frank Wall Street Reform and Consumer Protection Act Pub. L. 111–203). Revenue from sales of minerals from the Democratic Republic of Congo (DRC) (and adjacent nations) was funding rebel activities in Eastern DRC. The militias were terrorizing communities and violating human rights. The Dodd-Frank Act requires firms buying minerals from that region to publically identify the mines where their minerals were purchased. The idea was to "name-and-shame" firms—particularly consumer electronic firms that use the minerals mined in the DRC in their products—and deter them from buying minerals from mines where the payments ended up in rebels' hands.

If a GGE embraced a vision for addressing the problem of human rights violations in Eastern DRC, an RCA would likely indicate the underlying problem as the corrupt DRC military and government that tolerate, or are powerless to stop, rebel activities (Forrer *et al.*, 2012a). Given these circumstances, is there a change model that a GGE could embrace that would address human rights violations by bringing about major "good governance" reforms in the DRC government, its institutions, and its economy? Making such changes to the DRC government institutions would appear to be a task beyond any rational and sane hope for a GGE. Although it may be the root cause, it may also be an intractable condition; certainly beyond the scope of a GGE.

However, are there other actions a GGE might take to reduce human rights violations in that region of the DRC? Whatever actions are contemplated, they will have to give consideration to a deeply corrupt government and a fragile state (Foreign Policy, n.d.). GGEs do not have to attack root causes. They simply want to be impactful and purposeful. There might be other actions it could take to lessen human rights abuses in the DRC, even if it is not addressing root causes. Some advocacy groups have argued that boycotting electronics that use conflict minerals would be effective. Others have raised doubts about the effectiveness of a boycott. However, a GGE would want to make sure it had completed a thorough change model that could judge the likely impact of such a boycott on human rights abuses.

Too often people and organizations are advocating for solutions that are assigned to problems rather than the other way around. Some advocates have sorted out what they believe are proper approaches to solving problems (e.g., boycotts, public education campaigns, product labeling, etc.) but do not have rigorous, fact-based evidence to support the efficacy of their proposed actions. Contrariwise, the change model, combined with the vision, does not define what actions the GGE should take. It does set out an understanding for the partners as to what needs to be changed to achieve the vision, but leaves the action of the GGE to the future, based on who becomes a GGE partner and what they want to do. The change model does not identify the solution, but rather provides the information partners need to assess the trade-offs associated with many different possible actions and choose the one(s) they want.

Illustration of a Change Model: The Case of Sustainable Coffee Supply Chains

Interest in sustainable supply chains has grown rapidly since the mid-1990s. Numerous non-governmental organizations (NGOs) have formed to advocate for firms to purchase commodities and products only through supply chains certified as sustainable. Corporations have adopted procurement policies that set explicit product and supply chain standards for their purchases that promote sustainability. Governments have passed legislation and issued executive orders for government purchases to meet sustainability standards. Making supply chains more sustainable is an intriguing approach to making a better world. The complexity and interdependencies of global supply chains make them good candidates for GGEs on which to focus. An illustration of the type of information and analysis a change model would contain in support of a vision that seeks to enhance or expand the sustainability of global commodities supply chains is described below.

Your Morning Cup of Joe

Coffee is the second largest global commodity market after oil. The value of global exports for 2014 was $31.8 billion (Workman, 2015). Coffee is the world's most widely traded tropical agricultural commodity (2009/10). The Scandinavian countries lead the world with the most coffee drinkers at 9.4 kgs a year per person. They are followed by Switzerland (8 kgs) and The Netherlands (6.6 kgs). The U.S. consumed 4.1 kgs of coffee. Worldwide, about half a trillion cups are drunk per year (World Atlas, 2015).

The global coffee market is very mature, competitive, and demand-driven. The top ten roasters have 63 percent of the market share. Coffee is grown/

produced in over 50 countries. The leading producer is Brazil with 43,235 thousand 60 kg bags. It is not a new development, as Brazil has been the highest global producer of coffee beans for over 100 years. Brazil is followed by Vietnam (27,500) Colombia (13,500), Indonesia (11,000), and Ethiopia (6,400) (International Coffee Organization, 2016). Not only are coffee beans used for brewing a cup of coffee, but when put through a decaffeination process they provide caffeine for beverages (cola), pharmaceuticals, and cosmetics. Coffee production is a powerful engine of growth. An estimated 25 million families are directly dependent on coffee production for their livelihoods, and another 125 million indirectly (Bush, 2012).

Coffee is an important global commodity, including being the largest food import of the United States. Approximately 60 percent of the world's production is the Arabica bean, used for higher-grade and specialty coffees, and 80 percent of this bean comes from Latin America. Robusta coffee beans, which sell for half the price of Arabica, have more caffeine, and therefore a more bitter taste, but are easier to farm, have higher yields and are more resistant to insects than Arabica. Robusta is grown primarily in Africa and Asia (International Coffee Organization, 2016).

The global commodity chain for coffee involves a string of producers, intermediaries, exporters, importers, roasters, and retailers before reaching the consumer. Arabica and Robusta are the two principle species of coffee beans harvested today. Most small farmers sell directly to middlemen exporters who are commonly referred to as "coyotes." These coyotes are known to use their market power and pay farmers below market price for their harvests and to keep a high percentage for themselves. In contrast, large coffee estate owners usually process and export their own harvests that are sold at the prices set by the New York Coffee Exchange. Importers purchase green coffee beans (unroasted) from established exporters and large plantation owners. Only those importers in the specialty coffee segment buy directly from small farmer cooperatives. Importers provide a crucial service to roasters who do not have the capital resources to obtain quality green coffee from around the world. Importers bring in large container loads and hold inventory, selling gradually through numerous small orders. Since many roasters rely on this service, importers wield a great deal of influence over the types of green coffees that are sold in the U.S.

Global coffee markets are oligopolies for both trading and roasting. The dominant green coffee trading companies include Neumann Gruppe (Germany), Volcafé (Switzerland) and ECOM (Switzerland). Together they control approximately one-half of the world's green bean coffee market. Global coffee roasters rely on these trading companies for their coffee beans. With the merger of Mondelēz International and D.E Master Blenders 1753 in 2015 (now Jacobs Douwe Egberts [JDE]), the global coffee roasting industry now is led by two rival industrial giants: Nestlé (Switzerland) and JDE (the Netherlands). Most roasters buy coffee from importers in small, frequent purchases. Roasters have the highest profit margin in the value chain, thus making them an important link

TABLE 14.1 Largest Coffee Retailers and Chains

Largest Coffee Retailers	Biggest Coffee Chains
1 Keurig	1 Starbucks – $17.10 billion
2 Folgers	2 Tim Hortons – $3.16 billion
3 Starbucks	3 Panera Bread – $2.53 billion
4 Maxwell House	4 Costa Coffee – $1.48 billion
5 Dunkin' Donuts	5 Lavazza – $1.34 billion
Groden (2015), available at http://fortune.com/2015/09/29/top-coffee-brands-keurig/	http://www.mbaskool.com/fun-corner/top-brand-lists/13833-top-10-coffee-chains-in-the-world-2015.html?start=9

Global Problems with Coffee

- Tons of dangerous pesticides, herbicides, fungicides, and insecticides (South America).
- "Sun cultivation" techniques increases yields but results in the destruction of vast forests and biodiversity.
- Specialty coffee receives a "quality premium" price, but they never reach the farmer, and are held by the exporter.
- "Coyotes" are known to take advantage of small farmers, paying them below market price.
- Extremely low wages ($2–3/day) and poor working conditions.
- Coffee prices are set according to the New York "C" Contract market. The price of coffee fluctuates wildly in this speculative market.

in the commodity chain. The largest coffee retailers and coffee chain stores are shown in Table 14.1.

Retailers usually purchase packaged coffee from roasters, although an increasing number of retailers are also roasting their own beans to sell. Chains represent approximately 30 percent of all coffee retail stores. However, supermarkets and traditional retail chains are still the primary channel for both specialty coffee and non-specialty coffee, and they hold about 60 percent of the market share of total coffee sales (Global Exchange, n.d.).

Although coffee production generates very large economic value throughout its entire supply chain, global coffee supply chain practices raise a number of serious concerns about the consequences for people and the environment.

The global problems related to coffee production are associated with the absence of a sustainable coffee supply chain: damage to the environment, poor working conditions, low wages, and limited economic development impact. The way the planting, growing, and harvesting is conducted damages the environment. While coffee is traditionally grown in the shade, the coffee plants under the cover of other trees, "sun cultivation" increases productivity of the coffee crop. It requires clearing land and destroying the flora and fauna of the area. The destruction of forests also raises concerns over bio-diversity and a lessening capacity to sustain the full range of indigenous species.

Growing coffee in open lands can be accompanied by applications of chemicals to protect the crops from insects and diseases. These chemicals are often used without regulation and oversight, and many times excessively. Even with the best of intentions, applications of chemicals on farms can be irregular. The run-off threatens local communities and their water supplies.

The low wages typically earned by farmers for their crops are a result of their lack of negotiating power with buyers. Since commodities have a similar market value, coffee growers have to sell to a "buyer's market." If they feel the price offered is too low, the farmers have no other options. For some coffee growers who grow a higher quality bean that brings a higher price, getting the additional money from the cooperatives or the buyers can still be difficult. Corruption, weak governance, and a lack of information about markets put farmers at a serious disadvantage. For farmers who can capture higher prices for premium quality coffee beans, volatile market prices make securing loans for the additional resources they need to grow the higher quality bean risky and expensive.

All these issues highlight how unsustainable global coffee supply chains can be. The description also points out that the issues which affect the sustainability of global coffee supply chains are interconnected. Changing only one of the problems associated with unsustainable coffee supply chains could have limited effects on the other problems and therefore do little to improve supply chain sustainability. Want to raise wages for farmers? How can they grow higher quality coffee beans if volatile markets make business loans risky and expensive? Want to reduce the amount of pesticides, herbicides, fungicides, and insecticides used in coffee production (especially in South American countries)? How can farmers and cooperatives compete if they revert to shade grown coffee and lower levels of productivity? Want farmers to receive the true value of their premium beans? How do you dislodge powerful cooperatives and their corrupt practices?

Change Model Insights

The key to understanding the global problem of unsustainable global coffee supply chains is the nature of their interconnectedness. They are not only inter-dependent but they are mutually re-enforcing, and together they interact to perpetuate these conditions and the problems. Figure 14.2 shows the "Villainous Cycle" that all these factors create. The analysis could start anywhere in the cycle and run through the logical circuit over and over again.

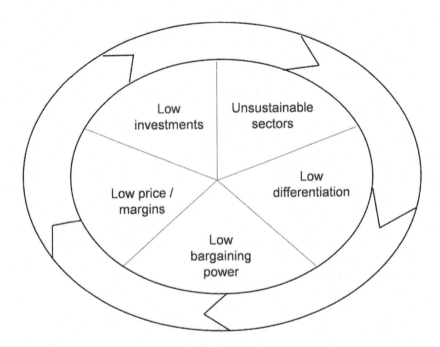

FIGURE 14.2 The Villainous Cycle

Source: Lucas Simons, NewForesight, lucas.simons@newforesight.nl.

Undifferentiated coffee beans create a "buyer's market." Farmers cannot secure higher prices because their product has no recognized value over any other farmer's coffee beans. In addition, because coffee growing is characterized by small landholders, they do not grow enough beans to have any influence on market prices. This means farmers must take the competitive low-market (or below) price. This also means that the coffee bean buyers do not put demands on farmers to adopt farming practices that are more sustainable.

These low prices for the farmer not only mean low income, but their situation is perpetuated. Higher coffee prices for the farmers could come from growing higher quality beans, but that requires an investment in different farming practices. Farmers have limited access to technical assistance and to loans, and such loans are high risk for banks due to the low margins, the volatility of global coffee bean prices, and a lack of creditworthiness profiles on farmers.

In many countries, there is limited infrastructure, farming knowledge, access to education, etc., to support improvements in the coffee sector. Governments are often weak and corrupt, with no effective social and environmental policies. There are good reasons for civil society to organize and bring pressure on governments, multinational corporations, or corrupt cooperatives to bring about change.

All these factors add up to an unsustainable coffee supply chain. Global coffee supply chains are a good example of how globalization has networked and integrated these conditions. Developing strategies for changing these conditions will be unique to coffee growers depending on their local circumstances, but one can see the shared experiences of coffee growers around the world. A similar experience is shared by others who grow global commodities. Coffee, cocoa, tea, cotton, metals, palm oil, soy, sugar, timber, fish, and others are all undifferentiated commodities that have similar global supply chain issues. They are a major source of income for many countries and support the livelihoods of hundreds of millions of families. Coffee is just one of many commodity supply chains that could be viewed as encouraging a "race to the bottom." The commodities are grown, harvested, and sold for money that barely sustains a family's needs, and yet is used for high value-added products that enrich firms and investors.

The integrated view of the Villainous Cycle of coffee supply chains makes clear the trade-offs that would come with making changes to bring about greater sustainability. For example, the low wages that farmers earn for growing and harvesting coffee translate into lower prices for coffee buyers, which in turn translate into the lower prices which consumers have become accustomed to paying for their Dunkin' Donuts coffee, Starbucks frappuccino's, and McDonald's lattes.

Such a description reveals that making global coffee supply chains more sustainable is going to take an integrated and multi-faceted approach. One possibility is to change the Villainous Cycle into a "Virtuous Cycle." This idea is represented in Figure 14.3. It illustrates a concept about how coffee supply chains could be made sustainable by taking into account the typical situation facing coffee farmers, commodity markets, marketing, retail firms, and consumers and finding shared interests in bringing about change. The Virtuous Cycle re-conceptualizes how markets might be organized for coffee supply chains, grounded in the full understanding of how business incentives are currently aligned and how any approach to increasing sustainability must recognize and respond to those incentives.

The Virtuous Cycle begins with setting standards for what constitutes sustainable coffee supply chains. The changes in farming practices and the resulting potential increased quality in coffee bean production adds value to farmers, lenders, buyers, consumers, etc. Credible auditing services of sustainable practices need to be instituted to ensure the integrity of the claims regarding beans coming from sustainable coffee supply chains. The potential of increased market value from adoption of sustainability standards is appropriated through communications to customers over brand value of sustainable products, typically through certification labeling (e.g., Free Trade) or product lines (Whole Foods 365). Brand awareness and consumer preference for sustainable products expands the demand for products from sustainable supply chains. Greater demand for sustainable supply chains increases rewards to farmers for growing sustainable coffee beans.

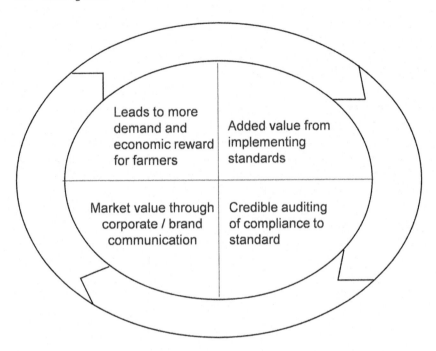

FIGURE 14.3 The Virtuous Cycle

Source: Lucas Simons, NewForesight, lucas.simons@newforesight.nl.

Just as the Villainous Cycle made clear the point that conditions judged to be antithetical to sustainability were self-re-enforcing, any actions that could change the situation would have to devise an approach that was consistent with the interconnected nature of coffee supply chains, but with different outcomes. Both "Cycles" are complex, befitting of descriptions of events that mean to capture the full complexity brought on by globalization.

One aspect of that complexity is the effort to see supply and demand issues in supply chains in terms of mutuality rather than opposition. Changing farming practices in ways that promote sustainable supply chains ends up raising the cost of commodities and the price of sustainable products to consumers (Forrer & Mo, 2013). This characterization puts farmers and consumers in a contest over higher wages and higher prices. However, the Virtuous Cycle builds value-added into its conceptual model. Since the products are worth more to consumers—being sustainable—increased product prices are acceptable, even welcomed.

Today, this approach has garnered a lot of attention. Some early GGEs, like Rainforest Alliance, were involved early on and now it is commonplace. Rainforest Alliance certifies nearly 100 brands of coffee consumers can buy, including Dunkin' Donuts and Caribou. Some Starbucks coffee is certified by Fairtrade (and supplemented by Starbuck's own (Coffee and Farmer Equity

(C.A.F.E) sourcing program). Over 30 billion cups of UTZ (based in the EU) certified coffees were sold in 2014 alone, and you can now drink UTZ coffee in over 64 countries worldwide (UTZ, n.d.).

Despite the popularity of certified coffee, it is just one proposed aspect of the Virtuous Cycle. For a GGE whose vision is to improve the lives of farmers, the track record on increased sales of certified coffee is not the proper measure; sales of certified products is the proposed measure for a GGE whose aim is to increase sales of certified coffee. The impact of certified coffee sales on farmers is far less clear. Anecdotal stories relate farmers who have done better by growing sustainable coffee. However, among some of the issues are that the premiums paid by consumers are not going directly to farmers, the quality of certified coffee is uneven, or certification only requires some portion of the product (minimum 30 percent for Rainforest Alliance) to be certified, and, finally, certified coffee has evolved from an economic and social justice movement to largely a marketing play for ethical consumerism (Haight, 2011).

Sustainable coffee supply chains offer good illustrations of the details and depth of understanding of the issues around global problems in order to construct a change model that supports a vision that is impactful and purposeful. Effective change models delve into conditions around global problems beyond the accepted wisdom or standard presentations. It explores possibilities and reasons why conditions exist that help guide partners to make the best decisions for the GGE.

Framing the GGE Change Model

Globalization has ramped up the complexity and interdependencies of our world to a point where we can no longer afford to think through issues and develop solutions confined by a single discipline or constrained by bureaucratic silos. If we do, the "solutions" that are developed to solve global problems will have limited application to real-world circumstances. The change model offers a clear and comprehensive perspective on conditions that need to be changed to achieve the vision. The discussions are framed when analyzing and describing such issues and developing potential ways to address them. These framings largely come from academic disciplines that have been used in support of the creation of problem statements, public policy analyses, and/or proposals. It is useful to identify clearly such framings when constructing the vision. Undoubtedly, there are an infinite number of framings that could be used to create a vision, but there are four popular ways to frame the thinking about innovative ways of bringing about change that matters:

1. improve and/or create markets;
2. greater access to public goods or services;
3. making supply chains sustainable;
4. honoring global commons.

There are of course, no wrong or right framings. People look at the world through different prisms of thought, depending on their experiences, culture, community, academic education, the media they follow, or politics. The choices that are made as to which framing(s) will guide the logic and the reasoning of the change model have profound implications for the future work of the GGE. Whatever frames are used—whether from the list of four frames described here or some others—it should be clear and explicit. Each of the frames will end up directing the discussion about the problems, solutions, and changes to particular rationales around why problems exist at all, what can or cannot be changed, what can bring about change, and what are useful actions that will bring about the vision?

Improve and/or Create Markets

The general perspective for this frame is that problems exist because of the absence of properly functioning markets. Markets create opportunities, but they do not always operate or provide products and services at the prices people want. In remote rural areas, markets are typically weak because it is easier, cheaper, and more profitable to provide services in urban areas where customers are concentrated. Or markets may offer products and services too expensive for certain populations or even whole communities to afford. Many of the Sustainable Development Goals (SDGs) would be considered classic "public goods" and would be seen as only being provided through government action because businesses cannot provide them *and* make a profit—so they would not.

So the efforts that would be associated with this framing are focused on facilitating markets to act (more) efficiently. In the case of market failures (e.g., natural monopolies, public goods, externalities, asymmetric information access), government regulation is one typical response to market failures. Market failures can also be addressed by improving the efficiency of markets or creating new markets. Markets can also be incorporated into government regulations such as carbon credit markets or cap and trade regimes for pollution emissions.

For GGEs to make changes through markets, a creative, innovative approach needs to be developed that explains why markets are not addressing certain global problems in the first place. What is inhibiting markets from forming or clearing properly? How can externalities generated by market exchanges be internalized or monetized? What empowering technologies and innovations can help expand markets? How can the provision of public goods and services and private goods and services be better integrated? How can "leapfrog technologies" be used to create new markets? Examples of the type of innovations GGEs may consider could include concepts such as Bottom-of-the-Pyramid and Creating Shared Value; social entrepreneurship projects run by Grameen Bank; micro-financing run by Kiva; and hybrid enterprise models like Coca-Cola's EKOCENTERs.

Access to Public Goods and Services

Reasons for global problems are often tied to the lack of access to basic public goods and services. Many of the SDGs speak directly to this point. A lack of access to clean water, energy, education, etc., is the way many global problems are framed. When framed this way, the implicit solution is embedded in the statement of the problem: if the problem is the lack of access to public goods and services, the logical solution is to provide that access. When framed this way, the solution may seem obvious, but in terms of framing the issue for a change model to address, it does not provide much guidance on why the situation exists or what might be changed to increase that access. A lack of access to public goods and services is more of an observation than the framing for an effective change model.

Framing the issue strictly as a lack of access to public goods and services may be accurate, but it is not dynamic enough for a GGE change model. Using this same framing can be beneficial when looking at other related issues. For example, immigrants often have trouble adapting to their new communities, particularly when they do not know the home language. Lack of access to education and training is cited as a major reason why immigrants have difficulty integrating into the community, cannot easily find work, be accepted by a bank for financial services, struggle in school, low engagement with community organizations, etc. The inability of immigrants to integrate into the home community is a concern for both the immigrant and local communities. Lack of access to education and training is a common source cited for many global problems, particularly related to global health issues.

For GGEs to make change by expanding access to public goods and services through a creative, innovative approach, an understanding is needed as to why public goods and services are not being provided in the first place. Is there a shortage of public funding available? Are the communities where the immigrants are located suffering already from poor education and training services? Is the immigrant community relatively small so there is limited demand for such services (regardless of how sorely they are needed)? Examples of the type of innovations GGEs may consider could include: eHealth and mHealth programs targeting remote communities; One Laptop Per Child; Global Education Partnerships; World Bicycle Relief; Water, Sanitation and Hygiene Resource Center Network Nepal (WASH_RCNN); and the Janicki Omniprocessor.

Making Supply Chains Sustainable

Global supply chains are so large and such a dominant feature of the global economy, many issues can be framed as a matter of sustainable supply chains. Corporations face increased pressure to make their supply chains sustainable.

Their actions can influence the economic, social, political, and environmental conditions in communities around the world. For example, human rights violations can be difficult to address when national governments are too weak or too disinterested to take actions. However, corporations with supply chains are called upon to ensure that the firms they are sourcing products and services from do not tolerate human rights abuses. Many high-visibility issues interact with company supply chains: human trafficking, land tenure, poverty, women's empowerment, etc. As brand reputation becomes an increasingly important asset for global firms, sustainable supply chains have become a way for firms to represent to their customers the positive effects they can have on society.

It is important to remember that corporations—even those who are deeply committed to adopting and instituting sustainable practices in their supply chains—can face limitations on the practices they can adopt. Supplies of products matching the characteristics of sustainability can be limited. Most commodity supply chains are not fully traceable all the way to a product's origin. Many commodities are blended in the early stages of processing and lose their identity altogether. Auditing sustainability practices can be expensive and are not always reliable or comprehensive. Sustainable products can be blended with non-sustainable products, but still retain certification as a "sustainable product."

For GGEs to make change through sustainable supply chains, a creative, innovative approach needs to be developed to address the issues above that explain why supply chains are not more sustainable. What prevents a firm from committing to sustainable procurements? How can better information about sustainability practices be monitored? What lessons can be learned about sustainability in one commodity supply chain that are applicable to other supply chains? How can firms support more sustainable supply chains without facing the prospect of needing to raise prices on their products? What businesses services could be applied to businesses activities within the supply chain that bring both lower-cost production and higher quality products? Examples of the type of innovations GGEs may consider could include Partnership for Indonesia Sustainable Agriculture (PISAgro), Responsible Down Standard, Yellow Seed, Heirloom Cacao Preservation Initiative, and The European Sustainable Tropical Timber Coalition (European STTC).

Honoring Global Commons

Making a claim for a global commons is a popular way to explain why global problems exist. Global commons occur when the collective actions of people are causing a problem for society, but there is no incentive for any individual to curtail the actions that are contributing to the problem. Overfishing is a good example: depleting fisheries harms all those who fish, affects other species, and can lead to species being under stress or even becoming extinct. Yet one person who stops fishing will not make a contribution to solving the problem if others continue to fish. This situation has been coined as a "Tragedy of the Commons" (Hardin, 1968).

When a commons occurs in a national or local government, policies can be adopted to take collective action through enforceable regulations that limit further elimination of the natural resource at risk. The weak powers of enforcement that characterize international policies can make the "enclosure" of a global commons difficult and sometimes impossible.

Another issue with global commons to contend with is that the source of the degradation of the natural resource can be indirect and the sources of the problem obscure. Coral reefs around the world have been bleached and their survival threatened. Causes are attributed to a rise in ocean temperatures and ocean acidification; both the result of global warming, which, in turn, is associated with anthropomorphic carbon emissions. The very indirect and diffused ways in which coral reefs are endangered makes it difficult to identify effective actions to take to reverse their degradation and restore their health.

For GGEs to make change through a global commons frame, a creative, innovative approach needs to be developed to address the issues above that explain how to establish global commons preservation. How can the real social, economic, and environmental costs of global commons degradation be reflected in market costs? How can efforts to restore degraded global commons generate revenue? How can alternative business models be developed that rely on access to natural resources without destroying the environment? How can substitute products be developed that reduce the demand for flora and fauna at risk of depletion? Examples of the type of innovations GGEs may consider could include: the concept of the Blue Revolution, Terrapass, High Seas-Areas Beyond National Jurisdiction program, Coral Triangle Initiative, Heart of Borneo Project, Open Sanctuary Alliance, and Carbonfund.org.

These four framings are not the only options future GGEs could select, but they are a common way of describing how we should think about global problems and could be used to structure change models. The choice of a framing has a profound influence on what a future GGE will look like and what actions it would take. There is no right or wrong framing to choose.

GGEs and Multiple Frames

Global policy is usually focused on one issue and one approach. It is much easier to explain and communicate. Plus, typically, frames are linked to political preferences for different policies. Picking one frame makes it clearer how to build coalitions in support of the global policy. Selecting a global policy with more than one framing could potentially deter support from some organizations. For instance, a global policy to protect tropical timber that used both creating markets and honoring global commons frames would likely put off both potential supporters—those who favor private sector solutions and those in favor of a global regulatory approach.

One major benefit of a GGE is that it can chose whichever frames and as many frames as it wants, adding multiple perspectives and considerations for GGE partners. Multiple frames can better reflect the complexity of issues due to globalization and help foster innovative solutions needed to address multiple aspects of problems. When a GGE looks at the possibility of addressing the issue of preserving tropical timber, three of the four frames described earlier could be employed.

As an issue of honoring global commons, portions of tropical forests could be set aside with restrictions on any lumbering in that preserve. Or a related approach would be to institute regulations and quotas that limit the amount of tropical timber that could be harvested every year together with requirements for reforestation. Linking harvesting quotas to actions that deter and lead to actual reductions in illegal logging could create an incentive for engagement with private lumbering companies. Creating a development fund that is allocated to regions and communities that cooperate in efforts to reduce illegal logging could create economic incentives to pursue business opportunities that rival logging.

A frame that looks to create markets suggests that economic values need to be assigned to the tropical timber and those who cut them down are charged accordingly. Determining the price of the tree could include consideration of the social and environmental value of the tree as well as the economic (e.g., market value). In this approach, the effect of cutting tropical timber on global warming, the local ecology, flora and fauna, diversity, economic and social implications for indigenous peoples could all be included in the price. Using a market perspective to frame the issue could guide a GGE to consider the issue from a perspective of more comprehensive land-use policies and practices, including the value of the land after timber is harvested, how the land is used, what revenues are (or might be) generated, and who benefits from these revenues?

A framing of sustainable supply chains would promote a collaborative effort where the interests of global lumber companies, indigenous people, local communities, and environmentalists are brought together voluntarily to develop standards around harvesting policies, how to combat illegal logging, and reduce tropical timber loss. It would also focus attention on the origins of the wood found in a firm's products and bring pressure to remove any illegal lumber from a firm's supply chains. It could also turn attention to recruiting other organizations that use products made from tropical timber and seek to reduce the demand for those products and/or identify alternative and more sustainable substitutes.

Change Model and GGE Actions

In Stage 2, the change model does not set out the actions to be undertaken by the GGE. That is a decision for future partners to determine. Having explored and described the problem and its sources in detail, governance options and approaches to making change are identified that would be consistent with vision although not predetermined. GGEs may initiate a number of actions to solve global problems: create voluntary multi-stakeholder standards, integrate service delivery operations across organizations, create markets for new goods and services, facilitate social entrepreneurs starting new enterprises, empower people with access to information, improve community safety and security, secure provision of services to communities at risk, and countless others.

Because GGEs are filling in a governance gap, they do many of the same things governments would do if those same governments had the capacity and will to do it. Governments have many different options when selecting their approach to solving global problems. Since GGEs are voluntary, they do not have the authority to tax, regulate, appropriate, authorize, or require anything. Since government agencies are often partners in GGEs, an agenda for action for a GGE could include a set of government actions, including funding support, policy changes, and/or creation of new programs that would advance the efforts of the GGE. Yet, tying the fortunes of the GGE to government actions is a poor decision. Even with the best intentions, the political dimensions of government operations always makes reliance on government actions problematic. In fact, this well-known constraint on government officials is one of the reasons why a GGE is so attractive: governance without government.

In practice, governments contribute to GGE efforts, but they are best when they draw on existing programs and funding, so it is a matter of coordinating GGE initiatives with existing government actions. GGEs also can improve the implementation of government projects as part of their action agenda, if they think it helps accomplish their vision.

Change models explain to potential partners how the GGE views the global problem and what factors have the greatest influence on that problem. If the vision of making the world a better place is to be realized, the partners need to have a shared understanding of what actions will bring about that change. When building a GGE, these matters are not topics of political or ideological debate, they are practical issues partners discuss and consider. The change model sets out a detailed map of the topography the GGE will need to transverse to make the destination articulated by the vision, but it does not dictate what roads will be taken, what forms of mobility will be used, how long the journey will take, and what else partners will do and see along the way. Those decisions are co-created by the GGE's partners when they confirm their agenda for action.

15

ATTRACTING AND LEVERAGING PARTNERS FROM THE GLOBAL GOVERNANCE LANDSCAPE

Armed with a vision, a clear and concise description of what the Global Governance Enterprise (GGE) will seek to make different, and an insightful change model that sets out the feasibility of success, attracting partners to join the initiative is the Third Stage. It is understandable that bringing together partners to support, co-create, and implement social innovations will encounter challenges such as inertial resistance to changing the status quo, perceived threats the new approach poses to current practices, identifying people in organizations willing to share the risks a new approach brings, identifying people who find inspiration in the GGE's ideas, and securing funding support for an emergent GGE. For those who are seeking to assemble partners into a GGE, the difficulties mentioned above should be assumed to be the norm, not the exception: building a GGE is not for the faint of heart. For that reason, understanding how to leverage efforts already underway and resources already committed is an invaluable skill for the governance entrepreneur.

Governance entrepreneurs have already accepted the risks of doing something different. They have determined that the potential for making the world a better place outweighs the costs and potential for failure. Sometimes the inspiration for a social innovation that will help achieve the Sustainable Development Goals (SDGs) is a spontaneous spark of insight. So therefore, it is only reasonable to expect that as the idea is shared as part of a GGE's vision, all the risks, downsides, and unintended consequences have not yet been exposed. Other times a social innovation comes out of many years of being marinated in, and influenced by, experience, frustrations, and lessons learned from trying to solve problems in ways that do not work very well and a deep understanding of what can bring about change in a community.

The popularity of partnerships is growing, but they are typically bilateral and limited to a specific, most often narrow, purpose. In fact, organizations are more likely to see themselves as competitors for limited resources and reputation for leadership than potential partners. The mission of many non-governmental organizations (NGOs), the scope of authority for government agencies and inside multilateral institutions, and goals for business corporate social responsibility (CSR) projects are siloed and single purpose. Those who search the global governance landscape for potential partners will find plenty of them. However, collaboration may not be their strong suit. Leveraging current global governance activities means identifying potential partners—which in fact is the easiest part—and of discerning which ones would make trusted partners in a future GGE.

The starting point for learning how to leverage the global governance landscape is to understand what the options are. The basic proposition is to choose from the business, government, and NGO sectors. Business offers technical and management expertise (and maybe funding), government offers legal authorization and legitimacy, NGOs offer local knowledge and lessons learned. The global governance landscape is so much more diverse than that and has much more to offer than the "traditional triad of collaborators."

Partner Prospecting

One of the challenges with mounting an effort to address the big global problems identified by the SDGs is not a shortage of resources, but rather the glut of organizations, programs, and funding streams, all trying to bring about change. As Murphy (2000) observed, global governance is poorly done and poorly understood. The massive efforts made to achieve the Millennium Development Goals (MDGs), the growth of corporate philanthropy addressing

TABLE 15.1 Potential Collaborators

• banks	• business and professional associations
• charities	• community development organizations
• cooperatives	• foundations
• global NGOs	• international alliances (e.g., NATO)
• international development agencies	• international organizations
• local community organizations	• local governments
• local NGOs	• micro-financers
• multinational corporations	• national development agencies
• national government agencies and ministries	• quasi-governmental agencies/authorities
• small- and medium-sized enterprises	• socially responsible investors
• state/provincial governments	• universities and colleges

global problems, expansion of CSR projects, socially responsible investments, and the creation of programs such as The Global Fund have expanded the overall global governance effort, but has also contributed to its crowded conditions. One of the paradoxes of recruiting partners for GGEs is not that there are too few potential organizations, but, in many instances, there are too many. Table 15.1 lists many potential partners to consider joining a GGE.

Partners from any of these sectors can bring a wide array of experiences, real expertise, and resources that can contribute to co-creating how the GGE will make a better world. They can also be a powerful resource to the governance entrepreneur in helping with the formation of the GGE itself. Most professionals have their own networks of other professionals they work with and admire. Finding a few strong potential partners can be a way to gain access to like-minded organizations and leaders who might be good candidates as partners for the GGE.

Finding Common Ground (What Partners Contribute)

One great advantage of the crowded global governance landscape is the richness of possible partners for a GGE. No GGE needs to start from scratch. The task is the assembly of organizations already concerned and active in the area of interest and adding to that the new energy, ideas, and activities that governance entrepreneurs can contribute. The goal is to find, across an array of organizations from many different sectors, a team whose efforts complement each other and produce real, tangible synergies. Of course, just because organizations are working on the same SDG does not mean they are compatible as partners in a GGE.

One of the challenges to implementing the GGE model is the differences in organizational cultures across sectors and the "clash of cultures" that occur when efforts are made to collaborate. These very same "clashes of cultures" are a challenge when multisector efforts are undertaken to develop or implement global policies addressing the SDGs. Under such circumstances, the differences are accommodated because it is a requirement of working on government policies and/or receiving grants and contracts to conduct their work. Because the differences in how government, business, and NGOs think about global problems can be vast, and measures of success can be as different as night and day, they all need to figure out how to cope with these differences if they want to collaborate. Of course, some groups do not participate in collaborations for these very reasons. Many NGOs do not want to work with large multinational corporations (MNCs), because they see a conflict in their mission and the values of MNCs. Many MNCs do not engage actively with the United Nations (UN) because they believe they do not have to answer to international agencies for the choices they make as a firm.

Since GGEs are voluntary, the trick is to forge an alliance of very different partners and get them to agree to work together to achieve a result they all want to accomplish. Along with these differences, the GGE anticipates that there are natural complements among the three basic sectors: each has strengths and attributes valued by the other sectors. Governments can offer political legitimacy, a coalition of stakeholders with a consensus around global problem definition and solutions, approval of regulatory requirements, and sometimes funding. NGOs bring the development expertise about local conditions, local context, and what type of actions will work in a given community. They also have the institutional knowledge of past efforts, both successes and failures. Business brings technical and managerial expertise, innovative strategic thinking, and the business-like approach to problem solving, and, sometimes, funding or other resources. In theory, the "clash of cultures" between different sectors can be overcome in a GGE by identifying a "confluence of contributions" built around a new GGE initiative.

Important differences exist between government, business, and NGOs: what roles they play in collaborations; what they consider as useful metrics of success; what political narratives are assumed; what are viewed as problems and opportunities; what is considered risky behavior, etc. An effective governance entrepreneur does not wait for these disputes to emerge, but anticipates them. Understanding the differences between partners is key to forging a workable and ultimately thriving GGE. Table 15.2 compares aspects of organizations from the three main sectors. Chapter 3 illustrated the differences between them to underscore the need to account for these differences when formulating a credible conceptualization of GGEs. Now, with the practical task at hand to build a GGE, Table 15.2 reveals where similarities may reside.

In practice, there are nearly limitless prospects for GGEs to attract as partners. Partners will have a range of assets, expertise, and resources to contribute to a GGE, separate from whichever sector they are from. In fact, pigeonholing any one of these three sectors into a specific role not only limits the GGE's potential, but also acts as a deterrent. For example, some NGOs may look at the prospects of collaborating in a GGE with a corporation as an opportunity for securing funding support for their activities. However, once the NGO learns funding from the corporation is not likely, they may lose interest altogether. The various strengths and resources of different partners are important to recognize and anticipate, but many partners will offer assets and resources that go beyond the standard attributions.

It is also valuable to keep in mind that some of these very same attributes assigned to different sectors are also antithetical to the collaborative nature of GGEs. Where government may bring a consensus on how to frame and address global problems, GGEs are about innovative approaches to overcoming difficult and sometimes resilient challenges. If a potential partner wants to join a GGE and claims the "solution" is known, that would be a problem. If a business brings too much of a "market-based approach" mindset, many NGOs and, depending on what political party was in office, some government officials, will not collaborate. NGOs may know what has worked well in the past, but if they are not willing to rethink some fundamental ideas about approaches to development, collaboration will not go far.

TABLE 15.2 Expanded Perspectives of Actors within Global Governance Enterprises

	Nonprofit	Business	Government
Types	• Indigenous/local, regional, state, national, international • Formal/informal community groups • Issue-oriented/task-oriented • From broad public interest perspective to private narrow focus	• Local, regional, corporations, and multinational • Micro, small, medium, and large	• Local, regional, state, national, international, and regulatory entities
Organizational goals	• Fulfilling mission and values • Pursue principled beliefs	• Profit • Pursue material interest	• Delivery of public goods and services/meeting public needs
Factors that limit actors' influence prior to GGE participation	• The size and diversity of the NGO community, leading to fragmentation • Financial resources • Representation, accountability, and transparency • Increased competition for limited resources	• Limited understanding of the social issue at hand • Potential distrust by NGOs, including watchdog and consumer groups • Suffer from negative stereotypes, such as being considered hegemonic and exploitative	• The traditional roles of government were no longer sufficient to carry out its responsibilities in an increasingly globalized world (Salamon, 2002) • Impediments include insufficient budgets, absent training, unreasonable policy expectations • "Hollowed-out" government (referring to a government with little or no capacity to manage its partners, let alone deliver services itself) (Goldsmith & Eggers, 2004) • Lack of financial and human resources

Perceived factors that inhibit actors to participate in GGE	• Distrust of business sector • Fear of mission being compromised • Fear of being used for public relations purposes • Fear of being overpowered by other actors in the network	• Shareholder objectives • Uncertainty about added value to the company's bottom line	• Limited ability to steer and guide agenda • Fear of losing authority
Benefits to actors from participating in GGE	• Compete more successfully for limited funding • Reach a larger geographic scope	• Gain a voice in the rules and guidelines of the particular issue • Decrease transaction costs (i.e., from voluntary standards vs. regulation)	• Coordinate resources for producing public value • Gain expertise from other sectors
Benefits to GGE from actors' participation in the GGE	• Bring the voice of a wider affected public to the global decision-making processes (Dombrowski, 2010)	• Enhanced employee skills and financial resources	• Brings legitimacy and accountability to the network • Funneling symbolic power • Contribute to the "democratic anchorage" (Koliba et al., 2011).
Governance functions of each actor in GGEs	• Serve the role of integrator, which serves to connect the components of the network, facilitate interaction, and resolve problems (Goldsmith & Eggers, 2004)	• Serve the role of integrator, which serves to connect the components of the network, facilitate interaction, and resolve problems (Goldsmith & Eggers, 2004)	• More choices for allocating resources • Serve as the administrative core • Serve as facilitators and conductors, rather than implementing and dictating policies and program approaches (Salamon, 2002). • Serves as the role of integrator, which serves to connect the components of the network, facilitate interaction, and resolve problems (Goldsmith & Eggers, 2004)

Why Join a GGE?

The basic proposition to partners is that they can accomplish more through a GGE than through alternative approaches, whether that involves acting unilaterally, in bilateral partnerships, or other types of collaborations. Because the GGE is co-created by its partners, they have a greater influence over its ultimate mission, goals, and activities. That influence means partners have greater opportunities to advance their own organization's strategic and operational goals. There are important differences in the reasoning behind a decision to join a GGE for governments, NGOs, and businesses. Understanding these differences is crucial to successful partner prospecting.

Government agencies will want to claim that participation in a GGE will improve its ability to achieve its programmatic goals and objectives. Therefore, the GGE will need to be aware of the performance indicators used by an agency and accommodate these performance goals into those of the GGE. Claiming that a GGE can provide services more efficiently can be helpful for local governments, but for national government agencies, such savings cannot be returned to the agency, and so it is a lesser selling point. A prestige factor is beneficial to government agencies in joining GGEs. When GGEs have partners with well-known reputations, that association demonstrates that expert NGOs and businesses think the GGE is a good idea and is a strong argument for the government to follow that lead. Politics also influence a government agency's decisions. A GGE with a strong presence of business can be attractive or a disincentive. Collaborating with business has become a more common theme for government agencies, irrespective of the political party in power. For example, the Global Alliance for Clean Cookstoves had the strong support of the U.S. Department of State under Secretary Clinton and she referenced it regularly in her speeches as reflecting her interest in empowering women and improving their lives (US Department of State, n.d.).

Like the government, NGOs would also like to claim that participation in a GGE improved their ability to serve the needs of their target communities. NGOs have also established outcomes and performance goals that must be met, so a GGE needs to take account of these indicators as well. Unlike most national government agencies, NGOs value cost savings. More cost-effective ways of providing services is an attractive program feature for donors. In addition, NGOs might join GGEs because it allows them to expand the ways they can assist their target communities. Many NGOs have a built-in daily frustration with not being able to do more for those in need and encounter barriers that prevent them from being more impactful. A GGE that offers innovative approaches to solving problems the NGO is already addressing can be an attractive incentive. Finally, like governments, many NGOs are not so adroit in adopting innovative approaches to problem solving. GGEs open up opportunities to innovate.

Motives for Businesses to Work with GGEs

- sustainable supply chains
- sourcing security
- social license to operate
- future trends
- risk mitigation
- corporate social responsibility
- stakeholder management
- market entry strategy
- leverage partnership resources
- reputation
- public relations.

Incorporating businesses into GGEs is one of the bigger challenges. For many, businesses becoming engaged in multisector collaborations to address and solve global problems appear to be a fish-out-of-water. The typical view is that businesses care most about making the biggest profit they can. If they are interested in addressing and solving social problems, it must be because they think they can make money doing it. This perception is an obvious barrier to meaningful collaboration. How are firms convinced to join a GGE? What would they gain by working with governments and NGOs helping solve global problems—accept some good credit and public relations? If that is all they would get out of it, they are not likely to be deeply engaged in the GGE or work very hard for its success.

This view that businesses have little to gain from participation in GGEs is not only inaccurate, but also unnecessarily limiting. Believing businesses are interested in GGEs only in terms of the potential to make a profit is too narrow a perspective. Of course, a business participating in a GGE will use it to look for business opportunities but it is a mistake to think that profit is the only, or even the main, benefit firms could get out of participating in GGEs. The following is a description of some of the very practical reasons why businesses should consider joining a GGE:

Sustained Supply Chains

Globalization has resulted in the diffusion and proliferation of global supply chains. Therefore, corporations are realizing new benefits as well as risks in managing the efficiency, reliability, security, and sustainability of supply chains. Clearly, the controls or standards of these components will typically fall beyond the complete control of any one government, corporation, or organization, thus making an attractive case for engagement through GGEs. By integrating best practices from the community and influencing relevant policies, businesses can advance their strategic goals and competitiveness through improved supply chain management.

A typical example is seen in corporations such as Bumble Bee Foods, which depends on a wide ranging, global, and cascading supply chain spanning many partners involved in harvesting (fishing) for tuna products to the end wholesalers and retailers. Any violation of acceptable standards including health or sustainability certifications jeopardizes the reliable flow of product through the entire supply and value chain, and the firm's brand value.

Sourcing Security

Businesses must protect their supply chains in order to continue a profitable business. If any portion of a business's resources is threatened, a business is highly motivated to take the necessary steps to protect this portion of their supply chain. The source of these supplies often comes into jeopardy because of global problems. In order for a business to protect its sourcing, it may collaborate with global organizations in order to address the global problem.

This effort is most often seen in environmental problems. There is an increased awareness of depleting natural resources and its impact on the source countries. Companies may choose to involve themselves in GGEs to remedy environmental problems in order to protect their supply chain. For a business, it may be easier to be part of a GGE-sponsored initiative rather than scrambling for new sources.

One example is the global problem of conflict diamonds, often called "blood diamonds." This global issue focuses on diamonds sold in order to fund violent conflicts. The Kimberley Process was started to address this concern. The Kimberley Process is a global network comprised of governments, businesses, and nonprofit organizations to create a certification system to ensure that diamond purchases are not financing violent conflicts. A key motive for businesses supporting the program is to ensure that access to diamonds continues and that jewelers can continue to purchase the key supplies for their business.

Social License to Operate

The idea of a social license to operate is in reaction to the negative impacts corporations have had on communities. The focus is on MNCs operating in developing countries, especially the extractives industry. Corporate involvement in global governance that is intended to have a positive effect on society is an unconventional idea for many people. Advocates of economic and social justice are more likely to anticipate corporate complicity in fomenting conflict: countries suffering a "resource curse"; supporting corrupt and autocratic regimes; and, causing extensive pollution and environmental damage.

Establishing a social license to operate isn't obtained from a government agency. It means convincing communities where corporations currently, or wish to, do business that can have a positive effect on people, society and the environment. The conventional approach is for firms to make the case that they are "doing good" and therefore should be trusted to take on responsibility for traditional government duties such as providing health care, clean water, or access to power. One well-documented example involves The Gap. Between 2003 and 2007, The Gap began to investigate labor abuses within its supply chain and began a series of stakeholder engagements to identify ways to mitigate the problems. Based on those engagements, The Gap adopted new practices and let the public know about their efforts. When child labor abuse allegations were made against a supplier of The Gap located in India in 2007, stakeholders voiced support for The Gap for having had made reasonable efforts to avoid such problems.

Of course, NGOs and media can be cynical and savvy, and criticize corporations for worrying more about making a good impression through their website, slick-looking sustainability reports, and other public relations as the real way they hope to achieve their social license to operate, rather than actually ensuring they produce positive outcomes for communities.

GGEs provide an opportunity for firms to earn their license to operate, but using a different tactic. Working with GGEs that are addressing SDG issues, firms do not so much earn the right to provide public services as they demonstrate their intentions to have a positive impact on communities through the provision of services that make the world a better place. The efforts made by firms to support the success of a GGE's efforts are demonstrable evidence of a business' concern for the social, as well as the commercial, consequences of their operations. That authenticity makes it much easier for firms to be accepted in countries where multinational corporations in general have an unfavorable reputation.

Learn About Future Trends

Another reason for businesses to join a GGE is to learn about future business and market prospects. Each company alone has their own individual knowledge and ideas about emerging opportunities; however, businesses can gain new insights from partners. With new perspectives and information from the partners or through the efforts of the GGE, businesses can acquire beneficial information on future market trends. These new insights can provide businesses opportunities and possibly a competitive advantage for positioning its own business efforts.

This information can provide market knowledge because of GGE efforts in a particular area, such as a geographic market, or provide insight through the experiences of the various partners in a market. Knowing these future trends can help the company decide where to take their ideas and what to expect. Businesses can develop more finely tuned strategies since they have a greater amount of knowledge to use going forward.

For example, the mHealth Alliance (see Chapter 9) is an alliance of companies, governments, and citizens working together to develop tools that will allow health information to be used in a different way. This information will improve responses to emergencies and the fight on diseases. The GGE is positioned to be at the leading edge of health care information. Businesses involved with mHealth Alliance are privy to new developments in this field that in turn allow the businesses to know how to position their own strategies to align with future health care trends. They will have a competitive advantage in the market as they work together towards developing the newest and greatest information tools in the health industry.

Risk Mitigation

When companies join GGEs it can help to mitigate risk for their individual company. Through a GGE, each partner is not assuming the sole responsibility for the effort nor the outcomes, risks (or negative results) could be spread among all participants. The risks of working to solve a global problem include several possibilities such as negative publicity, failing to accomplish GGE goals, or financial losses. Knowing that the other partners are assuming part of these risks, then the ultimate risk of choosing to work with a GGE is diversified. A GGE allows a business to become involved in activities that have higher risk profit than usual. That means more innovative (yet riskier) approaches to addressing a global problem.

GGEs help to mitigate risk because they are tackling a problem as an alliance rather than alone. The GGE works together to find the best solution for a problem. This teamwork helps to mitigate risk as they are taking action with all of their knowledge combined. They share information that allows them to have more facts upfront, and pooling this information together allows them to move forward in a strategic direction. If businesses acted alone, they may less able to discern as many of the risks before acting.

An example of a GGE where the partners mitigate risks is the Rainforest Alliance. This GGE was created to work towards conserving biodiversity and sustainable business practices. Rainforest Alliance offers farmers, forest managers, and the tourism industry the opportunity to benefit economically while meeting certain environmental and social standards. Since businesses work together under the alliance, they share any risks that would come from these practices such as loss of customers due to higher prices. Together, through the GGE, they can mitigate the risks of being criticized for not living up to responsible standards.

Corporate Social Responsibility

CSR has become a staple among many corporations as they look to be responsive not only to their shareholders but also mindful of their impact on the stakeholders and the communities where they do business. CSR is about integrating the business's values, beliefs, and ultimately, actions into their decision making regarding the best ways to increase shareholder value.

CSR has been ingrained in Tyson Foods, one of the world's largest processors and marketers of chicken, beef, and pork, as well as prepared foods such as appetizers and snacks. They have exhibited their willingness to use their own resources to promote campaigns that combat hunger. A project called KNOW Hunger is designed to encourage people to KNOW the scope of hunger in their own communities and get involved in relief efforts in the hopes of eradicating hunger. Through a network of nonprofits, Tyson is able to create awareness regarding the pressing issue.

In 2000, Tyson first partnered with Share Our Strength (SOS), a nonprofit to assemble a national campaign to teach families how to prepare affordable and nutritious meals. The program is called Cooking Matters and combines the resources and networks of both Tyson and SOS to provide an educational curriculum to help families understand a healthier lifestyle. This effort has been viewed as being a success and has been mutually beneficial for both organizations. Through this partnership, Tyson has been able to freely market their products in the educational meal preparation classes. It also provides Tyson with another market segment that would ordinarily not consider Tyson products. This campaign has multiple benefits for Tyson through the awareness of both their products and the global issue of hunger.

Tyson has been able to leverage their resources in a way that is mutually beneficial both to the company and its partners.

Since 2000, Tyson had donated more than 100 million pounds of food to hunger organizations across the United States. The company intends to continue food donations as it increases its efforts to raise hunger awareness (Tyson KNOW Hunger, n.d.).

Companies could engage in GGEs to enhance their CSR footprint by using these GGEs as a vehicle to exhibit their positive impact on different communities. As in the case of Tyson, brand differentiation was one benefit, as the effort allowed them to bring a unique value to the marketplace. Such relationships with GGEs could make a difference in winning potential new business or opening a market adjacency.

Stakeholder Management

A stakeholder is anyone who participates, manages, directly or indirectly contributes, or is affected by a program of work. Companies are extremely cognizant of their stakeholders. Stakeholder management for business is typically expressed through a strategy in which a company maps out their stakeholders and understands the positive and negative impacts their business activity has on the interests of each stakeholder.

GGEs are a real opportunity for businesses to engage stakeholders directly, or affect conditions in communities other stakeholders care about, through numerous possible avenues. Participating GGEs could be leveraged to do something good for a community or another global stakeholder, that otherwise would be very difficult to accomplish.

For example, Lockheed Martin is is an example of excellent stakeholder management. Their affiliation with the National Defense Industrial Association (NDIA), has allowed them the opportunity to be an active participant in the Business & Industry STEM (science, technology, engineering, and math) Education Coalition (BISEC). This coalition aims to join, enhance, and elevate the U.S. commitment to science, technology, engineering, and mathematics and facilitate STEM education through partnerships. Lockheed Martin supports a wide range of diverse and sustainable STEM activities that reach students and educators from elementary school through college. Through its Engineers in the Classroom, a STEM education outreach initiative, Lockheed Martin provides numerous opportunities for employees to interact with the next generation of engineers and technologists by serving as local school advisors, extracurricular activity mentors, and career role models for students in communities where they live and work.

Through involvement with GGEs, companies can contribute to solving a global problems, while cultivating the next generation of talented engineers that will solve the complex problems Lockheed Martin aims to solve. In a statement on the STEM program, Robert Stevens clearly illustrated this point, "As an industry leader, Lockheed Martin is proud to be doing its part toward easing the looming tech talent shortfall" (Lockheed Martin, n.d.).

Lockheed Martin has entered into a coalition with other defense contractors, nonprofit organizations, public schools, and various other entities to cultivate a solution to a potentially troubling program for the company. Without talented engineers, the company will be less likely to develop complex and innovative technologies. Lockheed Martin's strategy of participating in these industry coalitions with not only other competitors but with public organizations is critical to creating value for their stakeholders.

Market Entry Strategy

In order to remain successful in an increasingly competitive business environment, companies must constantly look for new markets to target. Markets are quick to become saturated as numerous companies begin to target the same segment of society. Businesses must constantly be looking for new profit generating opportunities, and one option is to enter new markets. Participating in a GGE provides businesses with a clear avenue to enter into a new market.

Foremost, the work of a GGE to solve a global problem introduces a business to the new market in a positive manner. By dedicating resources to a GGE, businesses will be able to garner public support, making their entrance into a new market less commercial and more widely accepted by the public. When companies are trying to help communities through GGEs this establishes a 'license to operate.' Entering a new market presents a business with new opportunities including but not limited to: first mover advantages, learn about consumers' preferences, and increased local partnership possibilities.

Nokia is an example of a company's decision to enter a partnership with the purpose of entering new markets. In 2003, Nokia partnered with World Wildlife Fund (WWF) to improve Nokia's environmental performance and promote Nokia's sustainability development. Even though the campaigns are focused on helping people make more environmentally friendly decisions in their everyday lives, the campaigns spread Nokia's brand name into new regions. As a result, Nokia was able to establish itself in new markets in a way that provides positive branding.

Leverage Partnership Resources

The global problems facing society require resources that cannot be marshalled unilaterally, bilaterally, or even regionally. The complexity of these issues, combined with constrained organizational resources and focused core capabilities compel participants to leverage the resources and strengths of partners within GGEs. Depending on the specific needs, leveraged partnership resources may take the form of direct funding, use of staff time, administrative support, data collection and analysis, use of equipment and/or facilities, contacts, relations, and networks, etc.

The International Seafood Sustainability Foundation (ISSF) was founded with the mission "to undertake science-based initiatives for the long-term conservation and sustainable use of tuna stocks, reducing bycatch and promoting ecosystem health" (ISSF, n.d.). Company mentions include Starkist, Bumble Bee Seafoods, and Chicken of the Sea. Clearly, the participating companies and environmental stakeholders have shared concerns that require resources beyond their individual capacities and capabilities. A specific area of leveraging of partnership resources is the data that are integral to fisheries' stock assessment and management. To accomplish this, the ISSF has passed and implemented a resolution to share all data within their control in a timely manner.

Public Relations (PR)

From the recent Volkswagen 'falsified emissions' disclosure to the notorious business scandals Deepwater Horizon oil spill, Enron, Worldcom, and Barclay's Libor manipulation, the public's perception of businesses is not always favorable.

Public opinion typically views businesses as profit seekers, and sometimes uneth-ical, in order to make 'profits over people'. Entering a GGE could improve a business's reputation with its target markets and the general public. By trying to show a commitment to society and wanting to play a role in finding solutions to global governance problems, businesses have a chance to improve their brand, image, and reputation.

Tide is partnered with Feeding America in the Tides of Hope Program. This program helps provide a mobile laundromat for communities that have been struck by disaster. Recognizing clean clothing as a basic human need, the mobile laundromat is capable of cleaning and drying over 300 loads of clothes a day. This partnership improves Tide's relationship with the communities that they service. The Tides of Hope Program is Tide's way of giving back to society and developing relationships with communities in need. Tide's product offerings are not significantly detrimental to the environment, but the com-pany is still making a conscious effort to develop a strong reputation and image with consumers.

Understanding Motives

Table 15.3 summarizes motives for businesses involved in GGEs and how they can benefit through their participation. While this chart looks at possible ben-efits only, it is important to note that positive and negative results are feasible within each motive.

The list of issues a firm might seek to address through participation in a GGE discussed above is not intended to be exhaustive. It is imperative that a firm's rationale for joining a GGE is understood. The reason(s) why a firm wants to join a GGE speaks volumes about what type of role they will play as a GGE partner. It should be anticipated that a business will have multiple ration-ales for joining a GGE. It may be leveraging the GGE to addresses multiple issues within the firm. There may be multiple offices within the firm that see advantages to joining. Alternatively, the firm may be hedging and hoping for one outcome from the GGE, but advancing other, lower priority outcomes, in case the GGE is not fully successful.

The more a GGE addresses core business issues, the better partner the busi-ness will be. It is critical not to dismiss the reasonableness of these motivations because they are more about business than helping people. GGE partners need to recognize and accept that the reasons why partners join a GGE will be very different. Building a GGE is not about why partners want to help, but what resources and commitments they are willing to contribute to achieving the vision. Organizations that make partnership decisions based on overly broad and sim-plistic generalizations about the worthiness of the activities of different sectors (e.g., business, government, nonprofit) will make poor prospects as a GGE partner.

TABLE 15.3 Motives behind Private Sector Participation

Motives	Businesses
Sustainable supply chains	Corporations are realizing new benefits as well as risks in managing the efficiency, reliability, security, and sustainability of supply chains.
Sourcing security	Businesses protect their ability to access resources in their supply chain in the future.
Social license to operate	Create a more favorable opinion about the firm.
Future trends	Provides businesses with greater knowledge and a view of future trends.
Risk mitigation	Risk is spread among the different businesses so individually there is less.
Corporate social responsibility	Positions private sector businesses to be viewed as "citizens" of the communities they operate in. Thus combating the typical profit motive impression that most people have of the private sector.
Stakeholder management	Participation in GGEs provides a greater network that increases the ability to create and develop new business ventures, partnership capacity, and strategic resource allocation. Not only reliant on their own resources and talent, but a participant in a GGE can tap the GGE's resource and talent pool to do things they would ordinarily be unable to accomplish.
Market entry strategy	Provides new markets to target with goods and services to keep the business operations strong.
Leverage partnership resources	A single business can leverage the resources and intellectual capacity of the cross-sector partners, thereby furthering their own.

Source: Jake Braunsdorf, Whitney Milliken, Kelly Pernia, Adriel Pond, Mark Vincent, and John Forrer.

Businesses are criticized by some for joining collaborations "just to make a profit" or "only for good PR." For a GGE, that would be a wonderful motivation to have a firm to be a partner. GGEs should celebrate firms that want to collaborate in a GGE to make the world a better place. The fact that a firm derives some benefit from the partnership is only reasonable. In fact, if there is not a valued benefit back to the firm, it suggests a weak commitment and lack of confidence in the GGE overall. Good PR and profits are important to firms. If GGEs advance a firm's interests in either of these two areas (among others), the GGE will be valuable to the firm. That is what GGEs want and need—committed partners who want the GGE to succeed. If the partners succeed when the GGE succeeds, that "governance glue" makes GGEs impactful, purposeful, and keeps these collaborations resilient.

With an understanding of real business motives, partners within the GGE can better recognize the influences behind the business's decisions. Understanding partners' intentions behind joining a GGE allows the organization to collaborate more effectively and develop innovative solutions to global problems. When partners become informed of the motives and potential consequences and benefits companies can accrue for participating in a GGE, it will allow for more effective and efficient decision-making towards a successful GGE.

GGE Value Proposition

If organizations are going to participate in a GGE, they need to have a good reason to do so. Of course, part of the motivation is to accomplish some results, some improvement in people's lives, advancing achievement of the SDGs, etc. These are all related to the effect a GGE can have on some problem, issue, or condition that a partner shares and wants addressed. For a partner to join a GGE, it needs to believe that the GGE can advance the partner's goals better than can be accomplished unilaterally or in some other partnership. It is a practical decision. That is the focus of the GGE: to bring about change and results that the partners all agree are important to accomplish. As a new approach to global governance, GGEs offer a compelling argument in their favor.

However, any proposed GGE has to see that it competes with scores of other options for potential partners to select. There are no shortages of partnerships and collaborations partners may join. The global governance landscape is crowded with organizations and initiatives. In addition, potential partners can choose not to join any collaboration or partnership. Any new GGEs need to look at how they can attract partners to choose to join compared to other options: it is a competition.

One area where the GGE can offer distinctive value to partners is by helping them adapt to the changes and challenges they face in a globalized world: events happen more quickly; the world is more connected and networked; problems are more complex and interdependent; there are more global problems and challenges; borders and boundaries are more porous; governments are less able to control and manage events from outside their boundaries affecting their own citizens and institutions; and problems in one community spread much more quickly to other parts of the world.

GGEs can help governments, NGOs, and businesses address the global problems they face in a more effective way. As a governance network, which means they are organized to be flexible adapters, they can adopt new partners and modify their activities as the collective learning of the network is enhanced and performance is adjusted, allowing partners to adjust and react to the issues they encounter. GGEs are the opposite of the traditional bureaucratic model that requires hierarchical accountability and is dedicated to executing the policies adopted by public officials. GGEs thrive through heterarchical relationships between partners. Activities are co-created and adjusted regularly to adapt to rapidly changing conditions and responding to new opportunities and obstacles.

Partners can benefit from joining and helping to build a purposeful and impactful GGE in many ways. For example:

- To foster coordination and integration among organizations in the delivery of services to communities. The coordination can be between NGOs, but also between NGOs and businesses. These arrangements can reduce delivery costs. They can also improve the efficacy of the services. Delivery of health care services and vaccines are a good example. Often, health care services and disease prevention efforts are undertaken by individual organizations addressing one disease or a set of health problems. Coordination and integration of services allows for a more holistic approach to providing services and medicines to people.
- To develop multisector consensus over business practice standards. Setting standards that are agreed by governments, NGOs, and business clarifies expectations for performance. They give businesses a target baseline for performance and give NGOs an opportunity to establish business practices that could not be achieved through public policy. Sustainable supply chains are a good example. Typically, one business or industry is not influential enough to set standards for the entire supply chain. Human rights and sustainability practices can be promoted as a part of the standards.
- To act as an interface between funders and implementing organizations. GGEs can propose program designs to funders that are effective and impactful and then administer funds to NGOs willing to adopt the established approach of program delivery. Disease prevention efforts are a good example. Different NGOs use different practices in the approach and dispensing of disease prevention services. Standardizing protocols across communities promotes continuity and better health across communities.
- To bring together partners that share values. Partnerships are often claimed to be forged around shared goals. However, the diversity of partners in a GGE makes this formulation improbable and unnecessary. However, organizations do value partnering with others that share organizational values. In addition, GGEs can be the vehicle for supporting that goal. A business can be mission-driven and making a positive impact on society a top priority, just as much as an NGO or a government agency.

To benefit individual partners in more general ways:

1. to identify new social innovations that improve performance;
2. to introduce current practices of one partner that becomes "new practices" to another partner;

3. to meet individuals from other organizations who might be good contacts for fostering partners on initiatives other than the GGE;
4. to attract funding from donors that support multisector initiatives, but not unilateral efforts or bilateral partnerships;
5. to engage the "unusual suspects" from other sectors that partners would not have an occasion to meet and engage.

A partner could take on each of these roles by itself, but doing so would be so much more expensive, risky, and uncertain. Joining a GGE is a risky proposition because it tries to make something out of nothing, like entrepreneurs do. Any alternative approach potential partners may use, comes with its own difficulties and challenges. GGEs have an advantage in their capacities to leverage the resources of partners and direct them to accomplishing the outcomes partners want. However, at the same time, GGE partners can accomplish their own organization goals through the activities of GGE by the leveraging of their own resources and combining them with the resources of other partners.

For those used to working on global policy and its implementation, such leveraging could be seen as a conflict of interest. If partners are allowed to advance their own organization goals through the activities of the program, the public interest could be compromised or even corrupted. It is one reason why the wisdom of inviting business to participate in global policy and governance is questioned. For GGEs, this possible difficulty becomes a major virtue. Rather than worrying about a conflict of interest, GGEs celebrate the discovery of a confluence of interests. Since the GGE is self-governed, concerns about conflict of interest are not ancillary, but central. The partners themselves decide what will be done and therefore are self-policing.

In this way, partners that are able to leverage GGE activities to advance their own organization's goals are not only acceptable, but also encouraged. The more a partner views its participation as a benefit, the more they will be committed to the GGE's success. The more partners are committed to a successful GGE, the more likely it will accomplish its aims to make the world a better place. A distinctive feature of GGEs is that they present an attractive win–win proposition. Partners collaborate and co-create activities the GGE institutes and manages, and bring about a better world: a shared interest of all partners. Any individual partner has an opportunity to advance their own goals through the activities of the GGE, themselves leveraging limited organizational resources.

16

CREATING AND CAPTURING VALUE

Stage four explores the opportunities for creating and capturing value. It serves two functions towards building a Global Governance Enterprise (GGE). The first is to drive commitment to undertaking innovative solutions to the global problem addressed in the vision. Creating and capturing value benefits the people and the community that is to be the target of the GGE's efforts. The second is to convince potential partners that the GGE will create value that they themselves can capture. Developing ideas about how value can be created and captured by partners is a discovery process based on looking at global problems through the lens of the change model and co-creating ways to bring about change that makes the world a better place.

Understanding what will be valued by the target community is reliant on a really good change model being developed in stage two. One of the main characteristics of a very good change model is a sophisticated understanding of the local context where the GGE plans to address a global problem. Generalizations and presumptions about what people in any given community may value have limited use to a GGE. The other characteristics are analysis, insights, and descriptions that convince potential partners that the actions could be taken by the GGE and would be purposeful and impactful. The extensive time spent drawing on experiences from the field and a thorough understanding of the conditions that explain why the global problem exists in the first place, is rewarded in stage four.

Understanding what will be valued by GGE partners is reliant on the thorough exploration of potential partners on the global governance landscape that might be interested in the GGE's vision. Pre-judging what partners may value based on political and/or ideological claims about different sectors (e.g., business only cares about profits) has limited utility to a GGE. Part of the calculation that should go into determining which organizations to collaborate with is what they can contribute to value creation possibilities associated with bringing about the GGE's vision. Equally important is appreciating the different reasons partners might want to join a GGE and how these motivations could be reinforced by creating value they can capture for themselves.

Winners and Losers

Global policies that are designed to solve global problems typically result in clear winners and losers. Those whose policies were adopted are the winners and those whose ideas were rejected are the losers. Different constituencies and communities also have winners and losers. Those who end up receiving the services are the winners and those who would have received the services from the alternatives not adopted are the losers. It is all part of the political process used to decide which policies should be approved and how much money should be spent on the activities. Creating winners and losers is not only an obvious consequence of global policy, but also an appropriate way of understanding the net benefits of the proposed policy. For GGEs taking actions that bring about change that creates a better world, it is no different: they create winners and losers too.

For some global policies, or actions by GGEs that bring about change, the "losers" are viewed as simply getting what is coming to them. For example, an employer who previously hired child labor and now has to pay higher wages for older laborers, due to efforts at eliminating child labor, is the loser. It is only right such employers should pay and the exploited children are the winners. Since child labor is considered wrong, there are no regrets that now these same people have to endure some cost to remedy the problem. In fact, it could be argued these same employers enjoyed the benefit of exploiting these children in the past, and taking those gains onto themselves through higher profits. It is only just and fair that they be compelled to make the situation right, and that some, if not all, of those tainted profits of the past should be redirected to pay for the cost of doing so.

Establishing livable wages for farmers who grow commodities has a similar narrative regarding winners and losers. Higher wages paid to farmers means the cost of the commodities will rise, which translates into higher prices firms must pay for the product, who in turn pass these increases on to consumers. The farmers win and the consumers lose. The low wages paid to farmers in the first place is what made the price of commodities so cheap. Corporations made higher profits and consumers enjoyed lower prices at the expense of farmers. It is only fair that consumers and businesses should have to pay more to provide a livable wage to farmers.

However, assessing the righteousness of making the world a better place and creating winners and losers may not always be so clear. A recent popular policy area is women's empowerment. Many programs provide support to encourage women entrepreneurs. Young Women Social Entrepreneurs, Ogunte, Women-sphere Foundation, Women for Women, Empower Women, 10 by 10 by 10, UN Women, and World Bank's Female Entrepreneur Resource Bank are a few samples of numerous such programs worldwide. Some programs provide micro-loans to women to start their own small enterprise. Others encourage women to organize and create products that could be sold as part of larger global supply chains. Selling products to a corporation is one way women can achieve stable employment, provide revenues for the women's family, contribute to the development of their communities, and strengthen their self-image and pride. Corporations involved in partnerships with non-governmental organizations (NGOs) that agree to buy products from women entrepreneurs are praised for meeting their corporate social responsibility (CSR) obligations and supporting the empowerment of women.

However, the story about these same programs that "empower women" could be retold without changing any of the facts. Corporations are constantly looking to reduce costs in their global supply chains. If they can identify alternative suppliers of products at a lower cost, this would be attractive and a competitive advantage gained over their competitors. Purchasing products from women entrepreneurs in developing countries could be viewed as nothing more than a smart business decision. However, the shifting of production of essential components by a global corporation in their supply chain from a developed economy to a developing country is also an example of relocating business to countries with lower wages and weaker bargaining positions. In this more conventional framing of such an alteration to a firm's supply chains, the previous accolades would be quickly hushed and the firm more likely condemned.

The confusion is understandable. The progress sought in the achievement of the Sustainable Development Goals (SDGs) would not only add immeasurably to the quality of billions of people's lives, but also eliminates unacceptable conditions in people's communities. In many instances, the "losers" were benefitting at the expense of others and their disadvantages, desperation, and suffering. Whatever losses are generated are good riddance. Of course, this view is applicable in many such situations, as it speaks loudly to the need to rethink the role of winners and losers when building partnerships. Understanding the role that creating value can play in rewarding partners and compensating those who will be disadvantaged by the changes the partnership is promoting, is a key to success.

Understanding who the winners and losers are as a result of a GGE's actions provides critical information that can be used creatively to build partnerships. Naturally, losers can be a powerful source of resistance to change. If a GGE vision were to result in shifting resources away from the community or a business; if NGOs were to have government contracts redirected to a new GGE; if prices or costs were made higher; and/or if revenues were charged for what was once provided for no fee, objections would be understandable. Rather than seeing such losers as the opposition to change, GGEs try to see them as potential partners. Even though some government officials, NGOs, businesses, and communities might end up losing from a proposed action by a GGE, helping these same organizations create and capture value is a pioneering way of getting them to join the effort to bring about the change from which they lose.

Perspectives on Value Creation

Government officials typically are not charged with the goal of creating value. They achieve program goals and objectives; stay within budgets; strive for efficiency, effectiveness, and equity, but value creation is not a typical mandate. It is not used as a metric for evaluating program performance. Government agencies tend to pursue actions that are in the "public interest." When developing a cost-benefit analysis, government officials are comfortable with "net social benefits" but not "net public value created." Only in the area of public–private partnerships has the concept of public value established a significant foothold.

Public Value

The notion of "public value" occupies a small and remote niche within studies of government. Given the ubiquity of the concept of private value, it is surprising its counterpart has not gained more traction. Moore's (1995) conception of public value equates managerial success in the public sector with initiating and reshaping public sector enterprises in ways that increase their value to the public, in both the short run and the long run. Just as the goal of private managers is to create private (economic) value for their shareholders, the goal of the public managers can be seen as creating public (social) value for citizens. The parallelism is not flawless. The relationships between private managers and their shareholders, and public managers and citizens, have profound differences. Still, the idea of a public manager seeking to make decisions in ways that benefit citizens (or even taxpayers) has merit. The definition of public value provides a unifying idea of what public managers should aspire to and what could guide decisions on the appropriate collaborative actions that meet a GGE's vision.

For governments, a goal for participating in a GGE could be thought of as an effort to create public value. Public value can be captured by citizens, whether through the services provided by the government, those provided through a GGE, or by additional spillover effects from the effort of other GGE partners. However, appropriate metrics still need to be developed to measure "public value" at both aggregate and disaggregated levels.

While the concept of public value remains underdeveloped, it provides a useful roadmap for government officials and NGOs who are participating in GGEs and want to leverage its activities in a way that advances their organizational mission and goals. Knowing that private sector partners will be thinking about how the GGE activities can generate private value that they might capture, other partners could be looking for analogous public value creation and capture opportunities.

As a rule, creating public value is not a concept that is explored at academic institutions or within government agencies themselves—with one particular exception: public–private partnerships (PPPs). The British version of PPPs—created in the early 1990s—called Private Finance Initiative (PFI) negotiates with private sector consortia to design, build, finance, and operate public infrastructure projects such as roads, prisons, hospitals, light rail, water systems, etc. In these negotiations, government officials call for bids and negotiate with bidders to optimize the public value projects can generate. The term-of-art used is "value for money (VfM)." It has a very specific meaning: what are the implications of changing a previous publically funded and managed project to a PPP? VfM is a concept and a calculation that investigates whether the theoretical benefits of doing PPPs will be realized in each specific case. Its general meaning is that governments should get the best deal they can when doing a PPP project.

Extensive and highly detailed analytic frameworks, measurement techniques, valuation estimation tools, and guidance for how to assess if VfM is met in a given proposal have been developed and refined over the decades. Popular in the rest of the world, VfM has not been integrated into U.S. procurement policy or practice. The experience of government agencies around the world attempting to optimize public value through the PPP procurement process offers useful guidance for quantifying the public value that might be created by GGEs.

Creating Value and Government Services

Many of the SDGs focus on the absence of government services, for example, access to basic needs such as water, sanitation, electricity or natural gas (power), education, and even mobile phone connectivity and internet access. Globally, many governments—particularly fragile states—do not have the resources to provide these services, or they are not made accessible to marginalized communities. The lack of government resources has become a major prompt for engaging business as partners to fill this gap and explore ways to attract private investment in the infrastructure through PPPs. However, providing government services through markets is an unattractive option for most private investors.

Typically, investors will earn their return on their investment in public projects from fees that are paid for the service. In poor, sometimes destitute, communities, they do not have the money to pay for these government services. The pure privatization of government services is not a reasonable option for these communities. In poor communities, the tax base is insufficient to fund the cost of utilities' real operating costs through service fees charged to users. In many countries, these services are subsidized by the government to make the price more affordable, but these same governments run deficits because they do not collect sufficient fees to cover the costs of the services. Alternatively, government services are provided, but collection rates from users are very low, and illegal connections to utilities services are high.

Trying to attract private investors and businesses to fill the governance gap related to government services under such circumstances is an improbable task. How could investors help produce and deliver services that by their very definition—public goods—business cannot produce and make a profit? Under these circumstances, a GGE that wants to address these matters will need to find a new and innovative way to produce and deliver such traditional government services. The private sector cannot produce and deliver public goods when organized and managed the way governments have traditionally done. GGEs need to find inventive ways of generating public and private value if it wants to engage the private sector in providing basic government services to the communities that are desperate for them. GGEs cannot simply replace governments and produce and deliver public services the way a government agency or utility would. Completely new forms of innovation need to be invented by GGEs if people who are most in need of basic services are to receive them.

Creating Value and Free-Riders

The "free-rider problem" is a well-recognized idea in public economics. The free-rider problem is the situation when someone "consumes" a service and did not pay their fair share (market price) for that service. It is a common issue with government services where services are consumed collectively or fees for services are set by government officials (not arbitrated by markets.) A common example is national defense. All citizens living in a country "consume" the national defense services provided by the government, but anyone who cheats on their taxes is a "free-rider": they are getting defense service benefits and not fully paying for them. Since economists believe in the ideal of optimal allocation of goods and service, the free-rider problem is vexing, and, when at all possible, should be eliminated.

As GGEs discover ways to create and capture value, free-riders are celebrated and encouraged. The root of many global problems is the absence of proper basic services, sufficient resources to support communities, and social and economic opportunities. The goal of the SDGs is to address these problems while recognizing that the communities at risk do not have the funds to pay market prices for these services. Discovering innovative ways to provide services to people who need them so desperately requires GGEs to create enough public and private value that those who are most in need can be "free-riders." GGEs search for ways to create and capture value that allow for the "free-rider solution": sufficient value is created by GGE partners working in collaboration that there is enough to pay for the services people need (not by them) and enough left over for the partners to capture that leaves them feeling it was worth the overall effort. Creating and capturing value is a motivational fulcrum for any GGE. It reinforces one of the core value propositions of any GGE: partners can gain more through collaboration than any other activities.

For NGOs, the value proposition of a GGE is in the improvements made in the lives of the people whose conditions and situations they are trying to improve. There is an intrinsic value in not being sick, in having access to water and electricity, in having secure and safe communities in which to live. The protection of the environment provides a similar value to the health of the overall ecology, promoting a healthy planet, and the health and welfare of all who live in it. The potential for GGEs to create value through expanding and enhancing services and opportunities that people and communities can capture is the allure. Since NGOs are dependent on grants, gifts and member support, GGEs offer a new opportunity to magnify their reach and impact that transcends the limits of government grants, philanthropy, and gifts.

For potential business partners, creating and capturing value is an everyday aspiration. Business conversations are peppered with phrases like "value propositions," "unlocking value," "bringing more value to customers," "creating shared value," and "co-creating value." All these phrases represent any type of value that will add to the long-term health and success of the business. Businesses find value creation a comfortable concept because they see it as something to be discovered and invented, rather than counted after the fact. Creating new products and services, providing existing products and services in a new way, stimulating demand for existing products and services, reducing the costs of producing and delivering the services, these and other ways create value for the firm. They can also create value for customers and society. It is more than simply creating economic value. It includes less tangible assets such as customer goodwill, employee satisfaction, supplier value, and managerial skills and experience. Business value can include intangible as well as tangible assets, such as intellectual property.

Value creation and capture resonates with business because of the allure of doing something smarter, doing something better, solving a problem, and being rewarded from the value the idea created. Asking businesses to think about creating public value is a seamless transition from creating private value. The business focus on customers and wondering about what they want and what they will pay for is an invaluable skill for identifying public value. It is this drive for doing something different, for providing people with products and services which improve their lives that is the inspiration that governments and NGOs can share with businesses in a GGE.

The Value of Creating Value for GGEs

Thurow (1980) coined the phrase "zero-sum society" that captured a prevalent despondent view of government gridlock and general feeling of malaise at the time. He noted how gains in one area, appropriated by one individual or group in an effort to solve a public policy problem (e.g., stagnant economic growth, inflation, environmental degradation), no matter how admirable, would be off-set by equal-sized losses for other individuals and groups. Political operatives are simply unwilling to impose current costs on constituencies (who will object and hold decision makers accountable) in order to generate future benefits (for which they are unlikely to receive credit) (Lee, 1982). When the action results in a redistribution of costs and benefits from those paying to those receiving, the problem is exacerbated.

This perspective on the intransigence of some groups to accept losses in order to solve problems affecting others is an underpinning narrative in debates about solving global problems. For example, designing global climate change policies in response to SDG 13 (Take urgent action to combat climate change and its impacts) would direct massive levels of investment in power, industrial, and transportation sectors to speed a transition from a carbon-based economy to a renewables-based one. However, resistance to such an effort comes from business leaders who view such an energy policy and the associated redistribution of resources as a direct threat to their survival. This feeling is often shared by the political leaders in whose jurisdiction carbon-based firms operate. It threatens to undermine their economies through the loss of business and jobs. These same concerns are shared by people who live and work in these communities. SDGs also create winners and losers on a global scale. Advocates calling for a reduction in coal-fired power plants as a way to achieve SDG 13—such as the Keep it in the Ground Campaign—see the benefits in addressing climate change issues. However, eliminating coal-fired power means the loss of the cheapest source of power in developing countries. The losses sustained by nations and communities by transitioning to a renewables-based economy are one reason why a comprehensive inter-national treaty on carbon emission reductions has not been accomplished after two decades of negotiations.

Global policy debates over the best way to solve global problems presume that change must be negotiated between the winners and the losers. It is assumed that those who will be the losers as the SDGs are achieved will resist and dig in their heels. As a result, change can come only when those who benefit from the current unacceptable state of the world are forced to abandon their current practices, accept their fate, and accept the losses they should rightfully incur.

In 1985, Thurow penned a follow-up book called *Zero-Sum Solution*. It proposed a range of government policies and programs that he argued would propel the U.S. to recapturing their position as a high performing, high pro-ductivity economy. It joined the ranks of similar books that recommended a re-industrialization effort by the U.S. in order to be competitive in the then emerging global economy (Lawrence & Dyer, 1983; Reich, 1983; Landau & Rosenberg, 1986).

Thurow's dalliance in U.S. industrial and competitiveness policy was less well received than his earlier work (his focus more on practice than theory). It does provide two valuable departure points for understanding the importance of creating and capturing value for GGEs. First, it looks to the familiar economic approach of addressing conflicts over scarce resources by "making the pie bigger." Thurow's suggestion that the U.S. grow its way out of its problems informs the approach used by GGEs to establish consensus around making change and reconciling the trade-offs of the fortunes of winners and losers. GGEs create value for the targeted communities they are looking to help, and they also create value that can be captured by their partners. As a result, value can be created that compensates those who end up losing from the actions of the GGE.

Second, Thurow's proposals for government policies and programs and the stinging rebuke they received by those who had long lists of government programs that proved to be ineffectual, underscores the attraction of the GGEs acting as voluntary organizations. Expanding productivity creates more value for everyone, but the decisions about who gets to capture those gains remains a political decision, resolved through public policies about taxation, accounting standards, regulations, trade laws and agreements, and other requirements. GGE partners work together to create value that advances the vision, but how much partners can capture beyond those requirements is an open-ended opportunity.

When looking to assemble a partnership, putting value creation and capture as top priorities serves several useful functions. When partners are able to see the value that could be created through collaboration, it offers a tangible enticement to participate and a strong incentive to ensure the partnership yields a sustained and productive GGE. Tangible value created in the near term has obvious attraction to all partners. The less tangible values have their own special attraction, especially for business. While uncertain and distant, the prospect alone of creating value may be enough of an inducement to some firms to make committing to a GGE worthwhile. For government and NGO partners, intangibles produced through partners will be more difficult to translate into tangible benefits.

Value creation and capture can be attractive ways to engage social entrepreneurs and local NGOs, and governments in the GGE partnership. Typically, large governments, NGOs and businesses would expect substantial impacts from their participation in a GGE. However, social entrepreneurs, and local governments and NGOs could utilize value creation in smaller amounts. Large and small organizations can complement each other in a GGE by being attracted to value creation that comes in all different forms and amounts. This situation supports a more dynamic process of value creation within the GGE. When the GGE's only partners are large organizations, they might bypass opportunities to create value that is expressed in smaller increments. In addition, social entrepreneurs and local organizations can be more flexible and adaptive than large organizations, taking advantage of opportunities to create value that are unexpected or fleeting.

Theories of Value Creation

Value has been a topic long debated and explored by philosophers, economists, and sociologists. Discourses on value seek to understand how we think about what something is worth. Classic divisions over what explains something's value began early. Plato regarded value as found inherently in an object, but Aristotle attributed value to an object's utility. The exploration of "value" through an economics and sociology lens informs the question about value discussed here and the questions GGEs must address. What is valuable to people and society? Adam Smith's exposition on the values and their distribution involved in market exchanges, and Karl Marx's "labor theory of value" (building on David Ricardo), set the idea that the value of an object is related to the labor expended in creating it (Dobb, 1973). Schumpeter (1943) added a dynamism to the idea of value through his thesis that "creative destruction" in which action unleashed capital and labor to be reformed in more productive ways through innovation. While change can bring about lost jobs, disbanded firms, and receding industries, economies grow more productive and richer in the new, reconfigured economy; and, citizens see the benefits of new and better products, shorter work weeks, better jobs, and higher living standards when capital and labor are allowed to find their next and logical constellation. While interest in the study of value has receded in economics, and the issue of "prices" has been of greater interest, concepts of value have found resurgence in the study of modern corporations and the study of management and strategy.

Shared Value

Businesses have long recognized the possibilities of generating benefits for themselves as they comply with government regulations or manage their stakeholders, and design and implement their CSR policies. Sometimes this is referred to as "strategic CSR": deciding how best to respond to stakeholder demands and claims by including the calculation of the associated benefits to the firm. For example, in response to advocates calling for "zero waste" to take pressure off landfills and being more sustainable, firms have adopted aggressive recycling programs. Ford Motor Company claims that its vehicles are 95 percent recyclable by weight, and feature unique materials that replace landfill-destined plastics (Ford, n.d.). One example is their use of old plastic bottles as feedstock for manufacturing the fabric covering the seats in their vehicles. The company's efforts have been a response to activists' demands, but Ford has saved money by also reducing manufacturing cost (Ford, n.d.).

The suggestion that businesses could be proactive—not reactive—in identifying ways to engage non-market partners, work together to address social issues, and create value for the firm was popularized by the concept of "shared value" (Porter & Kramer, 2011). Shared value is linked to a firm's management of its supply chains and refers to actions that generate both private and social benefits. Reducing costs and increasing value within a firm's global supply chains has become a bedrock business strategy for remaining competitive. Porter and Kramer argue that striving to create shared value was a better approach than simply looking to reduce operating costs or advancing CSR strategies. Shared value is a different way for business to help solve global problems. Companies can create shared value in three ways: reconceiving products and markets, reconfiguring supply chains, and enabling local cluster development.

The three approaches identified by Porter and Kramer provide insights on roles businesses can play in creating value. First, reconceiving products and markets means discovering innovative ways of selling things to people who are too poor or remote to buy current product offerings. If people do not have enough money to buy a bottled beverage in the traditional 12 oz/375 ml size, could that same product in a smaller container and therefore a lower price be marketable? For people who could not qualify for, or have access to, business loans, micro-financing may be an option. Inexpensive latrines, made locally with local products, improve sanitation and health. The possibilities are endless for developing new products and services that fit people's economic and social conditions. People gain access to products and services never before available and businesses make money. In addition, when those businesses are local, it stimulates development.

Second, reconfiguring supply chains has limitless possibilities as well. Relocating post-harvest commodity processing—such as cashews—to the country of origin reduces processing costs and provides local employment. Creating direct-to-home product distribution networks—often operated by women in poor communities—expands sales and increases family income. Replenishment of the water used by beverage bottlers improves sourcing security for the firms and improves access to water in those communities. The drive to create private value is done in tandem with solving global problems.

Third, enabling local clusters means engaging academic programs, trade associations, and standards organizations, as well as government and civil society. Good governance laws and policies are part of the "clusters" as well. Cisco trained over four million network administrators globally through its Networking Academy to overcome a constraint to expanding sales of servers. Nestlé provided substantial financial assistance to help expand small business in regions where it bought coffee. These business clusters strengthened the local business environment and resulted in improved productivity for Nestlé. Again, solving business problems was accomplished while addressing social issues.

The idea of shared value has many advantages for businesses and has helped firms to rethink how they should manage their engagements with their global supply chains. There are two key lessons to learn for governments and NGOs who seek collaboration with businesses in GGEs. Porter and Kramer (2011) criticized the convention about the trade-off between societal needs and economic success. They argue that scholars and practitioners need to step back from the suggestion that there is a trade-off between business and society. Businesses can pursue their commercial pursuits without any contradiction in helping to solve global problems. Of course, making money and helping people are not synonymous, but neither are they mutually exclusive. Successful GGEs have partners who believe the overlap of these two social spheres is not a mere sliver, but a nearly total eclipse.

Shared value is not about sharing value, which already exists—it is about expanding the current pool of value that benefits everyone. The trend of blurring profit/nonprofit boundaries is a strong sign that creating shared value is possible. Social entrepreneurs are leading the way on creating shared value because they are not locked into traditional thinking about boundaries between public policy and business. Real social entrepreneurship should be measured by its ability to create shared value, not just social benefit. Shared value is not about redistributing wealth and resources; it creates new value.

The concept of shared value has become immensely popular with business leaders to describe how their actions benefit society in a popular way. Its popularity notwithstanding, the shared value concept is open to criticism. First, shared value is such a broad concept that firms now claim shared value creation for nearly any business action that has a social benefit: job creation, employing the disadvantaged, providing health care to employees, using renewable energy, etc. Shared value claims are so ubiquitous that it now looks more like a PR gambit for firms rather than a marked change in their behavior.

A closer look at the concept shows that shared value is an idea of business, by business, and for business. Engagement and consultation with governments and NGOs is anticipated and expected as part of the process of creating shared value. However, in the end, the decisions about what actions to take are chosen by the firm to its advantage. This means that the firm is choosing what shared value it is willing to create. The shared value concept was developed by Kramer and Porter to help firms become more competitive while benefitting society. What value is created and "shared" is a unilateral decision by the firm. The three shared value approaches are directed at solving specific business problems; the social value creation is an add-on.

It is easy to see that nearly any business activity will have some positive impact on society (shared value), no matter what actions a firm takes—although not necessarily positive net social benefits. The question is not whether firms are creating shared value—they are, no matter what they do (along with a lot of negative impacts)—but who decides the form and content of that shared value. If business is going to acknowledge and celebrate its impact on society, who is to judge that impact? Against what standards and norms will that impact be judged? Who will establish these standards? What type of public and/or private value is created? How much? Who will capture it? Who benefits and who does not? In short, who wins and loses? Simply invoking shared value is not nearly enough of an answer.

Porter and Kramer (2011) do not stand alone in rethinking the connections and possibilities for businesses seeing the advantages of creating value that benefits more than themselves. Others have presented concepts of how to bring these two worlds—typically seen as separated—together in a synergistic way. Emerson (2003) has written extensively about the concept of "blended value" where the actions of NGOs, businesses, and investments are judged based on their ability to generate a blend of financial, social, and environmental values. Hart (1997) defined "sustainable value" as the contribution of any combination of economic, environmental, and social resources that are assessed based on their relative value creation. In the next chapter, the concept of "reciprocal value" will be introduced as a guiding principle for GGE partners to make decisions around creating and capturing value. The shared value concept adds to new thinking about how innovations can bring about change, such as "bottom of the pyramid" (Prahalad, 2006), social entrepreneurship (Bornstein, 2004), and Muhammad Yunus' microfinancing.

Creating and capturing value for a GGE takes on these issues directly and resolves them collaboratively within a framework of possibilities and expectations that is established by the GGE partners themselves. It should be clearer now why the recruitment of committed, diverse, experienced, and talented partners to participate in the GGE is so critical. Partners do not only share in the creation of value, they determine the type of value and its manifestations. That decision can be made collaboratively because of the agreement through the vision on what partners want to accomplish. The change model provides a coherent understanding of the situation and conditions they must consider and address in order to make decisions that are purposeful and impactful.

The concepts have opened up excitement about the possibilities for creating and capturing value. For firms it is valuable as they can transform that value into tangible benefits for itself. GGEs need to find more ways to create value and open up the opportunities for its capture by all of its partners—short term and long term.

Techniques for Creating Value

It is the prospect of value creation and capture that allows for a possible engagement, because the GGE is offering something to the partners that might be different or timely. GGEs should present themselves as a new opportunity for potential partners. The longer and more extensive the "value creation menu," the more possibilities that there will be a match for a GGE partner. In addition, an expansive list of value creation possibilities demonstrates to partners the capacities of a GGE and supports the prospect that the GGE will be in a position to respond to future interests of partners.

Creating Public and Private Value

There are no limits on the quantity or quality of value that could be generated by a GGE. The "value creation portfolio" of any given GGE is determined by its partners as they consider joining the GGE and what value they believe they will capture as a result. The more imaginative and inventive the ideas about how to create value, the more successful the GGE will be in attracting quality partners. Some specific ways to create both public and private value that would be commonly associated with the provision of products and services to help distressed communities as proposed by the SDGs are discussed below.

1. *Monetizing an Externality.* One person's waste is another person's valued feedstock. Technological innovations and or local market conditions can help transform goods with limited market value to valued products. Human and animal waste can be converted into methane gas and become a source of energy, as can landfill material. Human waste can be converted into drinking water through an Omni Processor and it evaporates solids that otherwise may be dumped on open land. Leftover food and material can be converted into high-quality fertilizer. Agricultural by-products, such as straw, rice husks, or sugarcane bagasse are converted into high value materials for building and other industrial uses. Plastic water bottles are recycled as materials in automobile manufacturing. In addition, carbon credits can fund the purchase of clean technologies that substitute for the carbon emissions that were curtailed in order to accrue the carbon credits.

2. *Create or Expand Markets.* New markets are created by businesses and entrepreneurs willing to take on greater risks or who believe risk assessments are misunderstood. Microfinance, microinsurance, and microbanking are all illustrations of seeing opportunities to create new markets. Expanding markets can make businesses with operating expenses that are too high and with a small customer base viable. Using extra room in vehicles travelling to other communities to carry products such as batteries charged by solar power expand markets for energy.

3. *Reduce Operating Costs.* Programs providing humanitarian relief are often dedicated to one or a limited set of services. This means multiple organizations, each with their own program and overhead costs, may be providing services to one community. Coordinating the delivery of these different services can reduce operating costs significantly. Coordinating some service deliveries—such as vaccines and medicines—can avoid administering a series of medicines by different organizations that have negative interactions if not dosed and taken properly. Coordinating and streamlining the administrative and operational aspects of programs' activities reduces the cost of overall services provided per person.

4. ***Higher Utilization of Capital***. Government or corporate philanthropy funding goes to equipment in support of program operations: refrigerators, vehicles, or computers. Rarely are these public assets fully utilized: refrigerators may not be full, cars may not be carry maximum passengers, and computers have excess storage or computational capacities. Some assets are left unused during non-working hours, like vehicles. These public assets have value and, if private sector partners were found that could utilize this excess capacity, a fee could be charged, reflecting their market value. Carrying products to destinations in vehicles with less than full payloads is a common example. In turn, private sector vehicles might be able to carry some goods destined for remote communities, acknowledging the marginal costs of transporting those additional public goods approaches zero. Sharing access to capital assets in increments means they are cheaper than buying the entire asset.

5. ***Redirect Public Funding with Better Results***. Finding more cost-effective ways to deliver services not only creates value for the community in need and for those that deliver the services, but such innovations can be leveraged to offer similar cost-effective savings for government funded programs. Governments that have contracted with vendors to provide services could find the GGE's approach cheaper than even the lowest bidder. The government would save costs by using the GGE as a lowest price option.

GGEs most often will use multiple techniques for creating value. A review of the GGEs profiled in Chapters 5 through 11 shows they use many of the techniques described above to create value to help achieve their vision and for their partners. These are summarized in Table 16.1.

TABLE 16.1 Techniques to Creating Value

GGE	Value Creation Techniques
GAIN	**Monetize externalities:** GAIN provides their employees with access to better nutrition, which in turn makes them healthier and more productive thus creating more relative wealth and allowing companies that are a part of GAIN to profit from increased sales.
	Create or expand markets: To mobilize the private sector in the fight against malnutrition and to ensure that the best ideas in agriculture and nutrition get to scale, GAIN has developed the Marketplace for Nutritious Foods.
R4	**Redirecting government funds:** R4 receives support from USAID (United States Government).

(continued)

TABLE 16.1 *(continued)*

GGE	*Value Creation Techniques*
mHealth Alliance	**Lower operating costs:** The R4 Rural Resilience Initiative brings together key risk management tools in a holistic approach that empowers food-insecure families. **Higher utilizations of fixed assets:** The Government of Nigeria invited the mHealth Alliance and other strategic partners to work with its Federal Ministry of Health.
Rainforest Alliance	**Lower operating costs:** To address the two health-related MDGs that lagged the furthest behind, namely those related to maternal and child health, the mHealth Alliance launched the Maternal mHealth Initiative. **Higher utilizations of fixed assets:** Rainforest Alliance Certified cocoa farms in Côte d'Ivoire produced 40 percent more cocoa per acre than noncertified farms. Productivity gains were shown to be due to greater efficiency.
GNNTD	**Create or expand markets:** In the Río Plátano Biosphere Reserve of Honduras, the Rainforest Alliance and local partners have worked with 12 community forestry cooperatives to provide technical assistance, training, and access to new markets. **Lower operating costs:** A Global Network partner developed a workshop in 12 West African countries that trained physicians on a specific operation. This workshop resulted in 3,000 patients receiving the operation to correct their disability.
HERproject	**Redirecting government funds:** GNNTD expanded their efforts to engage governments beyond the UK and US so that they could help support more cost-effective NTD programs. **Monetize externality:** HERproject in China has demonstrated the returns of loyal, healthy, and skilled workers through: an increased sense of belonging from workers; enhanced communication between workers and peers, line supervisors, and factory management; reduced absenteeism and worker turnover; and empowered women workers who play an important role in stabilizing the workforce of the factory.
INEE	**Redirecting government funds:** The Levi Strauss Foundation, Ministry of Foreign Affairs of the Netherlands, and the Swedish International Development Cooperation Agency all support HERproject financially. **Lower operating costs:** INEE contributed to the ongoing professionalization of their field through the launching of a peer-reviewed journal on education in emergencies and the development of a Conflict Sensitive Education Pack.
	Redirecting of government funds: Norwegian Ministry of Foreign Affairs and Deutsche Gesellschaft für Internationale Zusammenarbeit (German Society for International Cooperation) support INEE financially.

The examples provided in Table 16.1 are only a subset of activities the GGEs used to generate value. The five examples of techniques to create value are again a short list of possibilities.

The goal for the GGE is to discover as many options for creating value as possible. It is the value the GGE creates that could be captured by prospective partners which provides a powerful motivation for them to join the GGE. As a model of global governance, GGEs offer government, business, and NGOs an exciting alternative to conventional approaches and prospects for turning collaboration into a far more effective and impactful experience than other forms of partnerships. Each GGE is singular and must assemble their partners based on the direction and guidance set out by the vision and the change model.

17
ASSEMBLING THE GLOBAL GOVERNANCE ENTERPRISE

Stage five is the final step that assembles the Global Governance Enterprise (GGE). The efforts made during the previous stages have laid the foundation for securing agreement of the partners to participate in the GGE. The vision has been set out and states clearly and in terms that are quantifiable what the GGE proposes to change and how it will make for a better world. The change model describes the conditions that affect the global problem the vision is seeking to address in sufficient detail and in the local context. It provides a clear view of the actions partners might agree to so their actions are purposeful and impactful. Partners have been recruited from a wide spectrum of sectors: governments, businesses, and non-governmental organizations (NGOs). The partners that are directly affected by GGE actions have a broad range of experiences relevant to understanding the communities to be targeted, the global problem to be addressed, and a broad set of relevant skills. Finally, an investigation has been made about innovative ways public and private value could be created to advance the realization of the vision and be captured by the partners.

Principles for Assembling GGEs

Assembling the GGE needs to synthesize multiple ideas, interests, and partner intentions. The diversity of potential partners is the core strength of a GGE and a particular advantage over other forms of collaboration. It ensures that the very best ideas are being considered and discussed. The insights that come out of this discussion are continually used to adapt and refine the GGE's vision and change model. This process builds interest in and support for the GGE as it demonstrates how the partners ultimately co-create the GGE, just as they co-create innovative solutions to make the world a better place.

This same diversity is what makes GGEs a challenge to build in such a way that integrates partners' interests and generates a confluence of competencies. Principles to help guide the design and the collaboration of GGEs are discussed below.

Four Design Principles

The design of the GGE is a singular event. No two GGEs will be exactly alike. Designing a GGE takes account of the issues of what the GGE will be and what it will do. That includes matters of: what is its purpose? What is its vision? What is its mission? It includes the GGEs approach: what change will it try to bring about? What actions will it take itself? What support will it provide to others? Who are the beneficiaries? It includes how success will be judged: what metrics will be collected? What monitoring will take place? How will the information be interpreted?

All of these issues were addressed originally in stage one and stage two— creating a vision and establishing a change model. Those stages were the starting point of a process of modification and enhancement as partners were engaged, ideas and information exchanged, and levels of commitment from partners assessed. Although each GGE is particular, successful GGEs follow four design principles that reflect the findings of theory and the lessons learned of experience of how to leverage collaboration and identify social innovations that are impactful and make the world a better place.

Outcome-Oriented

Describing in detail what change the GGE will bring about is the fulcrum on which partners balance competing interests and ideas. How many people will be served? What are the specific characteristics of the services provided? What will be the standards used to assure the quantity and quality of service? How will access to the service for people in the target communities be provided? And scores of other details. It is a challenge to find the right level of specificity in the early stages of building. By the time the GGE is assembled, all questions should be answered, doubts erased, and the details explicated.

There are two counter pressures in presenting the planned GGE's outcomes to potential partners. One pressure is to present the details that potential partners need to understand the scale and scope of the GGE's efforts. These proposed outcomes cannot be casual; they come from the in-depth knowledge of those who have worked in the area and the field and understand the real barriers and opportunities for making a difference. On the other hand, the outcomes will be modified over time as partners become involved. Too much specificity too soon can be off-putting to some partners who do not want to commit to outcomes that they are not sure can be achieved or are the best ones from their point of view.

Government agencies need to explain what goals they will achieve to public officials approving their programs and budgets. NGOs need to convince donors and members that their programs have real impact. Businesses need to explain their profit potential to investors. GGEs need to be clear about what they will accomplish so partners can justify their own participation to their authorities and critical stakeholders. The outcomes need to be measureable and in ways that are relevant to their different partners: one-size metrics do not fit all. The metrics need to address the impact for the GGE's outcomes, but should also support measuring the creation and capture of public and private value of interest to the partners. Outcomes are the common touchstone which diverse partners with shared interests can work towards in a meaningful collaboration.

As partners begin to work closely together, new issues may arise, some of them potential points of contention or disagreement. The outcomes are the "vanishing point" that endures no matter what other future agreements or disagreements arise and for which collaborators continue to strive. The most important consideration is for the potential partners to believe that the specific outcomes agreed to by the partners will drive those activities of the future GGE. These outcomes may change as the GGE is built, but partners will ultimately settle on outcomes that align with the GGE's vision and the GGE will manage to those outcomes. Taking action that results in real change, achieves a desired outcome, and fills a governance gap are the characteristics that define the GGE's efforts as global governance.

Bundled Services

Services are more expensive to provide to remote communities. The cost of delivering service in localities that have little or no infrastructure can be prohibitive—particularly to smaller populations. Providing government services—directly or through NGOs—or creating markets for goods and services to remote communities face the same daunting economic realities. The "last mile" is a perennial services delivery problem. Using cross-subsidies is the conventional way for government agencies or utilities to address this issue. Rates are set for all customers and universal service is provided. Rates are higher for low-cost provision areas and those savings are used to pay for delivery in the high-cost areas. Many needy communities do not have the necessary infrastructure and their "fragile state" governments do not have fiscal or governance capabilities to provide access. Producing goods and services locally has many promising opportunities, but the cost of creating the local capacity to provide goods and services can make the cost-per-beneficiary prohibitively high.

The approach of bundling services means exploring ways to provide multiple services through fewer modes of delivery. Bundled services have several advantages. They expand the number of services that can be made accessible to needy communities by reducing the marginal cost of each additional service that is bundled. It takes advantage of the diversity of GGE partners and brings them together to deliver diverse services to communities in a more integrated way. For example, if a vehicle was transporting a nurse to a remote community to provide pre- and post-natal care services, the marginal cost of transporting a water purifier is very small. Alternatively, the cost of delivery for a water purifier alone might not be cost-effective. Each subsequent addition of another bundled service means ever lower marginal costs. The cost reductions in service delivery open up opportunities for social entrepreneurs and local micro-financed businesses to produce goods and services at lower costs. These lower-than-market costs help lower barriers to market entry for new business ventures and create opportunities for providing services at significantly lower prices.

Formally coordinating, let alone integrating, service delivery between organizations is difficult under the best of circumstances. Informal cooperation in the field is commonplace, but it is a challenge to blend organizations' activities and logistics in a manner that does not compromise or pose a potential threat to an organization's control over their mission and operations. Because NGOs compete for funding, working closely together can be difficult. GGEs provide the venue for exactly such collaboration, sharing resources and services at reduced costs to all partners. GGE partners can design their service bundling in ways that bring value-added to each of the partners. Once the original bundling arrangements are in place, new ways to combine and recombine the delivery of products and services are discovered. Bundled services can be used in support of building local capacity to create their own products and services due to significant cost reductions. For example, locating solar panels in remote areas means maintenance and inspection costs of the panels. Transportation used for eHealth programs can be used to carry personnel responsible for inspecting and repairing solar panels at a fraction of the costs of paying for transportation just in support of solar panels maintenance. Bundled services offer opportunities for recognizing the interactions and interdependencies of services and making modifications for higher quality services and better outcomes.

Reciprocal Value

The concept of reciprocal value is inspired by the theories of "shared value" that systematically look at the ways in which business actions—particularly through the management of their supply chains—can have a positive effect on society. The idea of shared value has been very helpful in convincing business and NGO executives, and government officials that businesses can contribute to helping to solve global problems while advancing their own business interests at the same. In short, creating public and private value are not mutually exclusive. In fact, they can be self-re-enforcing. However, the popularity of this approach notwithstanding, the shared value approach is incompatible with the co-creation undertaken by GGEs.

As described earlier, the concept of shared value promotes the idea that it is business—at times in consultation with others—that determines what type and form of value is to be created and shared. Shared value is a means to an end—makes a business more competitive. The success of the shared value approach is judged by how well the business solves the problem it was facing while simultaneously finding a way to generate some benefits for society. Where shared value starts with solving a problem faced by the firm, reciprocal value reverses the sequencing: it starts with the collaborative efforts of the GGE to provide services to underserved communities and making the world a better place. The success of the GGE is determined by its ability to achieve its outcomes and help to solve global problems.

The social innovations co-created by the GGE and the resources used to achieve its vision and create public value can be leveraged in turn to create private value. For example, eHealth services provided through a GGE include partners that make and sell medical diagnostic devices. These devices might be donated as part of a pilot project. Charitable funding sources may be approached to support the use of such devices. The use of the instruments improves the quality of health services people receive through greater access to more sophisticated diagnostic tools. The result is greater chances to identify conditions or precursors to diseases that, because they can now be diagnosed, can be treated as well. The need for medicines for these new treatments creates demand for the medicines. That demand creates a potential market for medicines to be provided to communities who had never been served by such a market before. The manufacturers of the appropriate medicines or local pharmacies might see new opportunities in finding a way to sell these medicines: directly to people or NGOs who might add those medicines to the medical care they now provide.

Leveraging public value creation to create private value can create a cycle that builds on itself: private value creation and capture by businesses and social entrepreneurs add even more to the opportunities for the GGE to expand its efforts, invite new partners to join and open up whole new opportunities for leveraging these assets to further expand and enhance services to underserved communities. The cycle of developing social innovations to address global problems and then leveraging that capacity to create and capture public and private value has no limitations. It all starts with the commitment of GGE partners—governments, businesses, NGOs, social entrepreneurs, community groups, investors, micro-financers, etc.—to make a difference in the world through addressing a global problem. The initial focus of the GGE on addressing a global problem exclusively brings together partners that are committed to improving people's lives. Once the GGE has decided how it will address the problem, new opportunities to create public and private value begin to reveal themselves.

Using the concept of reciprocal value also helps address a common concern by some GGE partners that business interests will corrupt the public value undergirding the GGE vision. By focusing first on addressing the global problem, trust is developed around the intentions of all the partners and their commitment to create a better world. Businesses and social entrepreneurs with an eye on opportunities to leverage the GGE's efforts and create private value can anticipate future efforts and look for ways to organize GGE activities that optimize the amount of public value created. The creation of more public value only expands the opportunities for partners to leverage it and create and capture private value. Reciprocal value is a new concept for building trust among partners in a GGE and leveraging resources in a way that perpetuates and propagates success in advancing the shared interests of GGE partners.

The Enterprise Case

GGEs justify their existence and operations through an enterprise case. It provides a justification for taking actions that provide social benefits, but operates in a way that is cost-effective and provides benefits to GGE partners. Establishing the enterprise case is analogous to making a business case, but there is an important distinction. First, a business case might suggest (erroneously) to government and NGO partners that the GGE cares only about making a profit. To that end, some infer it means that the people and communities receiving services will be charged a fee, akin to privatization: the concern is that GGEs will require payment in exchange for the services they provide. A proper description of the business case is a justification to decision makers to approve some kind of action in terms of benefits to the firm. An enterprise case is a justification to partners in terms of benefits to the GGE and its partners. Assembling a GGE around an enterprise case means the organization will run efficiently with low overhead, good management practices are valued, and resources are conserved and leveraged where possible. It means decisions are made on achieving the vision, and partners are accountable to each other.

The enterprise case does not have to be a formal document per se. It addresses the way the GGE will conduct itself and the basis for decision-making. When business participation in a GGE is based on achieving corporate social responsibilities (CSRs), alone it can make for a very weak partner. First, what makes for acceptable CSR activities by any given firm is a contested and sometimes contentious issue. Firms will be stuck trying to advance their CSR interests within a GGE while simultaneously debating with stakeholders the proper boundaries of their CSR activities, as well as debating internally what the best CSR initiatives are for the firm. This imposes heavy constraints on being flexible and adaptive with their other GGE partners. Firms should believe that the enterprise case of the GGE is well aligned with their own business case rationales for joining. Once the business partners understand the alignment of the approach of the GGE with a strong business case for a firm, then leveraging their engagement with a GGE to advance CSR, philanthropic, or other goals becomes easier.

Governments and NGOs are familiar with the notion of an enterprise case, even if they do not always use that term themselves. A "government-sponsored enterprise" is a common hybrid organization created to carry out some government functions (Kosar, 2007). Two examples are the U.S. Federal Home Loan Bank System and the U.S. Farm Credit System, owned and operated cooperatively by their borrowers. They carry out public policy goals, but are organized and run like an enterprise and not government. These are similar traits of GGEs, created to help solve global problems (not government policies), yet operated and supported by its partners. Large NGOs receiving corporate philanthropy must make extensive documentation about their program goals, activities, and outcomes and make the "enterprise case" that the funds will be managed in a business-like way. Activities are tracked and progress updated regularly. The enterprise case establishes an approach to governance that is familiar to all three sectors. It presents a persuasive rationale for diverse organizations to collaborate to achieve shared interests even though the goals, norms, and operating style of the different partners may be dissimilar and even at odds.

Four Collaboration Principles

For GGEs, collaborating to decide what it will do is one key task. The second is agreeing on how it will be accomplished. Successful collaboration involves several issues: how will the partners organize themselves? What decision-making processes and procedures will be adopted? How will membership be determined? What obligations and duties are assigned to partners? Can there be different types of partners with different expectations for responsibilities and contributions to the GGE? What will the leadership structure look like?

All these questions need to be sorted out and agreed to, but it is essential not to let the decisions about management, organizational, and governance issues of the GGE supersede collaboration among partners. The benefits of using a multisector collaborative approach and following the guidelines of being a GGE are the actual collaborations and what they produce. Decisions on how to organize and manage the GGE should single-mindedly be guided by what conditions will facilitate genuine exchange of ideas and information, honest critiques and authentic dialogs, earnest problem-solving efforts, and out-of-the-box thinking—all these activities conducted among diverse partners. The four collaboration principles promote the type of circumstances under which partners meet and set a tone and expectations for engagements that promote teamwork and fellowship in the efforts of partners and re-enforces the potential of the GGE partners to co-create something innovative, impactful, and important.

Trusted Partners

GGEs fully anticipate that partners will have to be negotiating and bargaining over what they see as the best course of action to take to make it a better world. It means securing concurrence on refinements (or wholesale changes) to the vision and the change model, agreement on which partners should be welcomed into the GGE, and which actions by the GGE make the most sense. The debate and discussions co-create the innovations for the GGE to adopt. Trusted partners are a type of collaborative relationship that fosters just this type of engagement and exchange.

When partnerships are transactional, it is about gaining whatever advantages one party can from another. Since all partners are attempting to maximize their own advantage, there is rough fairness about the results: some will gain more than others, but that is the expectation. Transactional partnerships are better suited to short-term engagements where collaborations are formed around achieving some shared short-term goal. Partners need to figure out the best arrangements and accommodations for success. Transactional partnerships serve the specific aims of the partners and no others. There are no shared values and no shared interests. As a result, there is no basis for co-creating innovations, one of the critical functions of a GGE.

Trusted Partners work together to the advantage of the GGE and the other partners. Trusted Partners look to optimize the impact of the GGE and simultaneously create opportunities for the partners to benefit. Partners of GGEs do not come together to solve a joint problem; they come together to discover the best way to bring about the change they all agree they want to see happen. This is accomplished through several mechanisms used to foster collaboration. First, voluntary disclosures of information are made that aid the individual partners and the collective decision-making capabilities of the GGE. It might include information about the partner's own organization, experiences relevant to the vision and/or change model, activities of other entities addressing similar issues, future plans of relevant organizations, opportunities for funding the GGE, and generally opening up one's network to other GGE partners.

Second, it involves a shared effort to allocate risks associated with GGE actions optimally among the partners. When deciding what actions the GGE should take, Trusted Partners determine which partner is in the best position to take on that risk and assigns accordingly. For example, government officials might be thought to be the best ones to maintain and/or establish favorable relations with other government officials. However, NGOs and businesses may have great relationships with a government official based on previous projects, and, in such cases, the NGO or business GGE partner would take on managing the risk associated with approval of actions by the government.

Third, accountability for the GGE's actions and impact are shared collectively. When GGE activities are successful, all partners can share the credit. But when problems arise, all GGE partners accept responsibility and take whatever actions they can to solve the problem. These actions can mean contacting a colleague and asking for a favor, or supporting the speeding up or slowing down of GGE activities, even when that is not to the advantage of the individual partner. It might mean spending more time on the GGE than had been previously antici-pated. Typically, these problem-solving actions do not benefit the partner, only the GGE, and require a strong commitment to make sacrifices without imme-diate benefit to individual partners. Shared accountability means partners are empathetic to the challenges faced by other partners, and efforts are made to help them overcome difficulties. It may be as simple as deciding what date to launch the GGE, mindful of accommodating high-level executives and public speak-ing events. It could involve an unexpected funding allocation shortfall during one partner's budget cycle and the partners agree to look for additional funding sources within their own organization. Trusted Partners cements the agreement of partners to work together to reach the outcomes described in the vision.

Three-Layered Partners

Multisector collaborations are most frequently discussed at the organizational level. We talk about governments, NGOs, and businesses, their general organ-izational missions and goals, and how those could be complements when collaborating within a GGE. We also talk about champions for GGEs within those organizations, the individual employees that become engaged in the ini-tiatives, participate in meetings, and represent the interests of their respective organizations. However, GGE partners are so much more complex than organi-zations and champions.

GGEs successful at fostering collaboration recognize the organizational complexities of their partners and expect that the employees who are working with a GGE have to account for these complexities as well. Partners should be viewed through three perspectives. The first perspective concerns the interests of the organization, both strategic and operational. Each organization will be different in the ways these interests are articulated and animated. Partners need to share how each of their respective organizations view their own interests, how the efforts of the GGE might be aligned with those interests, and the chal-lenges in getting the leadership of the organization to agree to join the GGE. It should be expected that some partners will be "all in" while others, even once a partner has agreed to join a GGE, may question the wisdom of joining, and the activities of the GGE may be under review by some partners for a while.

The second layer involves the interests of the office where the partner liaison to the GGE works. Each office inside an organization has its own goals and responsibilities to manage. It is valuable to explore and understand how the activities of the GGE or the other partners might be useful in helping contribute in some positive way to that office. Here it is a matter of helping to translate the action of the GGE into operational assets. For instance, by working with a GGE, one NGO might meet a businessperson with whom they do not have a current partnership. The NGO's affiliation with the GGE might lead to overtures from the business to explore partnerships outside the GGE. It is a very tangible asset for the business and the NGO that came from their GGE affiliation.

The third layer is the professional interests of the partner liaison. Participation in the GGE may lead to a promotion, greater exposure to executives within the organization, enhanced reputation as an innovator and risk-taker. The participant may believe in the GGE and want to change the culture and practices of the organization, even if it means challenging decisions within the organization. Understanding what opportunities and challenges the individual liaisons face helps link the benefits a GGE accrues from success to the benefits liaisons may accumulate.

All three perspectives are typical for managers to identify and reconcile as they carry out their responsibilities. As governance networks, the leadership team of the GGE will spend considerable time facilitating success by managing the network relationships at all three levels. GGEs that take into account these same considerations open up more opportunities for collaboration and can help build strong partnerships.

Co-Creating Social Innovation

The actions taken by GGEs should be "game changers." Building a GGE takes a lot of time and commitment. If an organization is going to go through all that effort, there should be a pay-off that is sufficiently impactful and sufficiently different to make it worthwhile. The vision and change model speak to ambitions, possibilities, and innovations. The GGE needs to demonstrate a proof-of-concept that brings together diverse organizations with shared interests and can create innovative solutions to pressing global problems.

Such important ideas for achieving the GGE vision cannot be generated unless there is openness among the partners to thinking in new ways, to reconsidering the accuracy of what has been given truth, and shedding dogmas. Co-creation is a pragmatic effort where partners learn about new ideas and are inspired to think "outside the box." One way to moderate and facilitate co-creation is to develop expectations that partners will commit resources in support of their ideas. Not all organizations have discretionary funds to redirect to a GGE, and it is understood some members will have greater resources to contribute. It is unproductive to have a partner advance ideas but then commit no resources. GGEs are about doing, not debating ideas. Partners that put forward ideas should back them up with support or ideas on how to attract support for their execution.

GGEs need to create an environment which makes new thinking and questioning convention the norm. This type of approach to problem solving is not conventional. That means being opportunistic and looking for a new idea or approach the GGE can adopt and upon which it can build. There are some risks in embracing new ideas with little vetting, but diverse and interesting partners provide sufficient due diligence to avoid lapses in judgment: GGEs cannot afford to be risk-adverse. GGEs facilitate interactions among members that discourage advancing current practices as possible action and celebrate revolutionary formulations of problem solving.

Take-Aways Linked to Outcomes

Partners need to intentionally and transparently link the benefits their organization plans to gain from their participation in the GGE—the value proposition—to the realization of the outcomes. The value that is created that helps achieve the vision has to be entwined with efforts to create value that can be captured exclusively by the partners. When the GGE is successful, the partners will be successful. All partners have to be clear about this ordering.

One of the biggest concerns of GGE partners, because it is innovative and has unfamiliar risks, is the time and effort that will be wasted if the other partners do not follow through on their commitments. Many government officials and NGOs worry that business partners in a GGE will allow their interest to make money to undermine the vision of the GGE. Business people have also had experiences of participating in government-sponsored initiatives that had great opening ceremonies, but led to little action—sometimes cancelled without advance consultation. Linking partner benefits to the GGE's outcomes encourages partners to remain faithful to their original agreements. Since each partner has substantial input into defining outcomes, they are the confirmation and validation of real shared interests.

Alternatively, as the GGE outcomes are being realized, the amount or form of value captured by other partners is not relevant to the GGE. Partners negotiate with each other to set the outcomes that are desired. One partner might be able to leverage those outcomes and gain access to new markets for very profitable products or services. Another partner might leverage the outcomes for a speech by a public official who claims credit for the GGE's success. Another partner might leverage the outcomes to attract a very large new donor. GGE partners should celebrate these results—it reflects on a very well organized and managed GGE. How partners leverage their success is not challenged as long as each partner makes a full-faith effort to meet the GGE's outcomes.

The Role of the Governance Entrepreneur

Building a successful GGE is a delicate maneuver and not for the faint-of-heart. They are fragile in their earliest days and dynamic and unpredictable as they take shape and self-identify. They demand patience and an enduring spirit to nurture. In the beginning, it can be difficult to find any funding to support such a nascent initiative. Potential partners are unlikely to offer money even if they are inspired by the vision and persuaded by the change model. Early questions will be asked about who are other potential partners. What will the GGE do? Where will they operate? The answers will all be the same—not sure yet, that is for the partners to determine. It can give an impression of not being well organized as opposed to the intention of this approach, which is to defer to the collaborative process. For potential GGE partners, the costs come up front, the benefits down the road. That is a difficult sales pitch to make to potential partners, who are themselves resource constrained and trying to implement their own programs. One asset the governance entrepreneur has is the spark of an idea about how to make the world a better place. It is the heart of the inspiration that gets people's attention and attracts them to learn more about the prospects and possibilities of a GGE.

The combination of thinking about global problems in a new way and taking action to make change is also appealing. There is no shortage of associations, NGOs, advocacy groups, and conference presenters who have great ideas about how to make things better. Actually doing something about it is littered with barriers. GGEs are dedicated to taking on that challenge and putting action to thought. GGEs do not ask potential partners for contributions to help them implement preconceived ideas. They ask partners to join them to help translate that flicker of a brilliant idea into the discovery of a new and exciting vision they can work on together to bring to life. That is a different approach.

As governance entrepreneurs guide potential partners through the stages of building a GGE, there is constant pressure to find the balance of keeping the potential partners engaged in further developing and refining the vision and the change model, documenting and sharing discussions and ideas that partners propose that enhance and advance the GGE, and keeping attention on the process of building the GGE that makes it attractive for people and organizations to stay engaged and learn more. A governance entrepreneur can benefit from a diverse skill set as they have many roles to play: facilitator, translator, teacher, skeptic, counselor, project manager, and visionary, among others.

All the skills a governance entrepreneur has at their command will be helpful, but the most important skill is the recruitment of extraordinary people who want to see a better world, want to make a difference, are willing to take reasonable risks, will travel to meetings or attend conferences on behalf of their organizations, and represent the interests of the GGE to their superiors. These liaisons to the GGE are accomplished at moving ideas within their own organization, across other organizations, and know how to secure support (e.g., political, financial, and reputational) for the GGE. They are "rebels with a cause," working within the system. When potential partners meet others who share their views and values, the enthusiasm and belief in the possibilities for the GGE builds momentum. There is a tipping-point in building a GGE when the governance entrepreneur has to quickly transition from being the lead person, advocating and pushing for the GGE, to being the one trying to keep up with the partners and their own ideas and emerging opportunities to help build the GGE.

Chicken and Eggin' It

As GGEs engage potential partners, there is an unavoidable tension that comes from starting something new and innovative: creating something out of nothing. On the one hand, the vision and the change model set out the basic ideas behind the GGE's future mission; on the other, a case needs to be made to partners that the future GGE has good prospects for success. The best way to communicate those prospects is by securing support of prestigious and interesting partners. At this stage of building a GGE, there is a continual iteration and consultation with possible partners: spending time developing in greater detail the operational aspects of the GGE, securing expressions of support, and assessing what more needs to be accomplished or confirmed to gain their commitment to join the GGE. The level of details and routines that are requested by potentials partners conflicts with leaving sufficient aspects of the GGE unspecified so partners can still co-create and shape it. Too much specificity and it turns off partners who think the GGE is pre-cooked; too little specificity and partners will think it is undercooked and too insubstantial.

Governance without Government

Nearly any GGE is going to need the approval of government officials to operate in a country. Having a representative from the government as a partner can be useful, but is not required. The key is to find the balance between getting the approval of government officials without being constrained by government policy and/or governance preferences. Of course, different government regimes will have their own policies, but the GGE needs to garner government approval while maintaining its autonomy. The point is not that government involvement and policies are always misdirected, but if government has too strong a presence, it can inhibit prospects of co-creating and instituting social innovations. An alternative approach is engaging an NGO that has good contacts with the government already in place. A GGE working with a well-regarded NGO gains a license-to-operate. Businesses may have such contacts with the government as well, but NGOs do not face the same skepticism about its intentions as will a business. In addition, taking on activities that advance an existing government program that is consistent with the GGE's vision and change model can help as well. GGEs will at times be in conflict with specific government policies, and sometimes that fact is unavoidable.

Funding the GGE

GGEs are not expensive. In the early stages, the major cost is "sweat equity" contributed by the governance entrepreneur and early supporters. Governments have hosted the formation of multisector collaborations. The United Nations Foundation mandate is to create multisector collaborations. This type of hosting is beneficial and offsets the costs of convening and preparing documents. However, such government-sponsored initiatives are inclined to be too conventional for a GGE. Some small levels of funding may be available from government agencies, but they will want to fund a concrete function linked to their mission. Foundations have planning grants, but asking for money to develop an idea (no matter how appealing) without the firm commitment of partners is not very compelling. Private philanthropists may be the best prospects in the early days, willing to support something interesting and new and take some risk that the GGE does not come to fruition. Leveraging the funds of partners that are currently used to support activities and projects and combine them with similar funding from other partners is another approach. When a GGE is built, then conventional funding sources of government grants, corporate philanthropy, and foundational support are obvious sources. GGEs can also leverage funding from the private value partners may generate to offset operating expenses.

The Hidden Costs of Collaboration

Most NGOs, businesses, and government agencies are willing to let an employee attend an initial exploratory meeting convened by a governance entrepreneur. The convener has to have some reputation and standing. Either securing the support of some hosting organization, or having some well-known advisors is always a plus. Attendees may return for a second meeting if there is sufficient potential in what is presented—whether it is a compelling new approach or a confidence-securing agenda with background documents that indicates the organizers know what they are doing. After the initial engagement, the justification for participating in follow-on events—rewriting the vision or reviewing and assessing the change model—becomes harder for potential partners. One challenge is the costs come up front and the benefits come later (if at all). One approach is to secure two or three potential partners who comprise an informal steering group or "brain trust." That means finding people who will commit the extra time and energy to help build the GGE in its infancy. They also have enough seniority and influence within their organization to forecast which ideas and approaches their respective upper management will support. These partners dedicate the time to work on shaping the GGE's vision and mission, represent it at meetings, and advocate for the GGE by explaining why their organizations believe in it. In addition, these "GGE first-responders" can draw on their networks and identify other potential partners who approach their work with a similar interest in finding new ways and approaches to address their organization's problems.

Measuring Success

Each GGE partner will have its own need for metrics to demonstrate to their own organization that participation was a success. Core metrics are needed that will measure the success the GGE has had bringing about the changes it sought. Quantifying impacts on people and society can be difficult: data are not always available and the cause of change in people and communities over time can be difficult to isolate. The best approach is to include specific measures of success in the vision. NGOs that are used to managing donor expectations have extensive metrics they report. These metrics may not be perfect, but they may measure the GGE's impact well enough and overcome many of the barriers to collecting and reporting success. Some government-sponsored multisector collaborations measure success by how many organizations have signed up to be members; or they agree to adhere to specific principles of conduct; or they add up the total pledges made by firms and NGOs to meet specific targets. Adding up targets has the additional burden of validating that targets have actually been met. In addition, some organizations pledge to accomplish targets they were already planning on achieving. These latter approaches are not well suited to what GGEs are attempting to accomplish.

Assembling the GGE is the Last Thing You Want to Do

By the time Memoranda of Understanding (MOUs) are ready to be signed to create the GGE, all the other issues that matter to the partners should have been discussed—countless times. The vision and the change model should have been reviewed and specifics changed, tweaked, modified, and refined. The vision itself may have changed noticeably. The shared interests of partners have been identified and described in quantifiable outcomes that are achievable and significant to the members of the community that will benefit. The reasoning behind the future success of the GGE's efforts has been proposed, critiqued, reformed, and improved several times. The resulting shared "theory of change" is embraced and provides inspiration about future possibilities to all. Opportunities for providing public services that have been neglected or under-provided have been explored and decided upon; innovative and inspiring ideas have been co-created to overcome what had been thought of as barriers, creating value. Market opportunities for partners have been discovered and integrated into the operations of the partnership, creating more value. As new opportunities are developed and vetted, new partners are undertaking new roles, complementing the founding partners' activities. New partners bring even more ideas and innovative approaches that get incorporated into the overall mission of the GGE.

A pilot project may have been added to provide a less ambitious but more specific set of actions to be implemented by the partners. Such a pilot provides an opportunity to demonstrate proof-of-concept. Even if the original vision of the GGE has been scaled back to a modest first effort, proving and exhibiting success can be a powerful recruiting tool for other partners who were not sufficiently convinced the GGE would be successful. Another reason for starting with a pilot is when potential partners believe the risks associated with participating and then falling short of achieving the GGEs objectives are too high.

The desire to work collaboratively with partners in the GGE is grounded in the relationships and trust that have developed among partners as the benefits

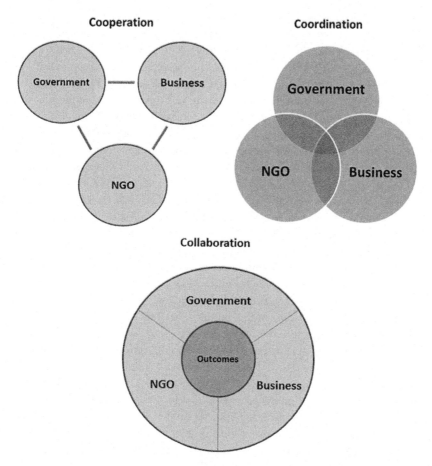

FIGURE 17.1 Different Levels of Partnership

Source: Author created.

that come from its planned accomplishments. The levels of teamwork among partners that is produced from going through the stages of building a GGE exceed typical partnerships. Figure 17.1 shows illustrations of different levels of possible partnership. In a cooperation mode, partners look for ways to work together, taking advantage of mutual activities, but their organizational mission and goals, their operations and activities may be modified marginally, if at all. Joint efforts to achieve the same ends and a willingness to help are characteristics of the cooperation mode. In a cooperation mode, partners modify their efforts to accommodate and complement each other. Goals are seen as shared, so such deference to other organizations can be a plus to achieving more together than separately. Cooperation also suggests some loss of unilateral decision-making and control, replaced by some shared responsibilities and obligations.

In the collaboration mode, the collective efforts are integrated into shared interests. The partners work together to an end that all deem to be worthwhile. Partners may have very different reasons for wanting the outcomes achieved and may stand to benefit in very different ways. The common bond is the desire for the outcome(s) that has been selected by the partners. In this approach, the participant's benefits from partnering are tied to the success of the GGE. GGE success requires a deep level of commitment. It is this level of commitment that motivates partners to spend the time and effort working out all the other stages so thoroughly. The success of the GGE requires an understanding of the prospects for success by potential partners. These same partners' understanding of the GGE's success requires serious work and dedication at all other stages.

If partners' own success is not tied to the success of the GGE, the level of effort made to ensure success will be guarded, understandably. That means that the exploration of partners to co-create an innovative and successful collaboration will be shortchanged, creating a greater risk of failure. There is an understandable self-gauging activity in the creation of any such partnership: the more the fortunes of the partners are tied to the fortunes of the GGE, the more investment in success they will make. But if the belief in the GGE's success begins to wane during different stages, the less risk partners will take, pulling back time and dedication to the building of the GGE, and further putting the whole effort at risk. The delicate tightrope act that is conducted during the other stages of keeping partners ever more interested at each new stage is rewarded in this fifth stage. The anti-climax of officially assembling the GGE is the sure sign of a successfully built GGE.

In many ways, a purposeful and impactful GGE is never completely done being built. Successful GGEs provide a platform to partners that allow them opportunities to put in place activities that meet their ideals for making the world a better place, while also achieving their own organization's goals. The power of collaboration to set its sights on a better world, develop a plan of action that achieves the desired change, while advancing the goals of the partner organizations has limitless possibilities to continually reinvent itself. GGE success fosters more success.

18

THE FUTURE OF GLOBAL GOVERNANCE ENTERPRISES

Globalization has transformed the world so dramatically and so rapidly, it is not a surprise that long-standing convictions about what constitutes good global governance and how it should be implemented properly, are losing their relevance. Whether conventional global governance, instituted through the international system and its institutions, is to be praised or criticized remains a contentious debate. What is undeniable is the changing global governance landscape, with a dramatically expanding role for partnerships of all shapes and sizes, which requires an updated and refreshed approach to achieving good global governance. Building Global Governance Enterprises (GGEs) that can help fill the global governance gap is a promising approach that begins to reimagine what good global governance looks like. Hopefully, additional approaches to good global governance will be developing as a response to the renewed efforts of the Sustainable Development Goals (SDGs) to address global problems.

Multisector governance in general and GGEs in particular, have been welcomed as an interesting and innovative form of global governance, providing a creative way to fill the global governance gap. Unfortunately, these efforts will be constrained from reaching their full potential until a closer alignment is established between how we practice good global governance and how we think about it. Such an alignment requires the further evolution of understanding what it means to have "governance without government" by both scholars and practitioners.

The collaborative approach, which makes GGEs an attractive global governance option for governments, non-governmental organizations (NGOs), and businesses, has been viewed by most scholars as an extension of existing forms of multisector collaboration where governments and non-state partners cooperate and coordinate. In fact, GGEs are a radical departure from past global governance practices (Forrer *et al.*, 2014). GGEs that help fill the governance gap, but are not accountable (at least directly) to governments are a misfit with conventional good governance principles. If they are autonomous from government, from where do they garner their legitimacy? The preponderance of research on network governance understands such partnerships as being a means for governments to achieve better results. Yet, it is the autonomy from government and its agencies that provides GGEs with the opportunity to achieve their potential. The tradition of the theories, practices, and norms that support the conventional approach to global governance is largely incompatible with the approach taken by GGEs (Weiss & Wilkinson, 2014).

There is an urgency to make the transition to a new paradigm on good global governance that reflects the realities of a globalized world and the emergence and growing importance of non-state actors involved in global governance and their engagement in non-state-centric models. GGEs are the avant-garde of good global governance, but the transformation globalization has brought means there is no going back to using conventional standards for arranging global governance and judging their efficacy. New ways to think about what makes for good global governance are needed if GGEs are to be understood fully and assessed fairly when put into practice.

The Theory and Practice of Good Global Governance

Enthusiasm over the promise of multisector collaboration and GGEs should not eclipse the rightful concerns that have been raised about their legitimacy (Rhodes, 1996). If GGEs are to be accepted as a credible and acceptable approach to global governance, they need to be viewed as a justifiable and effective alternative to conventional global governance. No matter how deserved the current reputation of global governance being done poorly, it does not by itself justify turning to new and relatively untested approaches to global governance (Murphy, 2000; Held, 2004; Easterly, 2014). At the same time, some of the critiques and concerns over GGEs compared to conventional approaches of global governance are misdirected. Standards and ideas about good global governance that have been developed over many decades are exactly the hallmarks from which GGEs have intentionally turned away. GGEs are inspired by the belief that there are better ways to help solve global problems. GGEs in particular are designed in opposition to many accepted practices of good governance.

If new principles, models, theories formulated, and the related empirics have yet to be generated and analyzed, how can the actual validity of GGEs be established in the tradition of democratic accountability? Figure 18.1 illustrates the current misunderstanding.

Judging the performance of GGEs against conventions of good global governance is not logical. Comparing the performance of multisector collaboration to the theories of conventional good global governance and finding that they fall short of established standards are misguided. Equally unfair is comparing

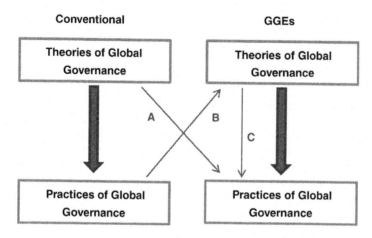

Conventional   **GGEs**

A. **GGE Critics Comparison**
B. **GGE Supporters Comparison**
C. **GGE as Good Global Governance**

FIGURE 18.1 Global Governance: Theory Informs Practice

Source: Author created.

the practice of conventional global governance with the theories of what multi-sector collaboration might accomplish. Comparing the theoretical prescriptions of multisector collaboration to actual global governance is also invalid. If it were a practical concern over rival approaches, comparing the performance of conventional global governance against the efforts of GGEs would be the right comparison. The proper comparison is theory to theory and practice to practice. Unfortunately, there is limited theory and practice of GGEs to make meaningful comparisons.

Therefore, what we are left with is the experiences of GGEs (and other multisector collaboration) that demonstrate it to be a promising and impactful approach to good global governance. However, the conventional global governance paradigm does not apply, and a new partnership paradigm is under construction. During this interregnum of making the transition from conventional global governance to a new partnership paradigm, careful attention needs to be given to those organizations that claim the mantle of GGEs. The definition of GGEs provided in Chapter 4 offers useful selection guidance, but arguments on what multisector collaborations qualify as GGEs (or some other partnership incarnation), will likely be robust (Waddell, 2012; Grayson & Nelson, 2013).

The most reasonable way to assure GGEs meet expectations is to set out strong theory that supports and justifies the global governance approach used by GGEs, and compare the performance of GGEs against the theory of what we believe it could accomplish. If GGEs act like GGEs should, that is a measure of their qualification as a good global governance approach. Greater attention is needed to developing a new partnership paradigm that is responsive to the changes brought about by globalization and frames what constitutes good global governance moving forward.

Emerging Partnership Paradigm

For some, the global governance gap represents a serious handicap to solving global problems. Without effective global governance institutions, properly resourced, fully legitimate, and with good leadership, prospects for solving major global problems as described in the SDGs are greatly diminished. However, as discussed in Chapter 3, GGEs present an opportunity, not only to help close the global governance gap, but to establish good global governance, superior to the conventional global governance practiced today.

The global governance gap should be embraced and accepted. The regime of failed and fragile states should be expected to persist for the foreseeable future, in a continual state of flux, moving in and out of the "buffer condition," the perpetual eruption of violent conflict (Forrer & Katsos, 2015). Globalization has left even the most developed and industrialized nations with lessening capacity to regulate effectively the flows across their borders or disentangle themselves from the consequences of myriad and unmanageable conditions and events occurring around the globe. Just as the global governance gap is a logical result of globalization, GGEs should be seen as a natural evolution of how good global governance is organized and conducted, responding to those same irreversible, transformational forces of globalization.

The capacity to make the world a better place exists, but we need to develop the aptitude on how to bring into harmony the new approach to governance offered by GGEs and an updated paradigm on what constitutes good global governance (Weiss & Wilkinson, 2014). Anticipating the need for a globalized world to accommodate the new realities of "governance without government," nearly 25 years ago, scholars began to develop the concepts and theories of such a condition (Rosenau & Czempiel, 1992). New governance and new public governance are the areas of research that study how to understand "governance without government" (Rhodes & Ruggie, 1996). To this growing literature, several elements of a new partnership paradigm are proposed based on the emergence of GGEs.

Blurred Lines: Public and Private Values

A distinction between "public values" and "private values" undergirds fundamental ideas about differences between collective action and individual choice, and assigned roles for government and business in the conduct of global governance. Where public values describe what is important to the community as a whole and its common use of resources and associated social benefits, private values pertain to what is important to the individual and the gains and losses incurred. These two value sets are typically cast as being in opposition to each other. Private values advance the interests of the individual; public values advance the collective interests of communities.

Without debating this classic distinction, the exclusive assignment of public values as the aspiration of governments, and private values as the motivators of business, is overly dogmatic and fails to recognize a more expansive role business can play in having a positive impact on the local communities where they operate, and on global communities more generally. Business can be adroit at creating and managing activities that advance public values and do so every day through community support projects and Corporate Social Responsibilities (CSR) activities. The logic of GGEs is predicated on the realization the business will take actions that are consonant with public values. This "blurred line" between public and private values should be recognized as an aspect of a new partnership paradigm. Business has the option of taking actions that reflect both public and private values, including actions reflecting a hybrid of both.

Asserting the primacy of public values does not exclude the productive participation of business. Demarcating private values as the sole motivation of business is a tired ideological assertion, countered by the increasing publicness of corporations brought about by globalization. Through the collaboration of GGEs, public and private values can be advanced, in harmony, by public, private, and nonprofit organizations. GGEs demonstrate that business can and do advance public values, and governments do not have an exclusive mandate in advancing them.

The Principal-Principal Problem

The Principle-Agent problem is a concept familiar and thoroughly parsed by legal, public, and private management scholars. It describes the dilemma of "agents" doing work on behalf of the "principal" and recognizing that the incentives of each party do not align. The results are that the interests of the agent can be advanced at the expense of the interests of the principal. It is a condition found in hierarchical relationships: agents doing the work have different motivations—and act upon them—than the principals who specify the work to be done. This is a common issue for governments contracting with other organizations. The principal-agent problem is amplified when the relationship is based on a multisector partnership. It is presumed that the interests of business and NGOs are not the same as government, and one global governance challenge is for governments to find ways to steer the efforts of their partnership towards achieving the public interests.

The traditional design of global governance efforts is to install government in a position of hierarchical authority to address the principal-agent problem in multisector collaboration. However, GGEs do not present a principal–agent problem; they present a principal–principal problem (Forrer *et al.*, 2014). Since GGEs are organized around a voluntary collaborative approach, it is a heterarchical organization. The actions taken by the GGE are agreed to jointly, not decided by one partner and implemented by the others. A new partnership paradigm needs to account for this new dynamic within GGEs.

GGEs collaborate not because of shared goals—the goals of governments, businesses, and NGOs can be disparate and, sometimes, in opposition—but because of their shared interests; partners self-select what they want to accomplish through working together, focusing on outcomes. If it becomes apparent that the interests of one partner are misaligned with those of other GGE partners, that partner does not remain a participant. Since partners in a GGE are all principals, government partners in a GGE have no authority or duty to direct the activities of the GGE. They act like all the other partners: working together to ensure the GGE's success in accomplishing the change it wants to bring about, while using those outcomes to advance their own organization's goals. As a heterarchical organization, GGEs confront the challenge of advancing the shared interests of the partners without allowing individual partners to advance their own interests at the expense of the other partners.

The Accountability Answer

The expansion of multisector collaborations on the global governance landscape poses a significant challenge for determining which ones are performing in a manner that meets the standard of democratic accountability (Forrer *et al.*, 2010). However, GGEs do not implement policies and programs on behalf of government. They choose their own activities and decide their own standards for measuring successful performance. Governments may be partners, but they participate in the GGE on a voluntary basis like all other partners. It is true that national and local governments could prohibit a GGE from operating in their country and, by extension, that is a type of accountability—GGEs could be prohibited from operating if they do not meet government expectations. Yet GGEs are often providing services just as people would want governments to do, if they could or would, so governments have many reasons to accept GGEs that improve the lives of their citizens. As a result, the idea of holding GGEs accountable, as governments would be is reasonable, but misdirected.

GGEs are defined specifically to address the "accountability question": if GGEs are not accountable to government, to whom are they accountable? The answer is to themselves (Forrer *et al.*, 2014). Each partner has a role to ensure that the GGE is "doing well" and "doing good." The role is not assigned to partners—they take it on themselves. The GGE being accountable to its partners is the best assurance it will achieve the change it wants to bring about. The definition of GGEs ensures that the outcomes of the GGE and the public interest are aligned. A new partnership paradigm needs to account for the approach used by GGEs to address the accountability question.

One of the defining characteristics of a GGE is for partners to represent a diverse range of interests and be held in high esteem by their peer organizations. The decisions of a GGE are co-created by partners. A diverse set of partners means a diverse set of interests are represented in GGE decisions. Partners who are respected by their peer organizations means the GGE benefits from a collaborative process that includes interests from a broad range of constituencies and decisions that would be considered to be appropriate and ethical. GGE partners ensure that the actions of the GGE do not contradict their own organization's mission or values. Since the actions of the GGE reflect upon the reputations of the partners, there is a strong incentive to ensure its actions would be viewed favorably from a perspective of good global governance—doing both well and good—as well as from the partners' own stakeholders. With such dynamics in place, GGEs are likely to be more accountable than the traditional approaches employed to ensure public accountability.

Unleashing the Power of GGEs

More scholarly research is needed to establish a new partnership paradigm that more fully justifies GGEs as acceptable players on the global governance landscape and articulates more robustly how GGEs' activities can embody good global governance. Practitioners also have a role to play in recognizing the different approach to good global governance taken by GGEs and modify their presumptions and implicit assumptions about how to work in successful partnerships. As mentioned above, GGEs are a radical departure from other multisector collaboration and partnership arrangements. Some equally far-reaching changes in the practice of partnerships are needed for GGEs to achieve their full potential for good global governance.

GGEs Should Be Self-Funding

The very heart of a GGE—developing unique social innovations to address global problems—makes autonomy invaluable. Being self-funded is the best way to ensure autonomy. It ensures the flexibility GGEs need and supports out-of-the-box thinking that gives rise to social innovations. Funding from governments through grants and contracts has been the conventional way of supporting development and humanitarian programs. As GGEs are not accountable to governments, it is reasonable to expect that government funding will be challenging.

GGEs strive to create both public and private value. Some of the private value could be monetized and used to offset the costs of operating a GGE. However, monetization could take some time to develop, so external non-governmental funding sources will be important in the creation of GGEs. Funding from sources that put a premium on social innovation and assured impact would be interested in providing initial funding support to GGEs.

Today, new sources of funding have emerged that could find GGEs an attractive initiative to fund. Traditional charitable foundations and philanthropic organizations are one possible source of GGE funding. In 2014, in the U.S., the top ten foundations gave nearly $10 billion (Foundation Center, n.d.). A study of corporate philanthropy for 2014 reported 271 companies, including 62 of the largest 100 companies in the Fortune 500, gave more than $18.5 billion in cash and in-kind giving (The Committee Encouraging Corporate Philanthropy, 2015). Of course, not all these funds would fit programmatically with GGE visions, but it provides a sense of the scope of non-governmental sources of potential funding. As a comparison, total U.S. foreign economic aid in 2014 was $35 billion (Rutsch, 2015).

In addition, a completely new opportunity for GGEs has developed through crowdsourcing. Crowdsourcing provides small amounts of funding for innovative ideas helping to solve global problems and are a perfect fit for GGEs. It is the embodiment of the growing feelings people have of being part of a global community and working together—even if virtually—to solve problems. Examples of crowdsourcing include Crowdrise, Kickstarter, GoFundMe, and Razoo. Micro-finance is a related opportunity, loaning money in small amounts for entrepreneurs to start an enterprise. These sources of funding, such as Kiva, Omidyar-Tufts Microfinance Fund, and Grameen Foundation, help build connections between GGE partners and social entrepreneurs. Once GGEs have secured enough funding to put their ideas into action, government funding might find them more attractive partners. When GGEs demonstrate their abilities to put in place changes that bring about the outcomes consistent with government policies, they become an asset to government in achieving shared interests.

Small Is Sustainable

There are many advantages to multinational corporations (MNCs), big international NGOs (BINGOs), large international organizations, and large national government agencies, working to solve big global problems. Large size brings economy of scale, a diverse skills base, long institutional memories, administrative capabilities to handle complex situations, and resilience. However, large organizations can be slow to adopt innovations, particularly when they originate from other organizations. Ambitious global solutions, developed to address global problems, tend to adopt a one-size-fits-all approach. GGEs develop innovative approaches to solving global problems aimed at changing very specific conditions and circumstances.

Economy-of-scale advantages of large organizations and large-scale projects can deter innovation in preference to approaches that have a proven track record and appear to be more cost-effective than smaller-scale projects. Social innovations need the flexibility to adapt to local conditions. Once implemented, small modifications can be a source of constant improvement in project performance. The failure of a new approach often shows a pathway to a modified method that succeeds. Small-scale projects, grounded in the norms, expectations, and resources of communities can be less at risk to volatilities characteristic of global networks. Many aspects of global problems can be addressed through small efforts, curated to accommodate local needs and circumstances. Large organizations working with GGEs need to find ways to support small-scale, innovative ideas. They need to develop flexibility in their governance and managerial structures and procedures if they are to create and capture the value GGEs can help generate in their pursuit of helping to solve global problems.

GGEs Should Franchise

Designing the actions a GGE could take to bring about the change it wants to see that results in making a better world is a challenging and resource-intensive effort. Substantial resources are required to develop a high-quality vision and a change model. Thoughtfulness and creativity are required to identify the actions that will be purposeful and impactful. Selecting measures of success needs an understanding of the complexity of the global problem being addressed. Once a GGE has established a proven track record of success, that same approach could be shared with others and quickly replicated. Franchising provides a way for global communities to adopt the GGE approach and replicate its success. Of course, the adoption of the activities of a GGE needs to be adapted to local conditions, but looking at how to model what a GGE has done so that the practices and lessons learned can be imitated with confidence of similar success will be much easier for new GGEs to be built, giving partners far greater confidence that successful outcomes are probable.

In business, scaling is one of the most difficult challenges as firms seek to grow (Sutton, 2014). It is one of the common reasons why small businesses fail—trying to become bigger businesses. Scaling a GGE faces no less a challenge. It has been designed to suit the specific circumstances and the capacities of the GGE partners. Encouraging a GGE to scale adds tremendous risks to its viability. The argument for scaling is it advances a cost-effective way to expand service provisions. However, given the risks associated with scaling, franchising is a more reasonable, lower risk approach to rapidly diffusing social innovations that can help solve global problems.

GGEs Should Bundle Service

Global problems are typically intertwined among several conditions and forces that transcend sectors, jurisdictional borders, and public policy subject boundaries.

The GGEs change model should clarify the relationships and correlations between these multiple factors and identify rational actions that will bring about the change the GGE wants to make. When such actions involve multiple global problems—even though the focus of the GGE may be only one in particular—addressing multiple global problems simultaneously may be the best way to achieve the GGE's outcomes. Engaging multiple partners with expertise in multiple policy areas (e.g., water, health, education, power) to address multiple (and interrelated) global problems through delivery of multiple services is an opportunity GGEs can take advantage of. However, it will require the desiloization of government and the development community.

Government agencies and NGOs operate in a competitive environment, sometimes more than business. Although mission-driven rather than market-driven, the nonprofit sector must compete for scarce resources, whether through appropriation bills, foundation grants, crowdsourcing, or membership fees. There is always the need to justify the continuation of funds that support their pursuit of public policy goals. There is always some other NGO or government agency who is pursuing the same or similar goals. There is always someone suggesting those funds would be better spent elsewhere. In such an environment, it is understandable that activities would be focused on particular ends where core competency claims could be supported. Working in silos may not be an effective way to make the world a better place, but it is an effective way for organizations to survive and, sometimes thrive, in a competitive environment.

GGEs will need to do more than argue that global governance underperforms when organizations work in silos. It needs to persuade these same organizations that it is to their advantage to move out of silos and into a collaborative mode. That is not always an easy sell. Bundling services is one way to desilo conventional global governance. Combining services that are provided requires collaboration among partners, which is a core competency of GGEs.

Global Governance Portfolios

Scholars and practitioners will need to make important contributions to understanding partnership portfolios for GGEs to reach their full potential as good global governance, but GGEs cannot address every global problem. Some global problems require specific governmental actions through treaties, laws, and existing international institutions. As volunteer organizations, there may not exist interest in organizing GGEs to address certain problems. GGEs are one more global governance option that should be used as the situation dictates: one more global governance tool.

Solving global problems as set out by the SDGs will require a complement of global governance options. Despite the frustrations and complaints, conventional global governance institutions and policies will be required. Their presence, funding, legitimacy, policies and processes, intimate knowledge of statecraft, institutional knowledge, and diplomacy will be essential. National policies, even given the challenges faced by failed and fragile states, are needed that address global problems as best they can in the context of a global perspective, not narrow national interests. GGEs are needed to create innovative solutions that approach the question of how to help solve global problems in a fresh and sophisticated way. Another form of good global governance that is now inchoate, but potentially powerful in the future, is global citizen governance.

Global Citizen Governance

People across the globe are organizing and bring pressure on governments and corporations to change their policies and priorities. Concerns over globalization mobilized these forces in large street protests early in the twenty-first century. The protestors were not representing the interests of one country, one religion, one ethic group, or one race: they were voicing their fears as global citizens. The large street protest ended, but the identity of people needing to think beyond national borders and look at issues from a global perspective remained and continues to grow today.

The emergence of an identity as a global citizen makes sense. Globalization has made looking at the problems people face through a nationalistic lens a blurred and artificial image. Many global problems require a global response and are insusceptible to the isolated actions of one nation. The lessening power of nations to manage events within their borders due to events outside their borders makes some citizens look to other institutions or global governance approaches that might be more effective at offering security and well-being. Of course, other citizens take the opposite approach and double-down on overtly nationalistic hopes and ideals. The expansion of global communities is another source of rising global citizenship. Through social networking, people begin to discover they may share more values with people on the other side of the world than those who live next door.

The potential for global citizen governance is greatest when the collective actions of individuals are the source of a global problem. Climate change is a good example. Actions of citizens emit greenhouse gases. Some actions are direct like using power lawnmowers, driving vehicles, burning fires, etc. Other actions are indirect like using products or household appliances powered by electricity generated from fossil fuels. Many people are inspired to take actions that reduce their own carbon footprints. Global citizen governance is the collective actions of citizens who act on their own, but identify that action as being part of a larger global community.

If all of the actions that are being taken today by individuals to reduce carbon emissions—off-setting carbon emissions when flying, installing solar power units, biking not driving, turning off lights at work—could be galvanized into a global campaign for each global citizen to take account of his or her global footprint, it would be a step towards addressing climate change. More and more people are ready to take actions as global citizens to help solve global problems, if they believed it would make a real difference. Social networks are the communication platform that could inspire, inform, and rouse global citizens to act in purposeful and impactful ways that would lead to a better world. The same energy and commitment that spurred anti-globalization protests could be harnessed today and magnified exponentially to serve the cause of global citizen governance.

GGEs are well suited to leverage and encourage an expanded role for global citizen governance in the future. Developing social innovations that make the world a better place could anticipate actions by global citizens that complement the actions of GGEs. They would have to be coordinated and integrated actions, but anticipating the possible initiatives of global citizens acting in concert to solve a global problem only creates more options and opportunities for GGEs to be successful in achieving its vision.

GGEs and Optimal Global Governance Portfolios

The global problems described by the SDGs are so daunting that it will take all the forms of good global governance we can muster to try to solve them. The addition of GGEs and the future role of global citizen governance create new opportunities for a portfolio approach to global governance. Global policies often must cast their efforts at solving the entirety of the problem being addressed. The SDGs take this approach in their call in SDG 1 for, "End poverty in all its forms everywhere" or "Ensure access to water and sanitation for all" (SDG 6) and even "Promote inclusive and sustainable economic growth, employment and decent work for all" (SDG 8). Given the global governance options available for addressing global problems, allocating particular portions or even aspects of actions addressing global problems to different global governance approaches, would align the actions needed to be taken with the form of global governance best suited to accomplishing it.

Financial investment portfolios diversify investments in an effort to optimize the overall return. Investment opportunities have a different mix of risk and return. Allocating the right balance of the total portfolio to the different investments ensures the optimal return on these investments, given the associated risks. Investment diversification would be a useful approach to be emulated by all those trying to help solve global problems. Just as risk-return trade-offs for investments, there are differing prospects for achieving good global governance depending on which form of global governance is employed. Ideally, the aspiration would be for an optimal good global governance portfolio where each global problem is being addressed with the right combination of global governance approaches.

There is a very practical application of the idea of an optimal good global governance portfolio. As GGEs grow and proliferate, the areas of their success and failure will begin to become clear. Which types of global problems

GGEs end up addressing positively can be modeled and their efforts franchised. Documentation of these successes will reduce the risks providing funding support from philanthropists, crowdsourcing, or even affect investors. As the practices of GGEs expand and mature, their impact relating to the SDGs can be quantified. The success of GGEs means other global governance efforts have proportionally less to do to achieve the goals. Even if GGEs could help achieve only 10 percent of the SDGs in a given country, it still leaves 90 percent to some other efforts; and 90 percent is easier than 100 percent. If GGEs were to have even more success—say 30 percent in a country—the approaches selected to address the remaining 70 percent might be different than if the task were to address 90 percent.

Conclusion

Multisector collaborations appeared on the global governance landscape as a curiosity. Business, NGOs, and government came together as voluntary, self-organizing groups, working together to solve global problems that governments were not solving. In recognition of the growing global governance gap, this new approach to global governance gained popularity and proliferated rapidly. Support for partnerships grew as reports and writings about their success were promoted uncritically, and enthusiasm for collaboration superseded a more in-depth grasp of how multisector collaboration could achieve the aspirations assigned to it. Over time, this new form of global governance became more gung-ho than know-how.

Fortunately, scholars had begun to notice the weakening of state powers in the face of globalization and the spontaneous populating of the global governance landscape with multisector collaborations. Over three decades of research on the dilemma posed by "governance without government," an emergent idea of network governance has provided a reasonable theoretical foundation to draw a distinction between multisector collaborations as a form of global governance and GGEs as good global governance. In addition, the creation of GGEs by pioneering governance entrepreneurs provides insight into the critical recognition of the important implications of the processes used to create GGEs on its ultimate success.

Building on the insights of research on network governance and the experiences of building and operating GGEs, the processes and activities that can be employed by a governance entrepreneur to build successful GGEs have now emerged. The five stages described in this book offer a template rather than a recipe. They are meant as a guide for making GGEs that are purposeful and impactful. No two GGEs will be exactly alike, but they share a common approach in their creation that produces the type of partnership dynamics that overcome the "clash of cultures" which comes from such disparate sectors co-creating solutions to global problems.

GGEs offer governance entrepreneurs an opportunity to channel their passions and beliefs into an approach of good global governance that can bring about real change. Whether acting alone, or in concert with other approaches to good global governance, they have an important contribution to make in conducting "governance without government." Realizing their full potential will require dramatic changes in the way we think about good global governance and ideas about how successful partnerships organize and conduct themselves. Today's global problems require urgent actions to be taken to create the social innovations that will improve people's lives and make for a better world.

REFERENCES

Agranoff, R. (2006). Inside collaborative networks: Ten lessons for public managers. *Public Administration Review, 66*(1), 56–65.

Agranoff, R. (2007). *Managing Within Networks: Adding Value to Public Organizations.* Washington, DC: Georgetown University Press.

Agranoff, R., & McGuire, M. (1999). Managing in network settings. *Review of Policy Research, 16*(1), 18–41.

Airbnb. (n.d.). About Us. Retrieved March 10, 2016, from https://www.airbnb.com/about/about-us

Barber, B. (1995). *Jihad vs. McWorld: Terrorisms Challenge to Democracy.* New York: Ballantine Books.

BBC. (2015). World Bank: Extreme poverty "to fall below 10%". Retrieved March 10, 2016, from http://www.bbc.com/news/world-34440567

Bentley, D. (2015). The top 1% now owns half the world's wealth. *Fortune.* Retrieved March 4, 2016, from http://fortune.com/2015/10/14/1-percent-global-wealth-credit-suisse/

Bevir, M., & Richards, D. (2009). Decentring policy networks: A theoretical agenda. *Public Administration, 87*(1), 3–14.

The Big Picture. (2003, April 21). Retrieved April 15, 2012, from http://www.unicef.org/nutrition/index_bigpicture.html

Bornstein, D. (2004). *How to Change the World: Social Entrepreneurs and the Power of New Ideas.* Oxford, UK: Oxford University Press.

Brilliant Earth (n.d.). Retrieved March 10, 2016, from http://www.brilliantearth.com/kimberley-process/

Bush, S. B. (2012). *Derivatives and Development: A Political Economy of Global Finance, Farming, and Poverty.* New York: Palgrave Macmillan.

Choyt, M. (2013). Why the Kimberley certification process for "conflict free diamonds" must be abandoned (part one). Retrieved March 10, 2016, from http://fortune.com/2015/10/14/1-percent-global-wealth-credit-suisse/

Cisco. (2015). Ericsson and Cisco partner to create the networks of the future. Retrieved March 10, 2016, from http://newsroom.cisco.com/press-release-content?articleId=1726935

The Committee Encouraging Corporate Philanthropy. (2015). Retrieved March 30, 2016, from http://cecp.co/measurement/benchmarking-reports/giving-in-numbers.html

Considine, M. (ed.). (2005). Partnerships, relationships and networks: Understanding local collaboration strategies in different countries. *Local Government and the Drivers of Growth*. Paris, France: OECD Publications.

Davies, J. S. (2011). *Challenging Governance Theory: From Networks to Hegemony*. Bristol, UK: Policy Press.

Derviş, K. (2005). *A Better Globalization: Legitimacy, Governance, and Reform*. Washington, DC: Center for Global Development.

De Senarclens, P., & Kazancigil, A. (eds.). (2007). *Regulating Globalization: Critical Approaches to Global Governance*. United Nations University Press.

Dobb, M. (1973). *Theories of Value and Distribution since Adam Smith*. Cambridge, UK: Cambridge University Press.

Dodd-Frank Wall Street Reform and Consumer Protection Act. 124 Stat. 1376 Public Law 111–203–July 21, 2010. Washington, DC: Government Printing Office.

Easterly, W. (2007). Was development assistance a mistake? *The American Economic Review*, *97*(2), 328–332.

Easterly, W. (2014). *The Tyranny of Experts: How the Fight against Global Poverty Suppressed Individual Rights*. New York: Perseus Books Group.

Easterly, W., & Easterly, W. R. (2001). *The Elusive Quest for Growth: Economists' Adventures and Misadventures in the Tropics*. Cambridge, MA: MIT Press.

Easterly, W., & Easterly, W. R. (2006). *The White Man's Burden: Why the West's Efforts to Aid the Rest Have Done So Much Ill and So Little Good*. New York: Penguin.

Easterly, W., & Levine, R. (2001). What have we learned from a decade of empirical research on growth? It's not factor accumulation: Stylized facts and growth models. *The World Bank Economic Review*, *15*(2), 177–219.

Emerson, J. (2003). The blended value proposition: Integrating social and financial returns. *California Management Review*, *45*(4), 35–51. Retrieved March 2, 2016, from http://www.blendedvalue.org/wp-content/uploads/2004/02/pdf-proposition.pdf

Finnegan, B. (2013). Responsibility outsourced: Social audits, workplace certification and twenty years of failure to protect worker rights. Retrieved March 2, 2016, from http://www.aflcio.org/content/download/77061/1902391/CSReport.pdf

Ford Motor Company. (n.d.). Choosing more sustainable materials. Retrieved March 1, 2016, from http://corporate.ford.com/microsites/sustainability-report-2013–14/environment-products-materials-choosing.html

Ford Motor Company. (n.d.). End of life. Retrieved March 1, 2016, from http://corporate.ford.com/microsites/sustainability-report-2014–15/environment-products-materials-endoflife.html

Foreign Policy. (n.d.). Fragile states 2014: Foreign Policy. Retrieved February 5, 2016, from http://foreignpolicy.com/fragile-states-2014/

Forest Stewardship Council. (n.d.). Our history. Retrieved February 29, 2016, from https://us.fsc.org/en-us/who-we-are/our-history

Forrer, J. Kapur, R., & Greene, L. (2012b). *Understanding Global Governance Networks Organization and Leadership*. Institute for Corporate Responsibility Working Paper.

Forrer, J., & Katsos, J. E. (2015). Business and peace in the buffer condition. *Academy of Management Perspectives*, *29*(4), 438–450.

Forrer, J., Mo, K., & Yeaw, J. (2012a). *Lessons Learned from Conflict Minerals Supply Chain Strategy*. Institute for Corporate Responsibility Working Paper.

Forrer, J., & Mo, K. (2013). From certification to supply chain strategy: An analytical framework for enhancing tropical forest governance. *Organization & Environment*, 26(3), 260–280.

Forrer, J., Robinson, L., & Wilkins, M. (2002). *Why Are People Protesting Globalization?* Washington, DC: GW Center for the Study of Globalization.

Forrer, J., Kee, J., & Boyer, E. (2014). *Governing Cross-Sector Collaboration.* San Francisco, CA: Jossey-Bass.

Forrer, J., Kee, J. E., Newcomer, K. E., & Boyer, E. (2010). Public–private partnerships and the public accountability question. *Public Administration Review, 70*(3), 475–484.

Foundation Center – Top 100 US Foundations by total giving. (n.d.). Retrieved March 30, 2016, from http://foundationcenter.org/findfunders/topfunders/top100giving.html

Fréchette, L. (2007). International governance, the G8 and globalization. Retrieved February 1, 2016, from https://www.cigionline.org/publications/2007/5/international-governance-g8-and-globalization

Fukuyama, F. (2004). *State-Building: Governance and World Order in the 21st Century.* Ithaca, NY: Cornell University Press.

Fund for Peace. (2015). Fragile States Index 2015. Retrieved February 15, 2016, from http://fsi.fundforpeace.org/

Gale, J., & Gokhale, K. (2014, December 21). In India, families pay bribes to receive the worst maternal care in G-20. Retrieved February 4, 2016, from http://www.bloomberg.com/news/2014–12–21/mother-s-death-shows-bribes-buy-india-worst-g-20-maternal-care.html

Gerencser, M., Van Lee, R., Napolitano, F., & Kelly, C. (2008). Megacommunities: How leaders of government, business and non-profits can tackle today's global challenges together. New York: St Martin's Griffin.

Giguère, S. (2003). Managing decentralisation and new forms of governance in managing decentralisation: A new role for labour market policy. Paris, France: Organisation for Economic Co-operation and Development.

Girerd-Barclay, E., de Menezes, C., & ACF International. (2010). *Taking Action Nutrition for Survival, Growth & Development.* UK: Actions against Hunger.

Global Alliance for Improved Nutrition. (n.d.). About GAIN. Retrieved April 29, 2012, from http://www.gainhealth.org/about/gain/

Global Alliance for Improved Nutrition. (n.d.). Alliances with business. Retrieved May 2, 2012, from http://www.gainhealth.org/about/alliances/#business

Global Alliance for Improved Nutrition. (n.d.). GAIN premix facility. Retrieved May 2, 2012, from http://www.gainhealth.org/knowledge-centre/project/gain-premix-facility/

Global Alliance for Improved Nutrition. (n.d.). GAIN project results. Retrieved May 2, 2012, from http://www.gainhealth.org/performance/project-results

Global Alliance for Improved Nutrition. (n.d.). Innovative finance program. Retrieved May 2, 2012, from http://www.gainhealth.org/knowledge-centre/project/innovative-finance-program/

Global Alliance for Improved Nutrition. (n.d.). Large scale food fortification. Retrieved May 2, 2012, from http://www.gainhealth.org/programs/initiatives/

Global Alliance for Improved Nutrition. (n.d.). Malnutrition. Retrieved May 20, 2012, from http://www.gainhealth.org/about/malnutrition/

Global Alliance for Improved Nutrition. (n.d.). Nutrition for women and children. Retrieved June 3, 2012, from http://www.gainhealth.org/programs/maternal-infant-and-young-child-nutrition/

Global Alliance for Improved Nutrition. (n.d.). Programs. Retrieved April 29, 2012, from http://www.gainhealth.org/programs

Global Alliance for Improved Nutrition. (n.d.). Universal salt iodization. Retrieved May 2, 2012, from http://www.gainhealth.org/knowledge-centre/universal-salt-iodization/

Global Exchange. (n.d.). Coffee FAQ. Retrieved February 6, 2016, from http://www.globalexchange.org/fairtrade/coffee/faq#1

Global Policy Forum. (n.d.). Kimberley process. Retrieved March 6, 2016, from https://www.globalpolicy.org/the-dark-side-of-natural-resources-st/diamonds-in-conflict/kimberley-process.html

Global Witness. (2011). Global witness leaves Kimberley process, calls for diamond trade to be held accountable. Retrieved March 11, 2016, from https://www.globalpolicy.org/the-dark-side-of-natural-resources-st/diamonds-in-conflict/kimberley-process.html

Goldsmith, S., & Eggers, W. D. (2004). *Governing by Network: The New Shape of the Public Sector*. Washington, DC: Brookings Institution Press.

Grayson, D., & Nelson, J. (2013). *Corporate Responsibility Coalitions: The Past, Present, and Future of Alliances for Sustainable Capitalism*. Stanford, CA: Stanford University Press.

Groden, C. (2015). Here are the 5 top-selling coffee brands. Retrieved March 6, 2016, from http://fortune.com/2015/09/29/top-coffee-brands-keurig/

The Guardian. (2012). Doha round trade talks – explainer. Retrieved March 2, 2016, from http://www.theguardian.com/global-development/2012/sep/03/doha-round-trade-talks-explainer

Haight, C. (2011). The problem with Fair Trade coffee (SSIR). Retrieved February 6, 2016, from http://ssir.org/articles/entry/the_problem_with_fair_trade_coffee#sthash.SxwwZk1G.dpuf

Hardin, G. (1968). *The Tragedy of the Commons*. Washington, DC: American Association for the Advancement of Science.

Hart, S. L. (1997). *Beyond Greening: Strategies for a Sustainable World*. Retrieved March 2, 2016, from https://hbr.org/1997/01/beyond-greening-strategies-for-a-sustainable-world

Held, D. (ed.). (2004). *A Globalizing World? Culture, Economics, Politics*. London: Routledge.

Held, D., & McGrew, A. (2002). *Governing Globalization: Power, Authority and Global Governance*. Cambridge, UK: Polity Press.

Held, D., & Koenig-Archibugi, M. (2005). *Global Governance and Public Accountability*. Malden, MA: Blackwell.

HERproject. (n.d.). Frequently asked questions. Retrieved May 15, 2012, from http://herproject.org/about/faq

HERproject. (n.d.). Where HERproject works. Retrieved May 15, 2012, from http://herproject.org/our-work/where-we-work

Hickel, J. (2015). Exposing the great "poverty reduction" lie. Retrieved June 18, 2016, from http://www.aljazeera.com/indepth/opinion/2014/08/exposing-great-poverty-reductio-201481211590729809.html

Inter-Agency Network for Education in Emergencies. (n.d.). About INEE. Retrieved June 1, 2012, from http://www.ineesite.org/en/about

Inter-Agency Network for Education in Emergencies. (n.d.). Advocacy achievements and updates. Retrieved June 1, 2012, from http://www.ineesite.org/en/advocacy/achievements

Inter-Agency Network for Education in Emergencies. (n.d.). Education in emergencies. Retrieved May 30, 2012, from http://www.ineesite.org/en/education-in-emergencies

Intercontinental Exchange. (n.d.). Chicago climate exchange. Retrieved February 29, 2016, from https://www.theice.com/ccx

International Air Transport Association (2013). New Year's Day 2014 marks 100 years of commercial aviation. Retrieved March 10, 2016, from https://www.iata.org/pressroom/pr/Pages/2013-12-30-01.aspx

International Coffee Organization. (2016, January). Retrieved March 28, 2016, from http://www.ico.org/trade_statistics.asp?section=Statistics

International Labour Organization. (n.d.). What is child labour? Retrieved February 4, 2016, From http://www.ilo.org/ipec/facts/lang--en/index.htm

International Organization for Migration. (2014). Global migration trends: An overview. Retrieved March 10, 2016, from http://missingmigrants.iom.int/sites/default/files/documents/Global_Migration_Trends_PDF_FinalVH_with References.pdf

Internet Live Stats. (n.d.). Total number of websites. Retrieved March 10, 2016, from http://www.internetlivestats.com/total-number-of-websites/

Investopedia. (2007). Free rider problem definition. Retrieved March 2, 2016, from http://www.investopedia.com/terms/f/free_rider_problem.asp#ixzz3wgq6giKQ

IRIN. (2009). Credibility of Kimberley process on the line, say NGOs. Retrieved March 10, 2016, from http://www.irinnews.org/news/2009/06/22/credibility-kimberley-process-line-say-ngos

ISSF. (n.d.). ISSF production. Retrieved June 29, 2012, from http://iss-foundation.org/

Jaffee, D., & Howard, P. (2011, December). Utilizing Fair Trade coffee. Retrieved March 28, 2016, from https://msu.edu/~howardp/coffee.html

Joswig, D., & Perez, S. (2011). *Rainforest Alliance: Twenty-Five Years and Still Growing 2011 Annual Report*. Allen, TX: ColorDynamics.

Kennett, P. (2008). Introduction: Governance, the state, and public policy in a global age. In Kennett, P. (ed.). *Governance, Globalization and Public Policy*. Northampton, MA: Edward Elgar Publishing, pp. 3–18.

Klein, N. (2007). *The Shock Doctrine: The Rise of Disaster Capitalism*. New York: Picador.

Klijn, E. H., & Skelcher, C. (2007). Democracy and governance networks: Compatible or not? *Public Administration, 85*(3), 587–608.

Koliba, C., Meek, J. W., & Zia, A. (2011). *Governance Networks in Public Administration and Public Policy*. Boca Raton, FL: CRC Press.

Kolko, J. (2012). Wicked problems: Problems worth solving. Retrieved March 6, 2016, from http://ssir.org/articles/entry/wicked_problems_problems_worth_solving#sthash.7mxh2bm1.dpuf

Kooiman, J. (2008). Governability: A conceptual exploration. *Journal of Comparative Policy Analysis, 10*(2), 171–190.

Koontz, T. M., & Johnson, E. M. (2004). One size does not fit all: Matching breadth of stakeholder participation to watershed group accomplishments. *Policy Sciences, 37*(2), 185–204.

Kosar, K. R. (2007). *The Quasi-Government Hybrid Organizations with Both Government and Private Sector Legal Characteristics*. Washington, DC: Congressional Research Service.

Kouzmin, A., Johnston, J., & Thorne, K. (2011). Economic SCADs: The dark underbelly of neoliberalism. *Public Integrity, 13*(3), 221–238.

Landau, R., & Rosenberg, N. (1986). *The Positive Sum Strategy: Harnessing Technology for Economic Growth*. Washington, DC: National Academy Press.

Lawless, M., & Moore, R. (1989). Interorganizational systems in public service delivery: A new application of the dynamic network framework. *Human Relations, 42*(12): 1167–1184.

Lawrence, P. R., & Dyer, D. (1983). *Renewing American Industry*. New York: Free Press.

Lechner, F. (2005). Globalization. In Ritzer, G. (ed.), *Encyclopedia of Social Theory*. Thousand Oaks, CA: Sage.

Lee, D. R. (1982). Review of the zero-sum society: distribution and the possibilities for economic change. *Public Choice, 38*(2), 219–222.

Lee, J. (2016). Your smartphone may be linked to child labor. Retrieved February 4, 2016, from http://www.triplepundit.com/2016/01/child-labor-amnesty-internatio nal/?utm_source=Daily Email List

Levitt, T. (1983). The globalization of markets. *Harvard Business Review*. Retrieved June 18, 2016 from http://www.lapres.net/levit.pdf

Lockheed Martin Aeronautics. (n.d.). Lockheed Martin celebrates national engineers week. Retrieved June 17, 2012, from http://www.lockheedmartin.com/us/news/features/2012/eweek-2012.html

Lomborg, B. (ed.). (2004). *Global Crises, Global Solutions*. Cambridge, UK: Cambridge University Press.

Malena, C. (2004). Strategic partnership: Challenges and best practices in the management and governance of multi-stakeholder partnerships involving UN and civil society actors. Retrieved March 6, 2016, from www.un-ngls.org/orf/partnership-carmen-malena.doc

Martin, M. (2010, September 28). Colleges see booming growth of international students. Retrieved March 10, 2016, from http://www.npr.org/templates/story/story.php?storyId=130188621

MBA Skool-Study.Learn.Share. (n.d.). Top 10 coffee chains in the world 2015. Retrieved March 28, 2016, from http://www.mbaskool.com/fun-corner/top-brand-lists/13833-top-10-coffee-chains-in-the-world-2015.html?start=9

Moore, M. H. (1995). *Creating Public Value: Strategic Management in Government*. Cambridge, MA: Harvard University Press.

Morris, S. S., Cogill, B., & Uauy, R. (2008). Effective international action against undernutrition: Why has it proven so difficult and what can be done to accelerate progress? *The Lancet, 371*(9612), 608–621. Retrieved May 22, 2012, from http://www.thelancet.com/pdfs/journals/lancet/PIIS0140–6736(07)61695-X.pdf

Mr Globalization – Tackling the paradoxes of globalization. (2010). Globalization: Origin of the word? Retrieved March 10, 2016, from http://www.mrglobalization.com/globalisation/252-globalization--origin-of-the-word

Murphy, C. R. (2000). Global governance: Poorly done and poorly understood. *International Affairs, 76*(4), 789–804.

National Oceanic and Atmospheric Administration. (n.d.). Basic questions about aquaculture. Retrieved March 10, 2016, from http://www.nmfs.noaa.gov/aquaculture/faqs/faq_aq_101.html

Nelson, J. (2007). Effecting change through accountable channels. Retrieved March 11, 2016, from http://www.brookings.edu/~/media/Events/2007/8/01sustainable-development/2007nelson5.pdf?la=en

Nixon, R. (2014). In Switch Development Agency welcomes business and technology to poverty fight. *The New York Times*. Retrieved March 6, 2016, from http://www.nytimes.com/2014/04/08/world/africa/in-switch-development-agency-welcomes-business-and-technology-to-poverty-fight.html?_r=1

Nye, J. S., & Donahue, J. D. (eds.). (2000). *Governance in a Globalizing World*. Washington, DC: Brookings Institution Press.

O'Rourke, K. H., & Williamson, J. G. (1999). *Globalization and History: The Evolution of a Nineteenth-Century Atlantic Economy*. Cambridge, MA: MIT Press.

Ostrom, E. (1998). A behavioral approach to the rational choice theory of collective action: Presidential address, American Political Science Association, 1997. *American Political Science Review, 92*(1), 1–22.

Ostrom, E. (1990). *Governing the Commons: The Evolution of Institutions for Collective Action.* Cambridge, UK: Cambridge University Press.

O'Toole, L. J., & Hanf, K. I. (2002). American public administration and impacts of international governance. *Public Administration Review, 62*(1), 158–169.

Pennington, R. (2014, September 21). Leading change isn't about the model. Retrieved March 28, 2016, from http://www.penningtongroup.com/leading-change-isnt-about-the-model/

Peters, B. G., & Pierre, J. (1998). Governance without government? Rethinking public administration. *Journal Public Administration Research and Theory, 8*(2), 223–243.

Pierre, J., & Peters, B. G. (2005). *Governing Complex Societies: Trajectories and Scenarios.* New York: Springer.

Porter, M. E., & Kramer, M. R. (2011). The big idea: Creating shared value. *Harvard Business Review, 89*(1), 2.

Prahalad, C. K. (2006). *The Fortune at the Bottom of the Pyramid.* Delhi, India: Pearson Education India.

Principles for Responsible Investment. (n.d.). UN partners. Retrieved March 3, 2016, from http://www.unpri.org/partnerships/un-partners/

Provan, K. G., & Milward, H. B. (1995). A preliminary theory of interorganizational network effectiveness: A comparative study of four community mental health systems. *Administrative Science Quarterly, 40,* 1–33.

Provan, K. G., & Milward, H. B. (2001). Do networks really work? A framework for evaluating public-sector organizational networks. *Public Administration Review, 61*(4), 414–423.

Provan, K. G., & Kenis, P. (2007). Modes of network governance: Structure, management, and effectiveness. *Journal Public Administration Research and Theory, 18*(2): 229–252.

Quelch, J. A., & Deshpande, R. (2004). *The Global Market: Developing a Strategy to Manage across Borders.* San Francisco, CA: Jossey-Bass.

R4 Rural Resilience Initiative: Five Year Plan—Summary. August 2011. Accessed March 10, 2016, from https://www.agriskmanagementforum.org/sites/agriskmanagementforum.org/files/R4%20Five%20Year%20Plan%20Summary.pdf

Rainforest Alliance. (2011). *Rainforest Alliance: Twenty-Five Years and Still Growing 2011 Annual Report.* New York: Rainforest Alliance.

Rainforest Alliance. (2012). Happy New Year from the Rainforest Alliance! Retrieved June 29, 2012, from http://rafrogblogus.wordpress.com/2012/01/05/happy-new-year-from-the-rainforest-alliance/

Rainforest Alliance. (n.d.). Alleviating poverty. Retrieved June 26, 2012, from http://www.rainforest-alliance.org/about/poverty

Rainforest Alliance. (n.d.). Curbing climate change. Retrieved June 26, 2012, from http://www.rainforest-alliance.org/about/climate

Rainforest Alliance. (n.d.). Ensuring our integrity. Retrieved June 30, 2012, from http://www.rainforest-alliance.org/about/integrity

Rainforest Alliance. (n.d.). Measuring our impact. Retrieved June 29, 2012, from http://www.rainforest-alliance.org/work/impact

Rainforest Alliance. (n.d.). Our history. Retrieved June 25, 2012, from http://www.rainforest-alliance.org/history

Rainforest Alliance. (n.d.). 25 years of conservation. Retrieved June 25, 2012, from http://www.rainforest-alliance.org/history

Rainforest Alliance. (n.d.). Keeping forests standing. Retrieved June 25, 2012, from http://www.rainforest-alliance.org/about/forests

Rainforest Alliance. (n.d.). Protecting wildlife. Rainforest Alliance. Retrieved June 26, 2012, from http://www.rainforest-alliance.org/about/wildlife

Rainforest Alliance. (n.d.). Transforming business practices. Retrieved June 26, 2012, from http://www.rainforest-alliance.org/about/business-practices

Reich, R. B. (1983). *The Next American Frontier*. New York: Times Books.

Reinicke, W. H., & Deng, F. (2000). Critical choices: The United Nations, networks, and the future of global governance. Ottawa, Canada: International Development Research Council.

Reuters. (2008). Bush signs expansion of global AIDS programs. Retrieved March 16, 2016, from http://www.reuters.com/article/us-aids-usa-idUSN3029275220080730

Rhodes, R. A. (1990). Policy networks: A British perspective. *Journal of Theoretical Politics*, *2*(3), 293–317.

Rhodes, R. A. (1996). The new governance: Governing without government. *Political Studies*, *44*(4), 652–667.

Rhodes, R. A., & Ruggie, J. G. (1996). The new governance: Governing without government. *Political Studies*, *44*(4), 652–667.

Riggs, F. W. (1991). Guest editorial: Public administration: A comparativist framework. *Public Administration Review*, *51*(6), 473–477.

Riley, C. (2016). Oil crash taking stocks down … again. *CNN Money*. Retrieved March 10, 2016, from http://money.cnn.com/2016/02/11/investing/oil-price-crash/

Ritzer, G. (2007). A "new" global age, but are there new perspectives on it? In Rossi, I. (ed.), *Frontiers of Globalization Research: Theoretical and Methodological Approaches*. New York: Springer, pp. 361–370.

Rizvi, G. (2008). Innovations in American government: Some observations and lessons learnt. Retrieved March 23, 2016, from http://unpan1.un.org/intradoc/groups/public/documents/caimed/unpan028993.pdf

Rosenau, J. N. (1995). Governance in the twenty-first century. *Global Governance*, *1*(1), 13–43.

Rosenau, J. N. (2002). Governance in a new global order. In Held, D., & McGrew, A. (eds.), *Governing Globalization: Power, Authority and Global Governance*, Cambridge, UK: Polity Press, pp. 70–86.

Rosenau, J. N. (2003). *Distant Proximities: Dynamics beyond Globalization*. Princeton, NJ: Princeton University Press.

Rosenau, J. N., & Czempiel, E. O. (eds.). (1992). *Governance without Government: Order and Change in World Politics* (Vol. 4). Cambridge, UK: Cambridge University Press.

Rutsch, P. (2015, February 10). Guess how much of Uncle Sam's money goes to foreign aid. guess again! Retrieved March 30, 2016, from http://www.npr.org/sections/goatsandsoda/2015/02/10/383875581/guess-how-much-of-uncle-sams-money-goes-to-foreign-aid-guess-again

Salamon, L. M. (2002). *The Tools of Government: A Guide to the New Governance*. Oxford, UK: Oxford University Press.

Satterthwaite, D., & Choularton, R. (2011). *R4 Rural Resilience Initiative: Five Year Plan*. Retrieved May 4, 2012, from https://www.agriskmanagementforum.org/sites/agrisk managementforum.org/files/R4%20Five%20Year%20Plan%20Summary.pdf

Save the Children. (2015). The urban disadvantage: State of the world's mothers 2015. Retrieved February 11, 2016, from http://www.savethechildren.org/atf/cf/{9def2ebe-10ae-432c-9bd0-df91d2eba74a}/SOWM_2015.PDF

Say, L., Chou, D., Gemmill, A., Tunçalp, Ö., Moller, A., Daniels, J., & Alkema, L. (2014). Global causes of maternal death: A WHO systematic analysis. *The Lancet Global Health, 2*(6).

Scholte, J. A. (2000). *Globalization: A Critical Introduction.* New York: St. Martin's Press.

Schumpeter, J. A. (1943). *Capitalism, Socialism, and Democracy.* London: G. Allen & Unwin.

Shontell, A. (2011). FLASHBACK: This is what the first website ever looked like. Retrieved March 10, 2016, from http://www.businessinsider.com/flashback-this-is-what-the-first-website-ever-looked-like-2011-6

Simmons, P. J., & Oudraat, C. de Jonge (eds.). (2001). *Managing Global Issues: Lessons Learned.* Washington, DC: Carnegie Endowment for International Peace.

Snell, P. (2015, March 12). The top five supply chain disruptions of 2014. Retrieved March 30, 2016, from http://www.cips.org/en/Supply-Management/News/2015/March/The-top-five-supply-chain-disruptions-of-2014/

Sørensen, E., & Torfing, J. (2009). Making governance networks effective and democratic through metagovernance. *Public Administration, 87*(2), 234–258.

Starbucks. (n.d.). Starbucks Coffee International. Retrieved March 10, 2016, from http://www.starbucks.com/business/international-stores

Statista. (2015). Number of MTV branded television channels worldwide in the fiscal years 2009 to 2015. Retrieved March 10, 2016, from http://www.statista.com/statistics/350527/number-mtv-tv-channels/

Statista. (2016). Leading social networks worldwide as of January 2016, ranked by number of active users. Retrieved March 10, 2016, from http://www.statista.com/statistics/272014/global-social-networks-ranked-by-number-of-users/

Statistic Brain. (2015). YouTube statistics. Retrieved March 10, 2016, from http://www.statisticbrain.com/youtube-statistics/

Stiglitz, J. (2002). *Globalization and Its Discontents.* New York: W. W. Norton & Company.

Stiglitz, J. (2006). *Making Globalization Work.* New York: W. W. Norton & Company.

Strange, S. (1986). *Casino Capitalism.* Oxford, UK: Blackwell Publishers.

Sullivan, H., & Skelcher, C. (2002). *Working across Boundaries: Collaboration in Public Services.* London: Palgrave Macmillan.

Sutton, R. (2014). Scaling up is a problem of both more and less. Retrieved March 30, 2016, from https://hbr.org/2014/02/scaling-up-is-a-problem-of-both-more-and-less

Thorne, K., & Johnston, J. (2012). Benign partners or partners in crime? Reply to Kee and Forrer. *Public Integrity, 14*(2), 203–210.

Thousand Days. (n.d.). About 1000 days. Retrieved June 6, 2012, from http://www.thousanddays.org/about

Thurow, L. (1980). *The Zero-Sum Society* New York: Pantheon.

Thurow, L. (1985). *Zero-Sum Solution.* New York: Simon and Schuster.

Tiwari, S. (2015, January 29). 2 women give birth in hospital toilet. Retrieved February 5, 2016, from http://indianexpress.com/article/cities/delhi/2-women-give-birth-in-hospital-toilet/

Trading Economics. (n.d.). Retrieved March 30, 2016, from http://www.tradingeconomics.com/china/gdp-growth

Tumbleson, M. (2015). 19 text messaging facts | Teckst | incredible textable tech. Retrieved March 10, 2016, from https://teckst.com/19-text-messaging-stats-that-will-blow-your-mind/

Tyson KNOW Hunger. (n.d.). Our commitment: Tyson hunger relief. Retrieved June 17, 2012, from http://www.tysonhungerrelief.com/our-commitment/

UN. (2008). Goal 2: Achieve universal primary education factsheet. Retrieved May 30, 2012, from http://www.un.org/millenniumgoals/2008highlevel/pdf/newsroom/Goal%202%20FINAL.pdf

UN. (n.d.). Sustainable development goals. Retrieved February 13, 2016 from http://www.un.org/sustainabledevelopment/sustainable-development-goals/

UN. (n.d.). Goal 4: Reduce child mortality. Retrieved February 19, 2016, from http://www.un.org/millenniumgoals/childhealth.shtml

United Nations Conference on Environment and Development (1992). Earth Summit Agenda 21, p. 329, from https://sustainabledevelopment.un.org/outcomedocuments/agenda21

United Nations Foundation. (n.d.). Who we are: The Turner gift. Retrieved February 18, 2016, from http://www.unfoundation.org/who-we-are/the-turner-gift.html

United Nations Foundation. (n.d.). What we do: Become a partner. Retrieved February 18, 2016, from http://www.unfoundation.org/what-we-do/partners/

United Nations Foundation. (n.d.). What we do: Campaigns and initiatives. Retrieved February 18, 2016, from http://www.unfoundation.org/what-we-do/campaigns-and-initiatives/

United Nations International Children's Emergency Fund. (n.d.). Immunization. Retrieved March 3, 2016, from http://www.unicef.org/immunization/index_42071.html

United States Department of State. (n.d.). Global alliance for clean cookstoves. Retrieved February 29, 2016, from http://www.state.gov/s/partnerships/cleancookstoves/

UTZ. (n.d.). Coffee. Retrieved March 28, 2016, from https://www.utz.org/what-we-offer/certification/products-we-certify/coffee/

Vidal, J. (2015). Water privatisation: A worldwide failure? *The Guardian*. Retrieved February 18, 2016, http://www.theguardian.com/global-development/2015/jan/30/water-privatisation-worldwide-failure-lagos-world-bank

Waddell, S. (2011). *Global Action Networks: Creating Our Future Together*. London: Palgrave Macmillan.

Walsh, J. (2001). Catalysts for change: Public policy reform through local partnership in Ireland. In Geddes, M., & Benington, J. (eds.), *Local Partnership and Social Exclusion in the European Union: New Forms of Local Social Governance*? New York: Routledge.

Weiss, T. G. (2000). Governance, good governance and global governance: conceptual and actual challenges. *Third World Quarterly, 21*(5), 795–814.

Weiss, T. G., & Wilkinson, R. (2014). Rethinking global governance? Complexity, authority, power, change. *International Studies Quarterly, 58*(1), 207–215.

Woods, N. (2002). Global governance and the role of institutions. In Held, D., & McGrew, A. (eds.), *Governing Globalization: Power, Authority and Global Governance*, Cambridge, UK: Polity Press, pp. 25–45.

Workman, D. (2015, November 19). Coffee exports by country: World's top exports. Retrieved February 5, 2016, from http://www.worldstopexports.com/coffee-exports-country/

World Atlas. (2015). Top 10 coffee producing countries (2014). Retrieved February 5, 2016, from http://www.worldatlas.com/articles/top-10-coffee-producing-countries-2014.html

World Bank. (2005). Commodity and weather risk management programs to be expanded. Retrieved May 4, 2012, from http://go.worldbank.org/06TQDNH750

WTO. (2012). Dispute settlement: Dispute DS27. Retrieved February 22, 2016, from https://www.wto.org/english/tratop_e/dispu_e/cases_e/ds27_e.htm

Yeager, R., & Goldenberg, E. (2011). HERproject women's health program delivers real business returns. *Global Business and Organizational Excellence Glob. Bus. Org. Exc.*, *31*(2), 24–36.

INDEX